Pentecostal Hermeneutics in the Late Modern World

Pentecostal Hermeneutics in the Late Modern World

Essays on the Condition of Our Interpretation

L. WILLIAM OLIVERIO, JR.

PICKWICK *Publications* · Eugene, Oregon

Pickwick Publications
An Imprint of Wipf and Stock Publishers
199 W. 8th Ave., Suite 3
Eugene, OR 97401

www.wipfandstock.com

PAPERBACK ISBN: 978-1-6667-1822-5
HARDCOVER ISBN: 978-1-6667-1823-2
EBOOK ISBN: 978-1-6667-1824-9

Cataloguing-in-Publication data:

Names: Oliverio, L. William [author].

Title: Pentecostal hermeneutics in the late modern world : essays on the condition of our interpretation / L. William Oliverio, Jr.

Description: Eugene, OR: Pickwick Publications, 2022 | Includes bibliographical references.

Identifiers: ISBN 978-1-6667-1822-5 (paperback) | ISBN 978-1-6667-1823-2 (hardcover) | ISBN 978-1-6667-1824-9 (ebook)

Subjects: LCSH: Hermeneutics—Religious aspects—Pentecostal churches | Bible—Hermeneutics | Pentecostal churches | Pentecostalism | Pentecostal churches—Doctrines | Bible—Criticism, interpretation, etc.

Classification: BX8762 O45 2022 (paperback) | BX8762 (ebook)

05/23/22

To Our Immanuel Church Family

Contents

Acknowledgments

These essays are not merely the work of a single author so much as they are the outworking of the Pentecostal tradition at various intersections of understanding. Too many to name here have touched these essays and their composition. Many of those who deserve thanks appear in the text and the footnotes, of course, while others remain behind the text. Especially among these are several formative communities I would like to thank here. Many of the words in this volume were originally written in my offices and also the nooks of Memorial and Raynor Libraries at Marquette University, my academic home for fourteen years, where I was also pastor of Immanuel Church in downtown Milwaukee for the second half of that era of my life. My friends in the worlds of teaching theology and other disciplines in relation to Pentecostalism—in the Society for Pentecostal Studies, the School of Urban Missions (SUM), and now at Northwest University—have been inspirations to my work just as they have been my people. Most centrally to my life and thought, the center context to my hermeneutic, are my beloved—Rachel, Nick, Josh, Mom and Ed. To all of these, thank you. I have stood on your shoulders.

My additional thanks to the following publishers for their permission to publish previously published work in these collected essays, which have been lightly adapted for the format of this volume:

1. "Toward a Hermeneutical Realism for Pentecostal Theological Hermeneutics." In *Theological Hermeneutics in the Classical Pentecostal Tradition: A Typological Account*, 315–54. Leiden: Brill 2012.

2. "Pentecostal Hermeneutics and the Hermeneutical Tradition." In *Constructive Pneumatological Hermeneutics in Pentecostal Christianity*, edited by Kenneth J. Archer and L. William Oliverio Jr., 1–6. New York: Palgrave Macmillan, 2016.

3. "Theological Hermeneutics: Understanding the World in Encounter with God." In *Routledge Handbook of Pentecostal Theology*, edited by Wolfgang Vondey, 140–51. London: Routledge, 2020.

4. "Contours of a Constructive Pentecostal Philosophical-Theological Hermeneutic." *Journal of Pentecostal Theology* 29 (2020) 35–55.

5. "Spirit Baptism in the Late Modern World: A Pentecostal Response to *The Church: Towards a Common Vision*." In *The Holy Spirit and the Church: Ecumenical Reflections with a Pastoral Perspective*, edited by Thomas Hughson, 44–70. London: Routledge, 2016.

6. "The Nature of Theology and Pentecostal Hermeneutics: On the Relationship among Scripture, Experience of the Spirit, and Life in Spirit-Filled Community." In *Pentecostal Theology and Ecumenical Theology: Interpretations and Intersections*, edited by Peter Hocken et al., 157–79. Leiden: Brill, 2019.

7. "'True Religion, in Great Part, Consists of Holy Affections': A Comparison of the Biblical Hermeneutics of Jonathan Edwards and Pentecostals." In *From Northampton to Azusa: Pentecostals and the Theology of Jonathan Edwards*, edited by Steven Studebaker and Amos Yong, 23–39. London: T. & T. Clark, 2020.

8. "Breaking Out of the Immanent Frame: A Review Essay of James K. A. Smith's *How (Not) to Be Secular: Reading Charles Taylor*." *The Pentecostal Educator* 2 (2015) 7–19.

9. "An Interpretive Review Essay on Amos Yong's *Spirit-Word-Community: Theological Hermeneutics in Trinitarian Perspective*." *Journal of Pentecostal Theology* 18 (2009) 301–11.

10. "The One and the Many: The Theology of Amos Yong and the Dissolution and Pluralism of Late Modernity." In *The Theology of Amos Yong and the New Face of Pentecostal Scholarship*, edited by Wolfgang Vondey and Martin Mittelstadt, 45–61. Leiden: Brill, 2013.

11. "The Theological Hermeneutic of Amos Yong, in the Prime of His Theological Career." *Australasian Pentecostal Studies* 21 (2020) 4–28.

12. "Reading Craig Keener: On *Spirit Hermeneutics: Reading Scripture in Light of Pentecost*." *Pneuma* 39 (2017) 126–45.

Pentecostal Hermeneutics in the Late Modern World

An Introductory Note

Pentecostalism is a Christian folk spiritual tradition that is indigenous to modernity, a set of diverse movements which functions, in aggregation, as a tradition that is simultaneously modern and anti-modern. Pentecostalism embodies the tensions of Christianity today, in late modernity. Pentecostalism might even be considered *the* indigenous modern folk Christian spiritual tradition of late modernity, though that could overstate the case. There are other indigenous modern folk Christian spiritual traditions with a similar modern-anti-modern dynamic—such as folk versions of evangelicalism and Catholicism. However, these two other examples, in practice, might exemplify the preceding point, as they have both often gravitated towards charismatic spirituality, practices, worship, and pathos, much because of Pentecostalism's influence, as Pentecostalism has embodied so much of the dialectic between modern experientialism and revelatory sources of Christian authority. At the center of my accounting for Pentecostal hermeneutics, I have contended is this very dialectic between experience and Scripture as operative with various Pentecostal assumptions. That is, the very back-and-forth is the thing itself so that this dialectic is at the center of Pentecostal hermeneutics and, as I have claimed, the very hermeneutic that originated Pentecostalism.[1]

Global Pentecostalism is now one of the four major traditions of Christianity, and it came out of almost nowhere at the turn of the twentieth

---

1. See chapter 2, "The Original Classical Pentecostal Hermeneutic," of my *Theological Hermeneutics in the Classical Pentecostal Tradition*, 31–82, which argues, illustrates, and explains this claim.

century.[2] While taxonomies of the tradition abound, attempting to account for its various layers, The *World Christian Encyclopedia* numbers 19,300 Christian denominations and fellowships it considers Pentecostal/Charismatic, with 644 million adherents worldwide, as of 2020; initial numbers for 2022 are ranging around 667 million.[3] Pentecostalism is the massive aggregation of these communities, socially and historically, and essentially includes charismatic wings of other Christian traditions which it shares in the *oikumenē* of the Christian faith, as a theological and ecclesial tradition.[4] Pentecostalism is also a tradition in the MacIntyrean sense, that is, as a running embodied conversation of large swaths of human communities with its own rationality, morality, and ways of life, as they interact with other traditions, as developed in the work of the eminent philosopher Alasdair MacIntyre. Its rationality, ethics, and way of life are embedded in the tradition itself. Simo Frestadius has explicitly identified Pentecostalism as a tradition in this way, resourcing MacIntyre here, considering Pentecostal communities and their narrative frameworks, with Pentecostal theologies as tradition-constituted.[5]

As a theological tradition, Pentecostalism has been rightly identified as a tradition of Christian spirituality. Steven J. Land's landmark work, *Pentecostal Spirituality*, cannot be acknowledged enough, if its location as the very first volume of the Journal of Pentecostal Theology Supplement Series did not already point to its significance, for its role in orienting scholarship on Pentecostal theology to the tradition's embedding of its theology in its lived spirituality—in its many songs, tongues, dances, fervent prayers, practices of faith, habits of Christian life—so that Land notably coined the

---

2. As considered in Jacobsen, *The World's Christians*.

3. Johnson and Zurlo, *World Christian Encyclopedia*, 5–8, 26. The Center for Global Christianity at Gordon Conwell Theological Seminary, which hosts the work of *The World Christian Encyclopedia* has published updated numbers on their website that has Pentecostal-Charismatics worldwide at the 667 million number (see "Annual Statistics").

4. For a recent reflection on Pentecostalism as a theological tradition from a leading figure, see Vondey, "Pentecostalism as a Theological Tradition." If the Pentecostal theological tradition is found in any particular text, it might be best found in a handbook made for the very purpose, in *The Routledge Handbook of Pentecostal Theology*, edited by Vondey, which included the contributions of forty-two leading Pentecostal theologians. More broadly, *Brill's Encyclopedia of Global Pentecostalism*, edited by Michael Wilkinson et al. and published in 2021 by Brill, represents another important contemporary representation of the global tradition.

5. Frestadius, *Pentecostal Rationality*, particularly 45–60. Among MacIntyre's significant body of works, his *After Virtue* and *Whose Justice? Which Rationality?* stand as central to developing this notion of tradition.

Pentecostal triad of orthodoxy, orthopraxis, and orthopathy, with right affections as the stimulating agency of Pentecostal life.[6]

Therefore, authentic Pentecostal theology—and correspondingly authentic Pentecostal hermeneutics—resists an ontology of abstraction into human linguistic categories, whether in scholastic or analytic theologies, insofar as these theological approaches use human languages to circumvent the work of God rather than point to the explosive Pentecost of being and meaning indicated by God's self-revelation in history. This is one way of putting the resistance of certain forms of Pentecostal theology to certain forms of evangelical Protestant theology. Yet the plank in the eye of folk Pentecostalism, where local theologies are often enough assumed to be the apotheosis of (uninterpreted) truth straight from biblical revelation, may elicit pause from any Pentecostal triumphalism on this matter. They are sometimes merely sloppy or looser forms of the same. Pentecostal theological hermeneutics has been best when it is considered in relation to authentic Pentecostal spirituality, robust interaction with the biblical text, contextual-linguistic self-awareness, and an ecumenical orientation—where theology is done together and with the Church, past and present. This all seems to entail, as the dialectic of the cataphatic and apophatic in the Church's tradition remind, the call to speak the deep mysteries of faith.

Pentecostal theologies and hermeneutics have been shaped by particular commitments that are productive of further understanding. As such, Pentecostalism is a large and varied hermeneutical tradition. My work has sought to account for the hermeneutics of the larger tradition that is the aggregation of so many varied movements, that is, a massive religious tradition of 667 million persons, 19,300 sub-traditions (and just in the organizational sense), a global collective effervescence, a people of the Spirit. Such a task, even as it types out and analyzes, can only point. Such work might be considered technical. I would contend, instead, that it is deeply aesthetic and moral, as well as truth-seeking. I hope that readers will find a deeply meaningful and evocative prodding in this collection of essays on Pentecostal hermeneutics in this volume. The probing into the ontic, the spiritual, the meaningful in the Pentecostal tradition is not a mere quest for truth. It is also a quest for the good and the beautiful in the many tongues of Pentecost.

Pentecost is the antithesis of Babel. The pride of the univocal quest to lord authority over others in a forced conformity is met by the explosion of God's Spirit in the fruitful multiplication of human cultures, languages, hermeneutics—each on their own Abrahamic journeys, in moments of hope and loss, hospitality and failed faith, in sacrificial love. Pentecost is,

---

6. Land, *Pentecostal Spirituality*.

ultimately, a hermeneutic of love, of the self-giving of the Triune God to the world. Pentecost is many—and one: "one body and one Spirit . . . one hope . . . one Lord, one faith, one baptism; one God and Father of all, who is over all and through all and in all. But to each one of us grace" (Eph 4:4–7a NIV). Pentecostal hermeneutics are the many witnesses of the common faith.

Babel mimics Pentecost among Pentecostals as an idolatrous attempt to capture the grace of the transcendent God in exclusionary and limited categories. It was manifested in Babylon and Simon the Sorcerer, and today in authoritarian regimes and profiteers who take advantage of the poor as well as religious leaders who serve narcissistic ends. Even as being in itself always already limits and determines in its ontic actuality, revelation and experience of God will always transcend its human interpretive experiential understanding, even the great witness of the *oikumenē* in its communal shared understanding and our shared linguistic statements formed about it. The actualities, for finite being let alone the infinite, far exceed the snapshots which are the linguistic claims which we humans make about them, since symbolic-linguistic understanding is always our way of knowing our world as embodied persons in the world. Babel seeks to capture and own this all. Pentecost points to the mysteries and serves God's purposes in the world.

Pentecostalism as the fourth theological tradition of Christianity has arrived in the midst of modernity. If what I have claimed in the preceding paragraphs is the case, then the culturally-situated, linguistic, traditioned understanding of Pentecostals in the modern world has shaped the many tongues of Pentecost today. Folk and anti-modern cultural traditions, technical and analytical modern traditions, postmodern and deconstructive traditions have all come to influence Pentecostal interpretation in the sea of late modernity in which we swim. The dozen essays in this volume represent accounting for just that, as varied entry points into Pentecostalism as a hermeneutical tradition in the midst of modernity. No such attempt can be comprehensive so much as it can be a series of accounts which create openings for the furthering of hermeneutical paradigms. These essays on the condition of our interpretation only seek to point forward towards goodness, truth, and beauty found in Pentecostal interpretations of God, ourselves, and our world.

PART ONE

Historical-Constructive Hermeneutics

I

Toward a Hermeneutical Realism

In examining the development of theological hermeneutics in the Classical Pentecostal tradition, and in line with the contextual-Pentecostal hermeneutic, I have already pushed the matter of what is interpreted beyond written or spoken texts toward a broader view of that which is theologically interpreted. What constitutes a 'text,' in this sense, is anything that is interpreted theologically. It is the self or anything 'other' that is understood in light of one's faith commitments and further interpreted in inquiry, reflection, and criticism upon those commitments and that which is interpreted. The range of the 'texts' cognizantly interpreted by Pentecostals has included Scripture, the world or nature, special religious experiences, general human experience, the human self, rationality, and tradition. Even when tacit, the uses of certain concepts of rationality and the role of tradition have each played significant parts in the interpretive ethoi of the Pentecostal tradition. This has been the case even when the philosophical assumptions were unstated or the theologian unaware of these assumptions. Only recently have they come to the fore to be consciously reflected upon.

Deeper philosophical reflection on human understanding and the processes of interpretation has been and will continue to be helpful to the future development of Pentecostal theology. My purpose here is thus to offer an initial constructive philosophical and theological proposal for Pentecostal theological hermeneutics that enlists the help of several philosophers and philosophical theologians in order to provide the best approach for the task of Pentecostal theological interpretation that I can propose at this time. My desire is to offer a modest and provisional proposal that works toward a broad affirmation of a 'hermeneutical realism' for future theological hermeneutics in the Pentecostal tradition, even if the scope of the subject matter is broad. My goal is that this proposal will attend to current and classical philosophical concerns with enough breadth to include a variety of approaches to the task of doing theology.

The 'hermeneutical realism' I am advocating differs from a similar approach to the relationship between human understanding and reality which has been deemed 'critical realism.' Hermeneutical realism is chastened in its accounts of reality in terms of a recognition that it is operating with a historically contingent hermeneutic rather than with a single, proper critical method. While critical realism is typically modern, hermeneutical realism is reflective of the concerns of late modernity or postmodernity. This means that I affirm the ubiquity of interpretation. Yet this does not mean, as I have stated and implied throughout, that I find one hermeneutic as good as another. I follow Charles Taylor's "best account epistemology" that finds some accounts, and thus some hermeneutics, better than others. And following James K. A. Smith, I find all accounts of theological understanding or knowledge to be human accounts of reality from a theological (ad) vantage point. Thus, while every account will always be limited and always only partially adequate, they can be very fruitful and, hopefully, bear the "fruit of the Spirit" (Gal 5:22–23). This means that, with Smith as well, I hold that those theological accounts which speak theological truth can only do so as they are graced by God, as they participate in God's incarnational actions in the world, guided by the Spirit and gaining understanding from the Word and through the common grace of the goodness of creation with its cultivation in culture and tradition.

That hermeneutics is ubiquitous and that it is necessary for offering cogent theological accounts of our world are convictions in line with the 'linguistic turn' in twentieth century Anglo-American analytic philosophy and the similar turn in the phenomenology of the Continental tradition. My approach to theological hermeneutics is chastened by this conviction. My thesis is that theological hermeneutics is best understood in terms of holistic paradigms, our best theological accounts of the reality of our world which intertwine the ontologies implicit in our hermeneutics, the specific discernments made concerning the truths of historical existence, and what has come to be the structures of the hermeneutics themselves.

The Linguistic Turn and the Rejection of a Foundationalism of Indubitable Beliefs

Richard Rorty considers Anglo-American linguistic philosophy and Continental phenomenology the results of the lack of success found in quests for neutral viewpoints or criteria external to one's method.[1] Recalling modern attempts to transform philosophy into a science which could be disconfirmed, he makes the historical claim concerning modern philosophers that "every philosophical rebel has tried to be 'presuppositionless,' but none has succeeded."[2] He further holds that "to know what method to adopt, one must already have arrived at some metaphysical and some epistemological conclusions."[3] But defending them by using one's own method brings charges of circularity, while, on the other hand, not defending them entails begging the question of the truth of one's system. Yet he recognizes that, of course, philosophy does "progress" in that ideas change. Be that as it may, how do we know we are going in the right direction? For Rorty, there is, essentially no solution beyond the proclivities of communities: "There is nothing to be said to this, except that in philosophy, as in politics and religion, we are naturally inclined to define 'progress' as movement toward a contemporary consensus . . . one's standards for philosophical success are dependent upon one's substantive philosophical views."[4] What the focus on linguistic philosophy in contemporary philosophy has done is to stir debates centering around "the view that philosophical problems are problems which may be solved (or dissolved) either by reforming language, or by understanding more about the language we presently use."[5]

This has entailed a turn to tradition and a contextualized understanding of rationality. And it has led, in the theological world like others, to approaches which understand theological discourse in relation to communities and language. For example, the postliberalism of George Lindbeck holds that doctrines function for the Church like "idioms for the construing of reality and living of life."[6] Not just for postliberals, but also for others who have made the 'linguistic turn,' language is not just designative—a tool for putting labels on objects—but also constitutive of the social nature of

---

1. Rorty, *The Linguistic Turn*, 1–39.
2. Rorty, *The Linguistic Turn*, 1.
3. Rorty, *The Linguistic Turn*.
4. Rorty, *The Linguistic Turn*, 2.
5. Rorty, *The Linguistic Turn*, 3.
6. Lindbeck, *The Nature of Doctrine*, 18.

human existence.[7] As Kevin Vanhoozer puts it, "'language' thus stands for the socially constructed order within which we think and move and have our being."[8] He links the 'linguistic turn' to postmodernism which, as a "philosophical and theoretical" turn, is identifiable by its rejection of 'reason' as a neutral and disinterested perspective for the pursuit of justice: "Specifically, postmodern theory rejects the following modern postulates: (1) that reason is absolute and universal (2) that individuals are autonomous, able to transcend their place in history, class, and culture (3) that universal principles and procedures are objective whereas preferences are subjective."[9] In Jean-François Lyotard's famous phrase, the postmodern condition is "incredulity toward metanarratives," as there is no one true master story that is substantiated by autonomous and universal reason.[10] Vanhoozer, though, questions Lyotard's dismissal of grand stories in a manner similar to my approach. Is not Lyotard's dismissal itself a "performative self-contradiction"? As Vanhoozer puts it: "Lyotard dismisses metanarratives, but does he not present his own account in metanarrative terms, that is, as the 'true' story of knowledge?"[11] Is it actually not more consistent and honest to recognize one's own accounts as ultimately relying on a grand story, though without holding that it is the only story that can be told which has been provided by universal, autonomous reason?[12]

Murphy and Brad Kallenberg consider this situation in the Anglo-American context, but in reference to its Cartesian background. Descartes' image of human nature as a thinking thing, somehow distinct but residing within the extension of the human body, is at the root of modern epistemological foundationalism: "the real 'I' is an observer in the mind, looking at mental representations of what is outside."[13] The 'Cartesian theater' of the solitary knower, they contend, was the result of the socio-political conditions as well as the corpuscular physics of his day.[14] They find that the

7. The use of the terms 'designative' and 'constitutive' here follow Charles Taylor's approach to language and philosophical anthropology as explained below.

8. Vanhoozer, "Theology and the Condition of Postmodernity," 13.

9. Vanhoozer, "Theology and the Condition of Postmodernity," 8.

10. Vanhoozer, "Theology and the Condition of Postmodernity," 9–12. Vanhoozer cites Lyotard, *The Postmodern Condition*.

11. Vanhoozer, "Theology and the Condition of Postmodernity," 10n14.

12. James K. A. Smith argues that Lyotard's criticism of metanarratives (*grand récits*) is not simply of all grand stories. It is of those which "also claim to be able to legitimate or prove the story's claim by an appeal to universal reason" (Smith, *Who's Afraid of Postmodernism?*, 65; see also 59–79).

13. Murphy and Kallenberg, "Anglo-American Postmodernity," 27.

14. Murphy and Kallenberg, "Anglo-American Postmodernity," 27–28. Murphy

critique of this picture of knowing and its attendant referential notion of language by Ludwig Wittgenstein has been key for the reconsideration of language and human understanding in the Anglo-American philosophical and theological worlds:

> Wittgenstein's point is that language does not *refer*, or *picture*, or *correspond to*, some nonlinguistic reality; there is no way for us to imagine that to which language corresponds ('a state of affairs,' 'the world,' 'reality,' etc.) except in terms of the very language that this 'reality' is supposed to be considered in isolation of. Rather, learning a language is an irreducibly social enterprise by which a child is trained in a communal mode of living.[15]

Rather than trying to overcome language, a futile effort, "clarity begins with an acknowledgment of the irreducibly social character of human experience and the intrinsic relation of human experience to the real world."[16]

But does this also rule out realism, that is, the philosophical conviction that has been traditionally construed as holding that our knowledge is reflective of a reality existing outside of our minds?[17] My contention here is that one would have to answer in the affirmative if, by realism, what is meant is one correct account produced by the engagement of a universally available reason, autonomous from culture, tradition or special revelation that corresponds to reality as it actually and statically is, even if it comes in a 'critical' form. But such a version of realism and its correlating rejection found in non-realism are not the only options. They could be exhaustive options if we take as the universally true perspective that of the tradition of modern philosophical anthropology with its attendant disengaged and atomistic notions of human agency, which, in turn, have given greater credence to the naturalist worldview.[18] A hermeneutical realism, I maintain,

---

and Kallenberg succinctly explain the socio-political background to Cartesian epistemology: "Stephen Toulmin and others provide a plausible account of why Descartes's quest for absolutely certain foundations seemed so important in his historical location: social and political life could no longer be based on the authorities of the past because these authorities' divergent claims had led Europe into the chaos of the Thirty Years War. The desire to find rational agreement beyond the bounds of religious and political parties led to a quest for knowledge that was general and timeless rather than local and timely—in other words, to the quest for universal theory" (Murphy and Kallenberg, "Anglo-American Postmodernity," 27). Murphy and Kallenberg cite Toulmin, *Cosmopolis*, and Meyering, *Historical Roots of Cognitive Science*.

15. Murphy and Kallenberg, "Anglo-American Postmodernity," 34.

16. Murphy and Kallenberg, "Anglo-American Postmodernity," 35.

17. Grenz and Franke, *Beyond Foundationalism*, 31.

18. See Taylor, *Human Agency and Language*, 1–12.

could answer this question negatively as it insists on the fallibility and finitude of human interpretation, of all understanding as creaturely and rooted
in traditions, while still insisting on the reality of dynamic presences which
are known, in some aspects or others, more adequately or less, honestly or
deceitfully, helpfully or problematically, and in vast and complex mixes of
the above. We conceptualize our worlds differently and thus categorize our
experiences differently, experiences which we are able to have in the first
place because of our ability to relate to that reality through language. So, in
the first place, we have different experiences based on our pasts and present
agendas. This means that multiple true things can be said. But also, untruths
and distortions can still often be distinguished from truths. And almost all
of our claims require contextual qualification, though theology is the domain in which the most universal truths are spoken, even as they always
come from particular contexts.

However, Stanley Grenz and John Franke find that much of conservative Protestant American theology has not taken this route but rather has
embraced the foundationalist approach of overcoming uncertainty by finding unquestioned beliefs or first principles from which to begin. Whereas
liberal modernists looked to experience to ground these principles, con-
servatives grounded the truth of Christian doctrine by a simple appeal to
the Bible's inerrancy.[19] The naïve form of this appeal can be seen in each of
my exemplars of the original Classical Pentecostal hermeneutic (in chapter
2 of *Theological Hermeneutics*), though the Bible's inerrancy or reliability
tends to be, but is not always, argued for in the Evangelical-Pentecostal hermeneutic (found in chapters 3 and 4). The foundationalist and common
sense approach is not so simply naïve. It seeks to avoid getting hung up
on epistemological problems so that real claims about the content of what
is true about our world can, in fact, be made.[20] And its insights that some
beliefs are dependent on others and that belief systems appeal back to certain basic beliefs or affirmations are claims with strength. Alvin Plantinga's
defense of a softer form of foundationalism, with others in the 'Reformed
Epistemology' camp, represent a sophisticated contemporary defense of
such a position.[21] But with Grenz and Franke, I find it compelling that what

---

19. Grenz and Franke, *Beyond Foundationalism*, 30–38.

20. This can be seen in Thomas Reid's work where, in giving his important modern
articulation to this position, he repeatedly criticizes the hang-ups created by modern
philosophy's system of ideas. According to Reid, holding that ideas mediate human
knowledge of the world creates problems which a common sense approach does not
have. See Reid, *An Inquiry into the Human Mind*.

21. Plantinga, *Warranted Christian Belief*. Grenz and Franke suggest that this soft
foundationalism is actually a communitarian turn (*Beyond Foundationalism*, 47).

is 'basic' is not a simple entity that is given and that precedes the enterprise of theological inquiry and reflection. Rather, "the interpretive framework and theology are inseparably intertwined."[22] I hold this to be the case even if what is 'basic', or, as I will model it, at the core of a paradigm, is engrained in us by the traditions from which we come. Our traditions provide this integration of habits and beliefs, forming in us our basic commitments.

The usual alternatives to foundationalism and its correspondence theory of truth have been coherentism or pragmatism. Coherentism justifies beliefs in their fit with other held beliefs, in their non-contradiction so that truth is in relation to a belief system as a whole. And pragmatism finds truth to emerge as predictions are followed by testing, observation and confirmation in a cooperative effort of a community of interpreters.[23] However, it is possible that the correspondence, coherentist and pragmatic theories of truth can and do function together.[24] And I find that they are best conceived of doing so in an embodied manner which recognizes the roles which physical embodiment, context, tradition and culture play, and thus do not problematically separate belief from experience or statically conceive of reality. Religious believing would thus be understood as a type of experience, an encompassing and massively broad category. Religious beliefs and all other religious experiences would then be, on the one hand, specific to religious traditions and not generic, yet, on the other, not incommensurable with the beliefs and experiences of other humans on account of our common humanity and common world to which we relate. Grenz and Franke, working with similar convictions, find:

> Experience does not precede interpretation. Rather, experiences are always filtered by an interpretive framework—a grid—that facilitates their occurrence. Hence, religious experience is dependent on a cognitive framework that sets forth a specifically religious interpretation of the world. . . . Christian theology, in turn, is an intellectual enterprise by and for the Christian community. Through theological reflection, the community of those whom the God of the Bible has encountered in Jesus Christ seeks to understand, clarify, and delineate its interpretative framework informed by the narrative of God's actions on behalf of all creation as revealed in the Bible. In this sense, we might say that the specifically Christian-experience-facilitating interpretive framework, arising as it does out of the biblical narrative is 'basic' for

22. Grenz and Franke, *Beyond Foundationalism*, 49.

23. Grenz and Franke, *Beyond Foundationalism*, 39–41. There are, of course, many varieties of each of these theories of obtaining true knowledge.

24. Amos Yong argues that this is the case in *Spirit-Word-Community*, 164–75.

Christian theology. As the intellectual engagement with what is 'basic,' theology is a second-order enterprise, and in this sense theological statements constitute second-order language.[25]

My claim is that it is inevitable that we operate with beliefs central to our understanding of the world, beliefs which function to help us gain *faith*ful understanding of our world, through our *epistem*ic, hermeneutic grid. Faith is at the core of a paradigm, though it is not an indubitable foundation. I find such paradigms as not only functioning to account for our world but also as constructive of it as they consider the goal of theology to be the community's response to God's call to participation in constructing a world that reflects God's own will for creation.[26] Likewise, my approach would be consistent with Vanhoozer's canonical-linguistic approach to Christian theology in that the relationship between beliefs and the experiences of Christian life are held to be embodied together in their interrelation:

> Doctrine seeks not simply to state theoretical truths but to em-
> body truth in ways of living. . . . The Christian way is fundamen-
> tally *dramatic*, involving speech and action on behalf of Jesus'
> truth and life. It concerns the way of living truthfully, and its
> claim to truth cannot be isolated from the way of life with which
> it is associated.[27]

The approach to theological hermeneutics in terms of paradigms which I am proposing is then not merely cognitive. It is what gives shape to the embodied and practiced lived experience of Christian *faith*fulness to the Triune God.

Paradigms and Best Accounts of Our World

Though I maintain that Pentecostal theology should not pursue a corre-lationist strategy, privileging other disciplines above itself and necessitat-ing that it meet their criteria, I hold that it is clear that theology can (and

25. Grenz and Franke, *Beyond Foundationalism*, 49.

26. Grenz and Franke affirm the constructive human aspect in developing theology and the practice of Christian living as it participates in God's work in the world: "We participate with God as we, through the constructive power of language, create a world that links our present with the future, or, we should say, as the Holy Spirit creates such a world in, among, and through us" (*Beyond Foundationalism*, 53).

27. Vanhoozer, *The Drama of Doctrine*, 15. Vanhoozer further explains that "the main purpose of doctrine is to equip Christians to understand and participate in the action of the principal players (namely, Father, Son, and Spirit)" in this drama as they insist on audience participation (16).

should) learn from other disciplines and incorporate their findings into its own paradigms. Indeed, the understanding of theological hermeneutics in terms of paradigms I am proposing here draws from philosophy of science.[28]

Thomas Kuhn's publication of *The Structure of Scientific Revolutions* in 1962 was a watershed moment in contemporary philosophy of science. It was in this book that Kuhn coined the use of the term "paradigm" as a view of some portion of the natural world which includes a set of beliefs, methods and values.[29] Paradigms thus provide not only the theories from which the scientist works, but they also provide the rules of the game. As a result, this approach does not consider facts and theories as categorically and permanently distinct. New paradigms emerge to confront the state of crisis 'normal science' finds itself in by reshaping theories and thus reinterpreting facts.[30] What is theory in one paradigm may become understood as fact by

28. The Pentecostal biblical scholar Jerry Camery-Hoggatt has already begun to apply a paradigmatic approach to biblical hermeneutics. Contending for the gravity for meaning provided by the origin of the biblical texts, he nonetheless notes the selectivity, inherent ambiguity, polyvalence and linear nature of human language in *Reading the Good Book Well*, 76–81. This entails that we interpret the Bible in terms of paradigms of interpretation (23–36). He cites Thomas Kuhn's influence on paradigmatic thinking here without noting his attendant claim to the ultimately irrational basis for construals of reality.

Camery-Hoggatt finds paradigms as including four categories in their functionality: predispositions, presuppositions, background information, and protocols. Some, he argues, are wrong while others are right. And while he gives compelling examples of better and worse of each, he only claims that what differentiates the good from the bad ones are that the good are critical, that is, rigorously examined, and that collegial consensus is important for recognizing right ones from wrong ones (32–34). The standards of scientific inquiry—predictability, repeatability, explanatory power and consistency—cannot work as well in biblical interpretation. He argues that, instead, the "master paradigm" for biblical interpretation should be one that seeks to have "replicated the activities the authors expected their readers would engage in" (35).

29. Kuhn, *The Structure of Scientific Revolutions*. *Structure* seeks to play out Kuhn's understanding of the progression (but not progress) of the human scientific endeavor. In it, he finds the history of science to be particularly informative. He utilizes the progression of physics from Aristotle to Newton to Einstein, of cosmology from Ptolemay to Copernicus and Galileo, of chemistry from phlogistic to modern chemists, and other such examples of paradigm shifts to provide pause for the contemporary scientist or philosopher to not be overconfident in the correspondence of her own paradigms with nature itself. Other great paradigms which were held up as representing reality in their own day have been the subjects of scientific revolutions which have overthrown the old paradigms, thus one should be careful not to regard current paradigms as beyond being usurped.

30. Kuhn finds paradigms to be closely identified with what he calls 'normal science' which is the accepted science given in a culture. He finds paradigms to account for nature at multiple levels, although he is vague in articulating this point. He notes that there are paradigms within paradigms. Further, he refers to pre-paradigm activity as a mode of human inquiry that has not yet attempted to pull together a vision of nature into a coherent whole but is instead fragmentary, thus acknowledging that human

a new one. Importantly, he sees sociological factors as also being crucial to this process. Ptolemaic astronomy had its chance to solve its problems, but then a competitor was given the chance at replacing it. He claims that in the history of science, a loyalty to paradigms exists so that the falsification of theories simply by a direct comparison to nature does not really occur. Instead, another candidate must first emerge. The decision to reject a paradigm is the decision to accept another. The comparison that occurs between the two competing paradigms is a judgment between the two as well as one between each paradigm and nature itself. Often times, adherents to a dominant paradigm simply have to die out for a new one to take its place because of the strength of their loyalty to the dominant paradigm.[31]

My conception of theological hermeneutics is similar to this "hermeneutics of nature." Kuhn has seen that the methodological structures of investigation of the natural world and the content which this methodology accounts for are mutually informative. He was reticent to deem one paradigm better than another because of the human inability to ultimately adjudicate this, until he was pressed by accusations of relativism. So, in his 1969 "Postscript" to *Structure of Scientific Revolutions*, added to its second and third editions, he clarifies his position by stating: "Later scientific theories are better than earlier ones for solving puzzles in the often quite different environments to which they applied. That is not a relativist's position,

---

understanding does not always exist in paradigms that are, at least in part, coherent (Kuhn, *The Structure of Scientific Revolutions*, 10–51).

31. Kuhn, *The Structure of Scientific Revolutions*. Ultimately, Kuhn denies recourse to rationality for adjudicating between paradigms. That does not mean that there is not a basis for faith in a paradigm. Rather, he asserts that it cannot be appealed to as rational or ultimately correct. Yet he still claims that there are logical factors involved, although he is vague about their place. But the decision for one paradigm over another must be attributed, primarily, to aesthetic, sociological and psychological factors. His understanding of a paradigm focuses the crucial adjudicator for epistemic decision-making within human communities, and not on some inherent rationality or autonomous reason. Epistemic decisions by individuals are usually the ramifications of these values found in his or her community (144–210).

Yet Kuhn does not adhere to a strong notion of incommensurability between paradigms, recognizing some place of contact between competing ones. He most explicitly does this when he identified five "characteristics," not criteria, for making judgments between competing paradigms: accuracy, consistency, scope, simplicity and fruitfulness (Kuhn, "Objectivity, Value Judgment and Theory Choice," 435–50).

However, there is an inconsistency in his theory because, in the end, his claim to an ateleology of the progression of scientific paradigms is supported by his belief in the ateleology of the evolutionary process, itself a belief formed within a paradigm of scientific inquiry. Yet he privileges this belief in ateleology in forming his theory concerning paradigms as functioning prior to them and not as an understanding itself derivative from a paradigm to which he subscribes.

and it displays the sense in which I am a convinced believer in scientific progress."[32] But he does not work this out. Thus, the modification of this approach produced by Imre Lakatos in his methodology of scientific research programs is a more valuable resource for developing a philosophically-informed Pentecostal hermeneutical realism.

Lakatos' proposal is that of his methodology of scientific research programs (SRPs) which provides a centripetal model of the structure of beliefs.[33] As someone who also drew his ideas from the later Karl Popper, he finds 'unscientific metaphysics' to most often serve as the stimulus for new scientific theories. This allows for both metaphysical and thus irrefutable cores as well as refutable ones. In either case, philosophical assumptions are understood as informing the hard inner core of a SRP. The hard inner core of a SRP includes the methods, theories, and core beliefs of that program that are non-negotiable. To give up a part of the hard core is to surrender the program itself. The hard core also serves as the positive heuristic of the program; the positive heuristic tells the program which paths to pursue, setting the agenda. Around the hard core of the program is the protective belt of auxiliary hypotheses which serve as the negative heuristic of the program. The negative heuristic protects the hard core from objections, whether theoretical or experimental. It seeks to forbid the directing of a *modus tollens* directly at the hard core. The auxiliary hypotheses thus adjust and adapt or are even replaced in order to defend the core of the research program. A SRP is judged by being deemed either progressive or degenerating. It is progressive if it is able to predict novel, new facts. Thus, good empirical predictions reflect theoretical progressiveness. For him, this is not justification but corroboration. It constitutes what he calls a progressive 'problemshift.'

But all of this is not a description of what happens to an isolated scientific theory. It is a description of what happens to a series of theories—to entire systems or research programs. A SRP begins to degenerate when it is unable to corroborate its predictions or account for well-documented observations. It also degenerates when its auxiliary hypotheses are forced to deal with observations in an *ad hoc* manner, thus displaying burgeoning inconsistencies arising in the hard core. Yet Lakatos also warns against reverting to falsificationism. The best theories live with known anomalies and unaccounted for phenomena. History has taught us that in numerous cases it has been unwise to kill a budding SRP because of known anomalies.

In the case of the natural sciences, two or more SRPs should be allowed to breathe, at least according to Lakatos, though one will usually win out. It

32. Kuhn, *Structure of Scientific Revolutions*, 206.
33. Lakatos, *The Methodology of Scientific Research Programmes*.

will win because it is able to corroborate excess empirical content over its rival, even content that was forbidden by the rival. Yet it must also explain its rival's unrefuted content. Experiments do not overthrow theories; rather, they demonstrate their inconsistency with nature. Pressing farther ahead than Kuhn, Lakatos holds that these decisions do involve rationality and logic as they are not just psychological or sociological matters. Thus, the Lakatosian approach affirms correspondence as well as coherence and pragmatic tests for truth claims. Going beyond Kuhn's vagueness on this point, Lakatos sees this progression not just as a series of revolutions but as an evolution. Research programs stand on the shoulders of others, in some cases they stand on the shoulders of programs with which they are inconsistent, yet they do make progress in accounting for the natural world.[34]

Although Lakatos' methodology of SRPs was formulated for a philosophy of science, it offers insights for understanding theological hermeneutics. Nancey Murphy has already appropriated Lakatos' methodology to theological method.[35] Within limitations and with some augmentation, I find that much of Murphy's appropriation of Lakotos is helpful. This is so if entire traditions and types of theological hermeneutics are understood similarly to SRPs. They are ways of understanding reality, as programs for accounting for it, given certain core affirmations and attendant agendas which fund these programs.

Murphy sees this as providing an approach to theology that differs from that found in the history of religions school, where religions are studied utilizing the methods of the social sciences, and that found among dialectical theologians, for whom theology is the science of revelation.[36]

---

34. Lakatos, *The Methodology of Scientific Research Programmes*, 8–101. Of his own method, Lakatos recognizes that he stands on the shoulders of others. He attributes three main streams of thought as sources for his reconstruction of method: "From the empiricists it has inherited the determination to learn primarily from experience. From the Kantians it has taken the activist approach to the theory of knowledge. From the conventionalists it has learned the importance of decisions in methodology" (38).

35. Murphy, *Theology in the Age of Scientific Reasoning.*

36. According to Murphy, the applicability of Lakatos' SRPs to theology is dependent upon: (1) that the description of SRPs is applicable to theological programs (i.e., that it shows there exists, in any given program, a coherent series of theories that have the formal properties of a research program), and (2) that, at least occasionally, some theological research programs are empirically progressive (Murphy, *Theology in the Age of Scientific Reasoning*, 86).

With (1), I affirm that while theology does function as a research program, the focus of her approach is too cognitive and I will affirm below an approach that focuses on human understanding as embodied and thus attempts to better account for the dynamic between living faith and developing beliefs in theological inquiry, reflection and criticism. Regarding (2), the *hermeneutical* part of the hermeneutical realism I am

Murphy uses Lakatos to show how theology can lay claim to knowledge of God "in the age of probable reasoning." But I can only affirm this with her in a modified manner since I am approaching theological hermeneutics in terms of qualitative and linguistic categories rather than the scientific and quantitative ones found in the language of 'probable reasoning.'[37]

Much of the need to borrow from an approach such as Murphy's is to account for the tension inherent in the type of hermeneutical realism I am proposing that must consider *how* theology is to make theological claims *about* the *realities* of God, God's revelation, the nature of our world, the human self and other subjects of theological interpretation, while still taking into account the inevitable contextuality and fallibility of all claims to theological understanding. Using aspects of Murphy's approach is possible even if I would not go as far as she does in her goal of making theology follow procedures quite similar to those of the natural sciences and become something akin to a social science.[38] Murphy and I share the conviction that Christian theology is not just the internal discourse of the Church that has, in the end, no real and transcendent outside referent. But I find that the contextual placement of the people groups among humankind exists "so that people might seek God, even perhaps grope for him and find him, though indeed he is not far from any one of us" (Acts 17:26–27). So, my contention is that while theology is a second order reflection on reality that occurs in programs of theological inquiry that are never neutral or objective, they are still attempts to account for the reality of God. Thus, my approach to

---

advocating entails, with Murphy's notion of 'data,' that what counts as empirical data is in part constituted by the knower and the relation of the knower to the known, and not just to the thing known.

37. Murphy, *Theology in the Age of Scientific Reasoning*, 86–87. Though Murphy more narrowly utilizes 'science' in terms of its Anglo-American sense, theology has been classically understood as *scientia*, as a certain disciplined inquiry into what is. This is a sense which can be understood more broadly and thus is better than the narrower Anglo-American sense which Murphy sees as, essentially, entailing an inquiry which makes empirical progress in terms of knowledge of the world. For Murphy: "Christian theology must begin with the Christian tradition (its revelation and the phenomena of the Christian religion), it must proceed to confirmation vis-à-vis reality external to the tradition—that is, to contemporary sorts of data—if it is to fulfill its role as a science of God . . . if theology is to be a science at all (in the Anglo-American sense of 'science'), then it cannot be merely a study of the Scriptures, but must seek and find some sort of grounding in contemporary empirical data (however 'empirical' may be defined)" (87).

38. See Murphy, *Theology in the Age of Scientific Reasoning*, 168–73. For example, Murphy states: "The judgments to which I have called attention meet all the standard requirements for scientific data. They will not be of the same quality (reliability, replicability) as those of the natural sciences; they may more justly be compared to those of the human sciences such as psychology. Furthermore, discernment being a practice available to any group of Christians, theological experimentation is not at all impossible" (173).

theological discourse assumes that theological discourse is something more than a human projection, refusing to grant the "neutral" ground to reductionistically naturalist criteria.

Murphy's utilization of Lakatos' methodology seeks to distinguish "data" that has a bearing upon the nature of God from that which bears only or primarily on the psychology or history of religion. While I do not think that these types of data are ever entirely distinct from one another, Murphy does helpfully lead the theological interpreter to consider what data is suitable for theology. But what entails data is not a neutral given: "The categories of appropriate data must be determined by the content of the research program itself."[39] And her categories of appropriate data which count for theology represent a broadening of that which counts toward an account of the world away from reductionistically naturalist ones. Her recurring suggestion is that the discernment of Christian communities provides key data for Christian theological research programs. "Insofar as devotion and morality reflect the intentions and actions of God, they provide evidence to support theories about the nature of God."[40] So "the crucial data for theology are the results of Christian discernment."[41] This means that "the practice of making knowledge claims about God's activity in human life on the basis of discernment . . . [is a] Christian epistemic practice."[42] She holds that discernment includes the one discerning and her language, and it would be a mistake to see data as simply external to the discernments themselves. It is also internal and found in the relationship between the discerning community and the things discerned.[43]

---

39. Murphy, *Theology in the Age of Scientific Reasoning*, 130.

40. Murphy, *Theology in the Age of Scientific Reasoning*, 131.

41. Murphy, *Theology in the Age of Scientific Reasoning*, 132. For example, Murphy examines and affirms as "data" the practices of discernment found in Jonathan Edwards' understanding of the discernment of experience of God from merely human experience; the Ignatian *Spiritual Exercises*, especially in relation to 'consolation' and 'desolation'; Anabaptist judgment for determining the Holy Spirit's work from one's own opinion by relying upon the community and Scripture; the early Church's need to determine the truth of matters of doctrine, ethics and discipline; and the contemporary Charismatic movement's internal discernment in recognizing the Spirit's presence in one's own life (133–57).

42. Murphy, *Theology in the Age of Scientific Reasoning*, 159.

43. This type of a relational view as similar to Yong's in *Spirit-Word-Community* (see chapter 5 of *Theological Hermeneutics*). As seen in the original Classical Pentecostal hermeneutic, especially in the hermeneutics of William Seymour and Charles H. Mason, and more recently as articulated by Yong, such discernment has been central to Pentecostal theological hermeneutics.

Murphy claims that theology's data is always interpreted according to the paradigm in which it is operating so that "all facts are theory laden."[44] Observations of the world are not simply observations that every other competent observer would have; rather, they are influenced by what one knows and by the language one uses in expressing that knowledge:[45]

> Theories provide patterns within which data appear intelligible. A theory is not pieced together from observed phenomenon; it is rather what makes it possible to observe phenomena as being of a certain sort and as related to other phenomena. This is not to say, of course, that theories create what is seen, only that theoretical knowledge allows the observer to organize the raw data of sensation into intelligible patterns. It does leave open the possibility, however, that there may be more than one intelligible pattern.[46]

As I have contended throughout, this does not apply just to the relation of formal theories and data but to all human understanding. Still, Murphy accounts for the multiple languages that one can speak, within which one sees and comes to knowledge of the world while still claiming that they are accounts of the real world. This broadens what can count as a legitimate inquiry into reality by not legislating criteria beforehand so that marginalized inquiries, like theological ones are in contemporary Western academic culture, might be allowed to compete.[47] And theological hermeneutics will especially use the communal data of discerning God's self-revelation:

---

44. Murphy, *Theology in the Age of Scientific Reasoning*, 163. Murphy finds the relationship between theory and data to be problematic in modernistic methodology: "What appeared to be lacking in the modernist program was a clear sense of how to isolate data that were independent enough of the theoretical structure to count as corroboration of it" (175). She rejects such a possibility in order to offer an alternative way, following Lakatos, of justifying a theory's claims.

45. Murphy, *Theology in the Age of Scientific Reasoning*, 164.

46. Murphy, *Theology in the Age of Scientific Reasoning*.

47. This also means that the authority of Scripture cannot be legislated beforehand either. In a theological research program, Murphy thinks that the authority of Scripture must be built into a program's hypotheses which support its 'hard core' of affirmations (Murphy, *Theology in the Age of Scientific Reasoning*, 168–72). Thus, a Christian theological research program will likely be called upon to justify the role and authority of Scripture and cannot simply beg the truth of such.

The acceptance of the earlier claim that data is always theory-laden levels the playing field for theology to claim that Scripture is an authority, but it is not a simple appeal to authority as self-evident, but one that requires justification, even if this justification is based upon its self-authentication, as for Barth, *CD* 1/1:213–17.

Observation of God's acts and hearing God's word involve various forms of perception other than vision. As in science and, in fact, knowledge generally, we have *theory-laden facts*. In the clearest cases Christians do not say that they heard the words of fellow believers and then interpreted them as God's; rather they hear God speaking through the human speaker; the community's discussion or response attempts simply to find whether others heard it as well. The experience comes interpreted, but this is no objection since that is the regular means by which observation becomes knowledge. The surest way to get from observations to hypotheses or theories that explain them is to begin with observations that are already expressed in language suggestive of the causes or of the explanatory framework. The value for theology of observations already communally described as acts of God is obvious. In short, if God does not appear in the facts, his presence in the explanation will always be suspect.[48]

Thus, the language of observation is intimately linked to the language of explanation. This leads to the question of how multiple coherent interpretations of their respective data concerning a thing can be judged, especially if it is given that there is no neutral arbiter.[49]

This is where the pragmatic test of 'empirical progress' found in the Lakatosian research program comes to the fore. On this model, the program which produces novel facts is progressive, and therefore a successful program, whereas that which fails to make confirmed predictions is degenerative, and therefore a failing program.[50] Despite the slow evolution of

48. Murphy, *Theology in the Age of Scientific Reasoning*, 164–65.

49. I find the question as to if one can participate in multiple paradigms to be an anthropological question which cannot be given a simple yes or no answer. The answer is no in the sense that, at the most basic level, one's 'faith' cannot be transcended without an evolution of a paradigm or a conversion in a paradigm shift. That is, there are certain things which one cannot even conceive of unless there are changes in one's belief-forming processes. Or someone can have experiences which engender new beliefs which were previously thought impossible or could have not even been conceived of beforehand.

On the other hand, the question can be answered affirmatively. It seems that commonly, humans can explore different approaches to reality, or even operate with different belief systems, at the same time. The depths of this psychological state could also vary. It could range from an ability to carefully seek to understand someone else in a manner, that one attempts to see what the world looks like based on the assumptions of another—what Miroslav Volf calls 'double vision' in *Exclusion and Embrace*, 212–20, 250–53. Or it could range towards forms of schizophrenia or, spiritually, what the Apostle James criticizes as "double mindedness" (Jas 1:8) about one's deepest spiritual commitments.

50. While I broadly affirm this pragmatic testing of a research program (or

Christian belief and the conservative tendencies of Christian communities, Murphy finds that there is (and she thinks there should be) openness to new knowledge. A novel fact is that which is not used in the construction of a theory but whose existence is first documented after that theory is proposed.[51] But this should not rule out those new articulations which, while they offer an expectation of new experiences (and how could they not?) provide the language which better accounts for and opens up new experiences of transcendence as producing novel facts. I find Murphy's Lakatosian approach beneficial for construing a way of deciding between approaches to reality—even if its focus is too cognitive and gives too little attention to the role of theology in spiritual formation and discipleship.[52] Approaches that

theological hermeneutic) as described by Murphy, its placement before Taylor's notion of superseding accounts is indicative of my finding the latter a better approach since I find its notion of a 'gain' to be a broader and better account than 'empirical progress.' This is especially because I find the Lakatosian notion of 'empirical progress' to be a notion firmly in the tradition of modern scientific reasoning whereas the simpler notion of a 'gain,' a change in which there is no profitable reason to turn back, allows for a wider notion of what progress can entail while still holding to a pragmatic and experiential notion of advancement.

For Murphy, Lakatos' distinction between progressive and degenerating research programs properly serves as a means of rational adjudication between systems so that she would hold to a 'loosely empiricist' worldview (Murphy, *Theology in the Age of Scientific Reasoning*, 206). I would claim, in conjunction with the articulation of the hermeneutical views I am espousing below, that pragmatic tests show the presence of a reality which bounds accounts of it in the connections one makes in second order claims about realities, theological, scientific or otherwise. These connections move from the level of hypotheses to those of claims to those of articles of faith through pragmatic testing in experience. Murphy could be criticized for employing that article of the 'faith' of the Enlightenment that is 'progress' as, in actuality, a 'criterion' for successful research programs. But denying the recognition of progress as a form of adjudication would not be so simple. Minimally, progress shows that one is on track in one's accounts of reality.

51. Murphy, *Theology in the Age of Scientific Reasoning*, 168.

52. The inattention to the role theology plays in producing religious experiences is understandable given Murphy's project of accounting for these experiences in a manner that legitimates them in relation to scientific forms of inquiry. She is making a way forward for an interdisciplinary hermeneutic as she proposes a "nonreductive physicalism" in her anthropology. See Murphy, "Non-Reductive Physicalism." In arguing for a multidisciplinary approach to anthropology, she holds that "The nonreductive physicalist account of religious experience is valuable in that it allows believers to accept research on the biological, psychological, and social realization of religious experience. However, without an account of divine action, religious experience will be reducible to these lower levels in the hierarchy (of disciplines). The nonreductive physicalist account of nature needs to be completed by a theological account in which descriptions of divine action supervene on descriptions of natural and historical events, but without being reducible to them. We need to conceive of the hierarchy of the sciences as incomplete without theology, and especially to maintain the nonreducibility of theology to other disciplines" (148).

produce new benefits and achieve new ends pragmatically demonstrate that they have in some way accounted for what is real in a productive manner.[53]

That the type of contextualized understanding of our world I am proposing would recognize that every understanding is always already dependent on a faith does not entail uncritical fideism since faith in anything can be challenged. Paradigms, based as they are on certain items of faith, can be found strong (progressive) or weak (degenerative). The objection that there is a hidden foundationalism in the hard core of a SRP or theological research program is thus more of an observation about the inevitability of one's assumptions in formal reflection than a cogent objection to this view.[54] The "hard core" of a program *can* be challenged and found wanting, though it is the most difficult part of the paradigm with which to do so with, and a successful challenge will lead to degeneration and the likely collapse of the paradigm for those other than its most faithful adherents.

If, as I have been asserting, a hermeneutic is always interconnected with an anthropology and buttressed by an ontology which are the result of one's epistemic judgments, then it can be seen that the process of interpreting one's world, theologically or otherwise, is not simply a linear process. It is not just a process of forming a correct methodology and then implementing it. While this does not entail disregard for method entirely, it does revise its role away from that of a first science to a more heuristic role.

Without neutral criteria, then how can I give a theological interpretation of reality as somehow a compelling account of reality, especially in relation to incompatible alternative accounts? And how does such a paradigm show it is better than others if it is not the result of a method which uses supposedly neutral criteria?

---

53. Murphy, *Theology in the Age of Scientific Reasoning*, 204. I see this in, for instance, the new reading of God's present work in the world and of Scripture found in the original Classical Pentecostal hermeneutic as it produced a new way of being Christian, one that has not only produced the Classical Pentecostal tradition but has also been the primary tributary to the Charismatic movement and global pentecostal Christianity worldwide, with such a reading of reality contributing to the shape of the Christian tradition at large. This has continued even as this original Classical Pentecostal hermeneutic morphed into the various other types of theological hermeneutics which I have accounted for above.

54. This objection to Murphy's approach is offered by Shults, *The Postfoundationalist Task of Theology*, 63–65. The claim that there are 'basic beliefs,' beliefs which are legitimate for one to hold to without resorting to other beliefs, including belief in God, has been notably advocated by Alvin Plantinga (*Warranted Christian Belief*, 175–86). Perceptions of the world or the laws of logic also form 'basic beliefs' in his version of Reformed epistemology. Such beliefs have 'warrant,' even if they are still susceptible to being 'defeated' by *de jure* or *de facto* 'defeaters' (*Warranted Christian Belief*, vii–xi).

Charles Taylor has both argued against such supposedly neutral start-ing points as found in the tradition of epistemological foundationalism and offered a pragmatically-testable alternative in terms of transitions.[55] He speaks of the normal modern model of foundationalist epistemological reasoning, especially as it regards moral reasoning, as the 'apodictic model' where common premises must be first assumed. While the early moderns found at least a few 'self-evident' starting points, late moderns saw all first principles as ultimately assumptions made on good faith. Thus, for either, it is only possible to use rational arguments with those whom one finds himself in agreement with on basic premises. Taylor sees this 'apodictic model' as having its roots in seventeenth century science which left modern culture with a naturalist bent that denied the place of human moral and spiritual intuitions in accounts of reality. This assumption of a neutral and flat universe "destroyed the Platonic-Aristotelian conception of the universe as the instantiation of forms."[56] In this vacuum, human moral and spiritual intuitions were then construed in either the terms of natural theology or ob-jected to in the terms of the projectionist objection exemplified by Ludwig Feuerbach.[57] But Taylor flips the projectionist objection on its head, even calling his alternative model the 'ad hominem model,' a phrase representing a move anathematized by modern foundationalist rationality, for "what in fact ought to trump the ontology implicit in our best attempts to under-stand/explain ourselves?"[58] And, for Taylor at least, reductionistic accounts or the 'subtraction stories' told by the partisans of modern secularization are not the best accounts of ourselves and our world.[59]

Taylor rejects the quest for criteria in order to adjudicate between ba-sic claims because this quest is inadequate to handle the moral conundrums faced by coming to terms with multiple basically assumed principles.[60]

---

55. Taylor, "Explanation and Practical Reason."

56. Taylor, "Explanation and Practical Reason," 38.

57. See Feuerbach, *The Essence of Christianity*.

58. Taylor, "Explanation and Practical Reason," 39.

59. See Taylor, *A Secular Age*, for his extended argument.

60. Throughout Taylor's writings, and especially *Sources of the Self*, he is often quick to point out that despite disagreements on this deeper level of moral sources, there is often significant agreement about moral claims, such as those concerning human rights from those who hold to different ontologies. He claims that these more fundamental disagreements are often masked by widespread agreements on matters like human rights, and because of the desire for peace: "there is a great deal of motivated suppres-sion of moral ontology among our contemporaries, in part because the pluralist nature of modern society makes it easier to live that way, but also because of the great weight of modern epistemology . . . and, behind this, of the spiritual outlook associated with this epistemology" (*Sources of the Self*, 10).

Rather, he thinks these dilemmas can often be better explained in terms of transitions.[61] One paradigm, with its own criteria not independent from its ontology, trumps another, superseding it:

> You move from A to B via the overcoming of some error-induc-ing factor, such as a confusion, an elision, a too-simple palette of possibilities, and the like. It is clear from the standpoint of B that outlook A was conditioned by this error. The way of A to B was in fact mediated by the recognition of this error, as one is confident that now we are waking and before we were dreaming, because getting from there to here involved waking up. There is an asymmetry here, because, to use Ernst Tugendhat's term, an *Erfahrungsweg* of this (error-reducing) kind leads from A to B, but there is no such way of going in the reverse direction.[62]

First, Taylor understands moving from paradigm A to B as an epistemic gain. Second, against the foundationalist approach of arguing that B is supe-rior to A through third party criteria (C), his supersession argument holds that it is not the result of neutral criteria but that the shift from A to B is error-reducing. Third, again against the foundationalist appeal to criteria, rather than having adherents to both A and B agree on C to adjudicate their dispute and then to observe who wins the contest, this transition model finds that what is really convincing for adherents to B is usually invisible to adherents to A. Moving from A to B involves some type of conversion, of abandoning A for B. But it is not just that there are good reasons which can only be seen from the standpoint of B and not from A, but that this transi-tion involves a change of faith, that is, a change in one's vision or ability to see which usually occurs as one recognizes that such a change will overcome previous errors or obstacles that one's previous paradigm could not.[63] Yet this is far from a claim of total adequacy for such an account, whether sci-entific, theological or moral.[64]

61. Here, Taylor finds significant continuity between his approach to transitions and Kuhn's paradigm shift, Taylor, "Explanation and Practical Reason," 47.

62. Taylor, "A Philosopher's Postscript," 340.

63. Taylor, "A Philosopher's Postscript," 340–42. An earlier form of this supersession model of transitions can be found in Taylor's "Explanation and Practical Reason," 43–53. In it, Taylor finds three models of such transitions. In the first, X and Y are checked against that which are taken as the facts, seeing which can best predict or explain them. The score is kept like a sporting event. The second is stronger, the ability of one theory to incorporate the other and explain both *on its own terms* explains the success of one over the other, of Y over X. The third and strongest is when Y can be shown to be not just as a gain over X but as the superior explanation, the one that can best all other known comers. See also Taylor, *Sources of the Self*, 72.

64. To those who would claim that continual supersession is inevitable and it thus

Taylor understands our epistemology to be that which functions in order to form our best account of reality, and this best account is what it means to best 'make sense' of our lives.[65] But he does not think of epistemology in terms of the self construed by the modern foundationalist tradition. In that tradition of clear and distinct ideas, the subject is, first, ideally disengaged from her natural and social worlds. Second, the self is punctual, ideally free and rational to instrumentally change and reorganize her world to secure a better world for herself and others. Third, as a result of the above, society is construed atomistically in terms of individuals bound together by a social contract.[66] Against the empiricist tradition in philosophy, Taylor finds the necessity of holding to transcendental conditions for knowledge such that there are indispensable conditions for there being anything like experience or awareness of the world. He finds this critique of the empiricists in Kant's transcendental conditions, which focus on the mind of the subject for having experiences, as well as in Heidegger's critique where the knower and the known are a complex together, a 'clearing' (*Lichtung*).[67]

> As subjects effectively engaged in the activities of getting to perceive and know the world, we are capable of identifying certain conditions without which our activity would fall apart into incoherence. The philosophical achievement is to define the issues

---

demonstrates the irrationality of such supersession, I find at least two rejoinders. First, pragmatic tests can and do give us compelling reasons, which we regularly base our daily lives upon, for seeing one paradigm as superior to another. But a paradigm that succeeds another is not necessarily superior because a situation could occur where there could be good reasons to revert to a previous paradigm as superior. And there is no definitive and final way for humans, with our epistemic finitude, to conclusively prove such superiority. Yet this does not preclude us from being compelled to see its superiority given our experience and understanding.

Second, this objection would be an instance of what Pol Vandevelde calls the "future-perfect fallacy" which consists in speaking in the future perfect. In response to Gadamer's use of this fallacy, that "I now qualify what I say because, fifty years from now, it will have been shown that I fused my horizon with the horizon of the text," Vandevelde says, "this future perspective, strictly speaking, cannot belong to interpreters. Thus, an interpreter cannot say, at the price of sinking into pragmatic difficulties, 'My interpretation is true, but of course I can be wrong.' To such an interpreter it could be replied that he does not know what true means, that he does not master what Ludwig Wittgenstein would call the grammar of the term true" (Vandevelde, *The Task of the Interpreter*, 31).

Accounts or interpretations are claims to speak of what is true, and they are usually not claims to total adequacy and are only occasionally claims to definitively accounting for something. In fact, claims to truth could be alternatively considered in terms of drawing out *aspects* of what is real, revealing truth about it to some measure or another.

65. Taylor, *Sources of the Self*, 58.

66. Taylor, "Overcoming Epistemology," 7–8.

67. Taylor, "Overcoming Epistemology," 9.

properly. Once this is done, as Kant does so brilliantly in relation to Humean empiricism, we find there is only one rational
answer. Plainly we couldn't have experience of the world at all
if we had to start with a swirl of uninterepreted data. Indeed,
there would be no "data," because even this minimal description
depends on our distinguishing what is given by some objective
source from what we merely supply ourselves.[68]

Heidegger further shows how we are agents in our world even while we
are investigating it, that we are always standing within language and within
a shared life with others in understanding our world.[69] Taylor, like James
K. A. Smith (see chapter 5 of *Theological Hermeneutics*), gives Pentecostal
theology the ability to follow Heidegger's insights on these matters without
falling into the methodological atheism and amorality embedded in Heidegger's thought.

Additionally, Taylor's notion of a strong evaluation is essential to his
approach here as such evaluations, which are always conditioned by communal and linguistic considerations, are discriminations about that which
makes life worth living. They go all the way down, or, as Taylor puts it, 'up,'
to that which may be called the 'spiritual.' They are discriminations between
"right or wrong, better or worse, higher or lower, which are not rendered
valid by our own desires, inclinations, or choices, but rather stand independent of these and offer standards by which they can be judged."[70] A moral
and spiritual realism is here met with a hermeneutical pragmatism concerning human understanding.

Such an approach can be beneficial for Pentecostal theological hermeneutics, and there are both biblical and experiential reasons for this. Along
the lines already developed by Smith in *The Fall of Interpretation*, a case can
be strongly made that it is modern epistemology that bows before the idol of
certainty in its attempts to overcome human finitude and in its aggrandized
vision of the human. This stands over and against the biblical tradition of
humility before the holy otherness of God and its confessions of the brevity

68. Taylor, "Overcoming Epistemology," 11.

69. Taylor, "Overcoming Epistemology," 12. Heidegger's 'ready at hand' where *Dasein* is always already taking things *as* something before one scientifically investigates
it as 'present at hand' redefines the situation of human understanding of the world so
that one can never simply stand apart from one's shared life with others. See his *Being
and Time*.

70. Taylor, *Sources of the Self*, 4. Taylor's sympathies seem to lay with the Augustinian trajectory of going inward to go 'upward.' See "In Interiore Homine," chapter 7 of
Sources of the Self (127–42). This is similar in some regards to James K. A. Smith's use
of Augustine.

of human life and the limitations of human knowledge.[71] Accounts of human understanding which claim to hold total and definitive claims to knowledge have tended to fail miserably and produce oppression throughout human history.[72] Yet this does not mean that human understanding, theological or otherwise, might be held with anything less than strong confidence.

But must theology always function in paradigms? Must it always be systematic? Is it legitimate, and even more truthful, at least at times, for theology to speak of fragmentation? Can it speak from a fragmented horizon? The multiplicity of paradigms and the truth found in fragmented knowledge function to properly constrain and raise questions, note anomalies concerning our paradigms, and offer reminders that our paradigms are simply our best accounts of our world. My view is not the only legitimate one that can be had or story that can be told.

This does *not* mean, though, that the Christian gospel is just one story among many others because the Christian claim is that it is—ultimately— not a human story but God's story. It is other to our paradigms though mediated by them, a story for which we give our own accounts which cannot, in themselves, simply be equated with God's story. Further, the Scriptures themselves give us sufficient reason to believe that God's story is not a simple and static reality but God's dynamic revelation in the economy of salvation history. And one way to conceive of this in relation to the question of truth in general is with Miroslav Volf, who has suggested that God's truth be considered 'panlocal'—that "God's truth is not simply one among many perspectives, but *the truth* about each and all perspectives."[73] The fragmentary can thus be more legitimate than the systematic if the systematic negates other legitimate perspectives. However, any approach to understanding that operates with any consistency begins to form a paradigm. Thus, paradigms are inevitable, as even a program for deconstruction or fragmentation is just that, a program or paradigm, even if it is one which has at its core noting and celebrating discontinuity and difference.

The Hermeneutic Responsibility toward the Real

As aforementioned, realism has come under significant criticism in contemporary thought as the denial of a one-to-one correlation between human concepts and the things conceptualized has gained ascendance since

---

71. I could equally criticize the opposite error of the total indeterminacy of meaning and utter contingency of reality as just as 'unbiblical.'

72. See Volf, *Exclusion and Embrace*, 193–231.

73. Volf, *Exclusion and Embrace*, 251.

Kant, and has become canonical in much of late modern and postmodern thought. My contention, however, is that some level of correspondence between our accounts of things and the things themselves is necessary, that non-realism is not an acceptable alternative. When pragmatically tested, non-realism is found wanting. I put forth, instead, that a hermeneutical realism is a much better alternative. Such a realism does not mistake its categories or its speech for the world in itself. In fact, this kind of realism recognizes the way in which language comes to constitute the world in which one dwells. On the other hand, it recognizes the otherness of the things of which it speaks and seeks to respect them in this otherness. Rather than allowing for a false epistemic humility to imply the simple indeterminacy of interpretation, it mandates engaging in acts of hermeneutic responsibility toward the real world in its otherness. Yet reality is understood as historical and finite, constituted in previous constructions of the past which are related to and interpreted in the present. Even God's self-revelation is incarnate, as Smith contends in line with Aquinas' principle (see chapter 5 of *Theological Hermeneutics*), so that revelation is received according to the mode of the receiver. In all interpretation of creation and culture, and of course qualitatively more so for God's self-revelation, there is surplus in our interpretation of the interpreted thing and of the thing itself in relation to our interpretation of it. That this entire approach entails that better or worse cannot be universally proven does not deny the truth of this ideal nor its pragmatic function, especially as such ultimately rests in all of creation's relation to God, and even if this may only be eschatologically verified.[74] In the meantime, it is justifiable to affirm the hard core of our faith as we seek to understand God, ourselves and our world as the limited and flawed creatures that we are.

Fides Quarens Intellectum: Faith and Theology

Anselm's classic formulation of theology as "faith seeking understanding" (*fides quarens intellectum*) affirms a helpful and necessary distinction between faith as a first order matter of experience and theology as a second order matter of sustained inquiry and reflection. Its importance for Pentecostal theological understanding has already been pointed out by Smith. In responding to criticisms of anti-intellectualism in the Pentecostal tradition coming from the Evangelical historian Mark Noll, he rejects Noll's identity for theology as that of the queen of the academic disciplines. He is

---

74. This concept of eschatological verification is notably found throughout the work of Wolfhart Pannenberg.

concerned that faith will be pushed under the grid of a narrow version of orthodoxy and not allowed to, in turn, serve to correct theology. Such an understanding like Noll's, Smith contests, conflates faith and theology in a problematic way.[75] He considers that faith is pretheoretical while theology is theoretical.

> When the pretheoretical/theoretical distinction is conflated, faith—which is not theoretical but precedes theory—is forced into a theoretical mode and eventually becomes equated with theological propositions or formulations. Further, the failure to make this distinction creates a confusion between faith and the theological formulations which attempt to articulate or express that faith.[76]

This distinction is even buttressed by psychological research.[77] Beyond this, Smith holds that theological formulations always are exceeded by the experience of faith.[78]

Such a distinction between faith and theology is necessary in the paradigmatic model of theology I am proposing as an understanding of the task of theology. The formal development of a theological hermeneutic is a theoretical project, but one based upon one's own commitments. A program occurs within the assumptions of one's own tradition and with the presuppositions of its participants, both on communal and individual levels, and both tacitly and explicitly. Faith (*pistis*) is that which a community and/or individual have found to be trustworthy through experience of the world. Since, in line with phenomenology's approach to formal inquiry, it is better

75. Smith, "Scandalizing Theology," 225–38. See Noll, *The Scandal of the Evangelical Mind*. The distinction between 'faith' and 'theology' or 'theology 1' and 'theology 2' in Smith's thought is recounted in chapter 5 of Oliverio, *Theological Hermeneutics*. In "Scandalizing Theology," Smith argues that Pentecostalism is not anti-intellectual in the sense of being opposed to disciplined inquiry, though he decries the absolutism of the Fundamentalism that has crept into Pentecostalism as being anti-intellectual. He contends that such is not at the root of Pentecostalism in its origins. Further, he suggests that the lack of interest in bourgeois scholarship among Pentecostals is a result of its traditional location among the poor and in its concern for the poor, which entails a lack of time and resources for leisurely scholarship. Hence Smith speaks of the "Book of *Praxeis*" (Acts) as the Pentecostal 'manifesto.'

76. Smith, "Scandalizing Theology," 232.

77. Daniel Kahneman, in his Nobel Prize winning research on decision making with Amos Tversky, has noted "two generic modes of cognitive function: an intuitive mode in which judgments and decisions are made automatically and rapidly and a controlled mode, which is deliberate and slower" (Kahneman, "A Perspective on Judgment and Choice," 697). The intuitive mode corresponds to lived experiences of faith and the controlled mode to theological inquiry, reflection and criticism.

78. Smith, "Scandalizing Theology," 245–46.

to claim that doing theology is a mode of experience constituted by disciplined inquiry, reflection and criticism concerning one's faith, but it cannot be done apart from or without faith.

The quest for understanding that is theology is a form of inquiry, reflection and criticism that not only makes faith explicit but develops a person or a community's faith. Thus, this distinction cannot be pressed too far but ought to be understood as a relationship between intuitive experience, which has already been established in a person's way of life, and inquiry, reflection or criticism about that faith or the faith of others. Theology relates itself back to faith when its findings become the assumptions or convictions that produce this way of life, which continue this dialogical movement as they again can later be revisited through inquiry, reflection and criticism.[79] The relationship between thought and practice can be well accounted for with another of Charles Taylor's concepts, that of the 'social imaginary.' As an implicit map of our social space, a social imagination is "something much broader and deeper than the intellectual schemes people may entertain when they think about social reality in a disengaged mode."[80] A key aspect of Pentecostal theological hermeneutics is a spiritual hermeneutics which cannot be conceived of individualistically but must be conceived of in relation to larger Christian communities. A spiritual imagination, like Yong's 'pneumatological imagination' (see chapter 5 of *Theological*

79. For example, the reflections of Charles H. Mason on his spiritual experience at the Azusa Street Revival (see chapter 2 of Oliverio, *Theological Hermeneutics*) is an instance where a spiritual hermeneutic, which sought to determine what was particularly occurring in the spiritual battle which he was a part of during his time in Los Angeles, moved into a theological hermeneutic in that he later had a formal experience of reflection where he drew theological understanding from his experience of spiritual discernment. Thus, the discernments he made coming from his spiritual hermeneutic, which was already informed by his theological hermeneutic to begin with, his Holiness hermeneutic, in turn provided further material for theological reflection, for forming his understanding of the baptism in the Holy Spirit. His spiritual hermeneutic served as a hermeneutic of Christian spiritual life which allowed him to reflect on the particularities of his experiences of (what was becoming) Pentecostal faith and, in turn, open up space for both more experiences of Pentecostal living and for his developing Pentecostal theology.

80. Taylor, *Modern Social Imaginaries*, 23. Taylor's notion of the 'social imaginary' differs from social theory, he contends, in three key ways: (1) it deals with how 'ordinary' people imagine their world, which usually comes in images, stories and legends, (2) it is shared by large groups of people and not just theory privy to a group of experts, and (3) it is common understanding, and as such it makes a wide range of practices possible through a shared sense of legitimacy.

Taylor observes that "for most of human history and for most of social life, we function through the grasp we have on the common repertory, without benefit of theoretical overview. Humans operated with a social imaginary well before they ever got into the business of theorizing about themselves" (26). Still, doing theology serves as a special mode of sustained reflection upon all in relation to God.

Hermeneutics), functions as both a subject matter for interpreting God's work in the world and as the horizon from which a Pentecostal interprets.[81] Such a background for understanding together in a social imaginary can never be adequately expressed or articulated in theories because of its very nature as unlimited and indefinite.[82] Though Taylor has shown that theory does, although not necessarily, trickle down into the social imagination, and that is why such a function as doing theology is necessary and profitable.[83]

Meaning, Reality and Hermeneutic Responsibility

Thus, theology seeks to speak, producing more and better understanding. But what it speaks is never simply a given. My contention is that it is the confession of embodied and contextualized actors who seek to speak for themselves and/or their communities concerning faith in that which is ultimate. My further contention is that its task is to speak meaningfully. To speak meaningfully, I contend, is to express a faith that constitutes a world. But it is also to claim that it is an account which can be called true, even if it is never comprehensive or complete in its understanding, that it is always finite and situated.

This means reframing much of the contemporary debate among Pentecostals over hermeneutics. The debate which ensued after some representatives of the contextual-Pentecostal hermeneutic criticized the author-centered hermeneutics of the Evangelical-Pentecostal hermeneutic (see chapter 5 of *Theological Hermeneutics*) assumed an unfortunate and unnecessary either/or choice. The assumption about where the "meaning" of a text lays was considered to be either—as in the Hirschian school of thought—in the author's intentional meaning or—as in the Gadamerian line of thinking—in the fusion of horizons of the reader and the text. The debaters talked past one another. The Pentecostals who followed the Hirschian school emphasized the moral implications of offering valid interpretations of a text which are faithful to the authorial intent that might be identified with regard to the text. The Pentecostals who followed the Gadamerian line of thinking, on the other hand, emphasized the phenomenological aspects of what takes place in the process of interpretation, especially where the

81. The entirety of part 2 of Yong, *Spirit-Word-Community*, 119–218, is the thickest development of such an approach by a Pentecostal theologian.

82. Taylor, *Modern Social Imaginaries*, 25.

83. Most notably, Taylor has argued that the social imagination of the 'modern moral order' in Western democratic culture can be traced to the theories of governance found in Hugo Grotius and John Locke (Taylor, *Modern Social Imaginaries*, 3–22).

reader's linguistic and conceptual horizon fuses itself onto the horizon of the text. But there is an alternative to the mutual exclusion assumed by some Pentecostals who have followed one or the other of these approaches.

In his approach to interpretation, the philosopher Pol Vandevelde has maintained that this either/or choice be rejected for a both/and affirmation. His approach does this by providing an understanding of interpretation as both act and event. He bases this claim on the way in which interpreters do in fact operate. "Most interpreters in their practice would assent to points made by monists and pluralists alike."[84] Those who champion pluralism do want to be interpreted according to what they meant while those who advocate monism are quick to concede in practice that they as interpreters come to texts, consciously and unconsciously, with questions, concerns and methods which they are not neutrally bringing to the text.

> I take this capacity for monism and pluralism to cohabit at the empirical level of practice of interpretation as an indication that the debate between monism and pluralism is formulated in the wrong terms. The two positions constitute not a dichotomy but rather two theoretical positions on two different aspects of interpretation. I call these two aspects act and event. By event I mean the fact that we as speakers and interpreters participate in a culture and a language that carry with them concepts, values, and habits of which we might not be aware, so that our interpretation is also something taking place in a tradition. By act, I mean an act of consciousness: someone interpreting a text makes a statement or an utterance and through his or her act is committed regarding the truth of what is said, his or her truthfulness, and the rightness or appropriateness of what is said, so that, if prompted, the interpreter must be ready to defend the interpretation made regarding these claims.[85]

He thus tempers the claims of the constructivists, that is, those who understand interpretation as a projection of one's own horizon onto a text, and other forms of pluralism, with the moral impetus necessary in the act of interpreting communicative actions.[86] Interpretation is to be assessed from

84. Vandevelde, *Task of the Interpreter*, 3.

85. Vandevelde, *Task of the Interpreter*, 4.

86. Vandevelde explains this in light of interpretation being both event and act: "Interpretation is also an act of consciousness where an intention is expressed through statements, so that interpretation is a performance by a real person who relates to other people. Through their performance (writing a series of statements, presenting those statements in an ordered fashion, justifying the validity of those statements, etc.), interpreters are implicitly bound by what they wrote and committed to their audience, so

both a third-person perspective where what happens during interpretation is examined *and* a first-person perspective where the interpreter has responsibilities in her task.

Seeing interpretation from each of these perspectives alone has entailed a view of "meaning" that has conflicted strongly with that of the other. Vandevelde, instead, offers an alternative account of the meaning of "meaning," a three-fold account. There are three *levels* of the meaning of a text:

> (1) the author's intention—what someone meant by writing the text to be interpreted; (2) the literal meaning—what the text says, given the individual meanings of words and the composed meanings of sentences; (3) the representative content—what the text as a whole means in the sense of what it represents.[87]

This is based on there being both semiotic and intentional aspects to meaning:

> When we put together these two levels of meaning, semiotic and intentional, it appears that these two levels of meaning in one sense precede the speaker: she has to make use of words as existing in her language and she has to borrow what are acceptable intentional states in her community; however, because there is on her part a choice both of words and intentional states, she is accountable for what she said and expressed. When we apply these considerations to a text, its meaning cannot just be either what the words and sentences mean or what the author meant. Meaning, in other words, cannot just be either semiotic (language speaks) or mental (the author's thought). The meaning of the text is both semiotic and mental: it is what the sentences mean as made up of the words written and as chosen by the author as conveying those intentional states that a speaker of this language would understand. Because we have this interaction between two levels of meaning in the text itself, we cannot simply distinguish between two moments—for example, a verbal meaning and the significance this meaning has for readers—as Hirsch does, or between what lies in the text and what we impute to the text, as in Margolis. Before any significance (Hirsch) or imputation (Margolis), we already have two moments, semiotic

---

that, if prompted, they must be ready to justify their interpretation. The mistake of many advocates of pluralism is to focus exclusively on the event of interpretation and overlook the pragmatic aspect of interpretation as act" (Vandevelde, *Task of the Interpreter*, 4–5).

87. Vandevelde, *Task of the Interpreter*, 11.

and mental. The significance or imputation is in fact a third level of meaning, what I call the representative content of the text.[88]

Such an account of meaning offers a much stronger account for the hermeneutical realism I am advocating for Pentecostal theological hermeneutics than the trajectories laid out by the projects of Hirsch or Gadamer.

This is because, I claim, the location of the "meaning" of any thing to be interpreted is a claim which is supported by an entire approach to reality. The theories of meaning which focus on interpretation as event tend to work in an immanent frame which seeks to describe the "is" of an interpretation without prescribing any "oughts" about such acts. The claim, such as that espoused by Hirsch and the Pentecostal hermeneuts who have followed him, that the meaning of a text is in the author's verbal intent is a claim about the moral obligation of interpreters to the origination of a text. It is a metaphysical claim that meaning resides in the author's intent, and it is a moral claim that an interpreter should respect this place as its locale. But it does not sufficiently account for *langue*, the communally available language, nor for the expressive-constitutive role of language which Taylor has argued for and I will recount below.

But this is not to say that the authorship of a text does not have an important role to play in the text's otherness and the responsibility an interpreter has in interpreting it well. Rather, it is to hold that the author is not autonomous but is interconnected with the language she is using and the subject matter which she is disclosing. But the view of the meaning of a thing interpreted which I am promoting here for Pentecostal theological hermeneutics is one that holds that it is something other than what an interpreter herself produces in an interpretation, itself a subsequent meaning-producing activity. My interpreting a written text or other sign comes in relation to my understanding the subject matter (relating to Vandevelde's third level), the *langue* in which the *parole* occurs (relating to his second), and how the author uses the words chosen to articulate his understanding of the matter at hand (relating to his first).[89] By calling what I construct, using these elements, an interpretation, I am making a relational and moral statement that my understanding is not identical with the author's intention nor can it claim authority over the text as its meaning. Rather, I am responsible for it as my understanding or interpretation.

Vanhoozer has pointed out that "author" is etymologically linked to "authority," as both terms are rooted in the concept of origination. The

---

88. Vandevelde, *Task of the Interpreter*, 10–11. The references to Margolis are to Joseph Margolis, "Works of Art" and *Art and Philosophy*.

89. The *langue/parole* distinction comes from Saussure, *Course in General Linguistics*.

modern concept of authorship, he suggests, is related to the Enlightenment "turn to the subject," the author is an autonomous maker of meaning. On such a view, the author is the "Master" and language his "Slave." The rise of historical consciousness and the "linguistic turn" have critiqued this approach by countering that the author (and reader) is really "Slave" to his "Master" language. Instead, he suggests as an alternative that we are, and should view ourselves as, "Citizens" of language. With similar effect as Vandevelde's distinction between "event" and "act," Vanhoozer emphasizes the difference between *langue*, that is, language as a formal code, and *parole*, language in its actual use. While the former refers to the conditions of understanding and interpreting, the latter deals with the function of language in communication.[90] Heidegger, Gadamer, Derrida and the post-structuralists have overemphasized *langue*; Hirsch and author-centered hermeneutic theorists have not sufficiently recognized it. Offering helpful alternatives, both Vandevelde and Vanhoozer make moves toward recognizing what is publicly available in determining "meaning" by working with Jürgen Habermas' notion of communicative action.[91] If, while interpreting, someone is so bold to say what the text "means," as it is normal to do in our colloquial language, the interpreter is usually still implying that there is a difference in the meaning he has constructed in his interpretation and, in its technical sense, its meaning (at any of Vandevelde's three levels), and I am responsible for justifying why my interpretation is a legitimate one, even if I in no way claim that it is the only.

90. Vanhoozer, *Is There a Meaning in This Text?*, 203–4.

91. See Habermas, *Moral Consciousness and Communicative Action*, 43–194. Habermas relies on the structures of intersubjectivity in communicative action in order to develop what he sees as the rules of discourse ethics which will bring about proper and non-manipulative modes of rationally redeeming one's moral claims. His theory of communicative action provides an ethical structure for moral discourse. He recognizes the claims of the linguistic turn by granting that moral discussions are rooted in tradition and language; however, he argues that tradition can and must be criticized.

Habermas proposes that there are three criteria which competent speech acts must meet in order to be valid communicative acts: truth, rightness and truthfulness. A speech act in the objective world, that is, '*the* world' of scientific investigation, is valid if it is true. Sense perceptions lead to constative actions, that is, statements about states of affairs. To perform a competent communicative act in the objective world, one must speak what is true about the objective world. But in the normative world, that is, '*our* world' of human interaction, a speech act is valid if it is right. Rightness, according to Habermas, exists in an analogous manner to truth. The third criterion is that of truthfulness in the subjective world, "*my* world," the aesthetic world of self-expression. This requires sincerity in expression by the communicator. For helpful discussion of Habermas on this matter from a theological perspective, see Vanhoozer, *Is There a Meaning in This Text?*, 217–18, 223–24, 343–45, 400–401.

Yet such a move must still not overestimate the human capacity for understanding. Nor can it shirk its responsibility to seek to understand as it is for another. Recognizing the expressive-constitutive dimension of human language helps, I contend, to better frame the situation of hermeneutics. Taylor has done this by differentiating between two dimensions of meaningful objects or signs: the designative and the expressive. With the designative we explain a sign or word as having meaning by pointing to what it designates, that to which it has reference.[92] Yet this is contested by an expressive-constitutive dimension, anticipated before its wider recognition in late modernity by several German Romantics, especially by Johann Gottfried von Herder,[93] where something is embodied in a way that it is made manifest.[94] And this is the dimension Taylor argues is primary, not the designative. On this view, the whole web of language and its particulars are interrelated and inseparable.[95] And it understands the constant changing and shaping in language as opening a new non-static dimension of understanding reality.

If language serves to express/realize a new kind of awareness; then it may not only make possible a new awareness of things, an ability to describe them; but also new ways of feeling, of responding to things. If in expressing

---

92. Taylor, *Human Agency and Language*, 215–47. Modern post-Enlightenment philosophy of language came to see thought mirroring or representing things and that the role of language ought to strive for transparency. Taylor sees the roots of this theory in Medieval nominalism's rejection of essentialism. Language groups particulars into classes which do not exist as universal essences or Platonic ideas. But an Augustinian (an expressivist theory of meaning) also held the world as a meaningful order, where everything is a sign of God's speech, if we can see it properly. Yet the post-Enlightenment theory came to see language as an instrument of control in the assembling of ideas in mental discourse, mirroring nature. This is why definitions became so important in modern thought (222–27).

93. Taylor, *Human Agency and Language*, 227; Taylor, "The Importance of Herder," 79–99.

94. Taylor, *Human Agency and Language*, 219.

95. Taylor elaborates: "This expressive doctrine thus presents us with a very different picture of language from the empiricist one. Language is not an assemblage of separable instruments, which lie as it were transparently to hand, and which can be used to marshal ideas, this use being something we can fully control and oversee. Rather it is something in the nature of a web, and to complicate the image, is present as a whole in any one of its parts. To speak is to touch a bit of the web, and this is to make the whole resonate. Because the words we use now only have sense through their place in the whole web, we can never in principle have a clear oversight of the implications of what we say at any moment. Our language is always more than we can encompass; it is in a sense inexhaustible" (231).

our thoughts about things, we can come to have new thoughts; then in expressing our feelings, we can come to have transformed feelings.[96]

This occurs in speech communities where the activity of language creates self-understanding in dialogue so that our speech about ourselves also comes, in part, to constitute ourselves.[97] Our naming of ourselves, our world, our experiences, and so on, is itself expressive and constitutive. Taylor thus considers that the activity of language does three primary things. First, we formulate things in language and thus articulate ourselves, bringing things to our explicit awareness, focusing what is expressed and then delimiting its boundaries. Second, it enables us to place things in public spaces and thus creates public, shared space. Third, and critically, it provides the medium for our most important concerns, especially, for Taylor, the moral.[98] On this approach, language does not just point to things; it also discloses worlds, cultures and faiths.

Drawing upon this understanding of language, my claim is that the Classical Pentecostal tradition itself is in part constituted by its expression of faith in its theological language as a response to God's actions. The birth of the Pentecostal movement (which has since become a tradition) itself occurred with the articulation of the expectation of an action of the Spirit in relation to believers as baptism in the Spirit. Since its first articulations, it has since engendered a broadened and (still) developing complex of belief and experience.[99] Even the various articulations about the relation of *glossolalia* to baptism in the Spirit—as "the sign," or "Bible evidence," or "initial, physical evidence," or "a sign"—have variously invoked different expectations and experiences.

On the one hand, I would argue that a chastened form of realism must be maintained as each of these articulations cannot be simply held to be as good of an account of the Spirit's ways as the next. On the other hand, my approach to theological hermeneutics in terms of paradigms also entails the possibility that multiple accounts may, and most often do, provide a better

96. Taylor, *Human Agency and Language*, 232–33.

97. Taylor's understanding of language, and thus human identity, is dialogical: "If language must be seen primarily as activity, if it is what is constantly created and recreated in speech, then it becomes relevant to note that the primary locus of speech is conversation. We speak together, to each other. Language is fashioned and grows not principally in monologue but dialogue or, better, in the life of the speech community" (Taylor, "The Importance of Herder," 98).

98. Taylor, *Human Agency and Language,*" 260–63.

99. This point is illuminated by the manner in which, right at the origins of Pentecostalism, baptism in the Spirit came to constitute something different for Parham and Seymour after Parham's rejection of Seymour's practices at the Azusa Street Revival (see chapter 2 of Oliverio, *Theological Hermeneutics*).

and fuller account of the varied work of God in the world. This is to make the Pentecostal claim that God does not always act in the same ways among all peoples, though God's people are one body and have one Spirit, one Lord, and one God and Father of all (Eph 4:4–5). But we articulate and testify to our lived experience of faith differently.

Such a hermeneutical realism is ultimately an eschatological realism and, as such, is provisional. Since reality itself is dynamic and human understanding finite, our speech concerning it can in no way be conclusive and entirely definitive, grasping it as Vanhoozer's "Master." While the real world is experienced presently, in the Christian understanding what is real in the fullest sense is the future that is in God, in God's kingdom that has already begun to break in, not the immaterial realm of the forms or the effects of matter. It is the coming of the kingdom of God in its fullness. This approach thus stands in line with Grenz's vision for Christian theology that seeks to articulate the truth of God's revelation and future kingdom both faithfully and provisionally.[100] In the meantime, the recognition of the contextuality of the composition of texts, their transmission and their interpreters is the best way to achieve both faithfulness and responsibility in interpretation. Interpretation itself is a secondary meaning-producing event which, as an action of an interpreter and community of interpreters, implies responsibility to the text and those involved with its composition and their communicative actions, as far as such can be construed. The theologian thus works with written texts and other signs as texts to constructively articulate understandings of the world in light of God. Yet these understandings are not just cognitive but are also embedded in the embodied practices of faith in God. Yong envisions this in his understanding of truth in dynamic terms, combining pragmatic, coherence and correspondence notions of truth. Truth is understood as both *aletheia*—as unveiling and manifesting that

---

100. Grenz articulates the implications of Christian eschatology for theological understanding: "The divine eschatological world is the realm in which all creation finds its connectedness in Jesus Christ (Col 1:17) who is the *logos* or the Word (John 1:1), that is, the ordering principle of the cosmos as God intends it to be. The centrality of Christ in the eschatological world of God's making suggests that the grammar that constructs the 'real' world focuses on the narrative of Jesus given in Scripture. Further, the dynamic in the construction of this linguistic world is the Holy Spirit, who by speaking through Scripture creates the eschatological world in, among, and through us. The Spirit seeks to bring us to view all of life in accordance with God's creative program in fashioning a universe in accordance with Jesus Christ, the eternal Word, so that we might inhabit a world that truly reflects God's purposes for creation. In short, in contrast to the driving vision of much of modern science, the Christian faith refuses to posit a universe without recourse to the biblical God who is 'the Creator of the heavens and the earth.' And the only ultimate perspective from which that universe can be viewed is the vantage point of the eschatological completion of God's creative activity" (Grenz, *Renewing the Center*, 255).

which is, and as performative—as one lives truthfully and faithfully. I thus concur with Yong that the full truth of things can only be known in the "infinite long run."[101]

As seen in the Evangelical-Pentecostal hermeneutic, Pentecostals have often embraced—and, perhaps largely still do—an approach to theology that is primarily concerned with developing the right doctrines or belief system. But even a key figure for this hermeneutic like Robert Menzies acknowledges that systematic theology is itself contextualized, differentiating it from biblical theology where our task is to listen to the biblical authors:

> In systematic theology we frequently begin with the agenda and questions of our contemporary setting. We bring the pressing questions of our day to the biblical text and, as we wrestle with the implications that emerge from the text for our questions, we seek to answer them in a manner consistent with the biblical witness. In systematic theology, we do not simply sit passively, listening to the discussion at the round table. Rather, we bring our questions to the dialogue and listen for the various responses to be uttered. Ultimately, we seek to integrate these responses into a coherent answer.[102]

While I affirm that it is Scripture which is meant to norm and guide our theologizing, there is no compelling reason to think that we do not do the same with the biblical texts. In fact, I contend, that we do a better job listening to and interpreting the biblical text when we seek to clarify what questions we are in fact asking of it. So, it will be better to add several other key aspects to the explicit practice of doing theology as Pentecostals. We should also recognize that we draw upon creation, culture and tradition in our theological understanding, as well as on the Word of God, with Scripture being the form of the Word that witnesses to the eternal Word and norms Christian understanding and living. But we do this faithfully only as we allow the Spirit to be our guide.[103]

---

101. Yong, *Spirit-Word-Community*, 164–75. Yong is using Charles Sanders Peirce's term.

102. Menzies, *Empowered for Witness*, 245.

103. Oliverio, *Theological Hermeneutics*, 354–61.

2

Pentecostal Hermeneutics and the Hermeneutical Tradition

Drawing from a number of tributaries, especially nineteenth-century Romanticism, the twentieth century saw the emergence of the hermeneutical tradition in philosophy which moved beyond the Enlightenment's quest for neutral viewpoints and criteria with its situating of epistemology as "first philosophy."[1] For the hermeneutical tradition, the contingent factors of human existence in communities, and the languages that human communities use to express their understandings concerning all human noetic domains, have meant that all human understanding is irreducibly finite, social, linguistic, and contingent, and thus tradition is inevitable rather than an old city to be bulldozed in order to begin (again and again) from a supposed neutrality or nowhere.

That is, the hermeneutical tradition has worked with the strong affirmation that all human interpretation is rooted in traditions and communal understanding which are limited and human, and it has held that this claim is, essentially, a tautology. From the nineteenth-century Romantics to the "linguistic turn" in the twentieth century through the later Ludwig Wittgenstein and Martin Heidegger to Hans-Georg Gadamer to the post-structuralists and Jacques Derrida and the postmoderns, and in philosophy of science through Michael Polanyi and Thomas Kuhn as well as Imre Lakatos, the hermeneutical tradition in philosophy has couched all human understanding as human, finite, and communal. There are certainly large

1. Taylor, "Overcoming Epistemology," 1–19; Westphal, *Overcoming Onto-theology.*

differences in the hermeneutical tradition, yet there is enough continuity to speak of it as a major philosophical approach to the manner in which human interpretation occurs. It is in fact a tradition because it includes such continuity and difference.[2]

Hermeneutics has also had a long history in Christian theology and practices, as the interpretation of Scripture has continually been a major issue for Christian thought and living. From the New Testament's hermeneutics of the Old to Patristic allegorical approaches and Augustine's semiotics to the Medieval "four senses," and then from modern historical-critical exegesis to postcolonial approaches to the contemporary theological interpretation of Scripture movement, biblical hermeneutics has been a central discipline for Christian theologians and practitioners.[3] Late modern consciousness and the hermeneutical tradition have broadened the understanding of what inevitably happens in interpretation and the necessary sources that come into play in biblical interpretation. That is, contemporary biblical hermeneutics has recognized the interdependence between theological hermeneutics, general hermeneutics, and biblical hermeneutics, so as that the failure to recognize their interdependence will result in a less than adequate Christian hermeneutics.[4]

Further, contemporary Christian theologians, like James K. A. Smith, have been pressing the case that a more genuinely Christian theological anthropology and resulting approach to human knowledge will affirm the basic conclusions which the hermeneutical tradition has come to concerning the limitations it places on the finitude and situatedness of human understanding.[5] Speaking of the "literary turn in contemporary philosophy," Kevin Vanhoozer, with attention to its implications for Christian biblical and theological hermeneutics, characterizes this transition where:

> Hermeneutics has become the concern of philosophers, who wish to know not what such and such a text means, but what it means to understand. . . . Implicit in the question of meaning are

---

2. For leading contemporary overviews of the hermeneutic tradition in relationship to theology, see Porter and Robinson, *Hermeneutics*; Thiselton, *Hermeneutics*; Vanhoozer, *Is There a Meaning in This Text?* See Heidegger, *Being and Time*; Gadamer, *Truth and Method*; Derrida, *Of Grammatology*; Kuhn, *The Structure of Scientific Revolutions*; Polanyi, *Personal Knowledge*.

3. See Brown, "Hermeneutics"; Porter and Robinson, *Hermeneutics*; Thiselton, *Hermeneutics*; Vanhoozer, *Is There a Meaning in This Text?*

4. Jeanrod, *Theological Hermeneutics*; Yong, *Spirit-Word-Community*; Zimmerman, *Recovering Theological Hermeneutics*.

5. Smith, *The Fall of Interpretation*; Smith, *Speech and Theology*. Similarly, see Long, *Speaking of God*.

questions about the nature of reality, the possibility of knowledge, and the criteria of morality. . . . We now look at hermeneutics not only as a discipline in its own right but especially as
an aspect of all intellectual endeavors. The rise of hermeneutics
parallels the fall of epistemology. . . . It was not always so.[6]

Hermeneutics is no longer just a matter of philology or technique, but understanding and its conditions. And epistemology no longer rules the day,
and in many realms has been surpassed by the hermeneutical paradigm.
Classical Pentecostalism began with hermeneutical developments which re-
framed regnant interpretations of Scripture and developed the interpretive
quest for deeper fillings of the Holy Spirit which sprang from holiness and
revivalist movements.[7] I have accounted for the Classical Pentecostal tradition as having begun with the development of an original hermeneutic that,
working with new theological constructions that were constructive of this
new tradition, focused on the dialogical interaction between understanding Scripture and interpreting human experiences.[8] Yet as Pentecostalism
further emerged in the twentieth century, the movement-become-tradition
engaged Evangelical and Fundamentalist hermeneutics, which predomi-
nated at the time, and Pentecostals created a hybrid hermeneutic. This
Evangelical-Pentecostal hermeneutic worked with an Evangelical approach
to theology that had most often turned to a scholastic rationalism to defend the legitimacy of Evangelical theological interpretations in the face
of modernisms and liberalisms, though the Evangelical rationalism was
an odd and unwittingly modern form to merge with Pentecostal content
and experience. In this hybrid form, Pentecostals retained their doctrines
but turned to a much different interpretive ethos than in their original
hermeneutic, and their theory even conflicted with what was commonly
practiced in Pentecostal preaching and piety.[9] Later twentieth-century and
now contemporary forms of this Evangelical-Pentecostal hermeneutic often
sought to reconcile this tension by developing a strong pneumatic element
in Pentecostal hermeneutics in order to authentically account for the Pentecostal ethos and tendencies.[10] Other versions of this hybrid hermeneutic,
commonly taught at Pentecostal denominational institutions of higher

6. Vanhoozer, *Is There a Meaning in this Text?*, 19.

7. Dayton, *Theological Roots of Pentecostalism*; Menzies, "The Non-Wesleyan Origins of the Pentecostal Movement."

8. My detailed account can be found in *Theological Hermeneutics*.

9. See Jacobsen, "Knowing the Doctrines of Pentecostals"; Stephenson, *Types of
Pentecostal Theology*, 11–27.

10. See Arrington, "Hermeneutics"; Ervin, "Hermeneutics"; Horton, *What the Bible
Says about the Holy Spirit*.

education, drew more strongly on author-centered hermeneutic theory in the vein of its leading hermeneutic theorist, E. D. Hirsch Jr., and significant emphasis was placed on biblical interpretation in the form of historical-critical approaches that are often characterized as "believing criticism."[11]

Two contemporary counterapproaches responded to Evangelical-Pentecostal hermeneutics as insufficiently accounting for, respectively, the hermeneutical insights of the hermeneutical tradition and the wider agenda of Christian theology. A contextual-Pentecostal hermeneutic arose that began to turn the insights of the hermeneutical tradition to the concerns of Pentecostal hermeneutics. Though at first this resulted in largely unfruitful debates,[12] more fruitful constructive hermeneutical work quickly emerged.[13] Such a contextual-hermeneutic considers all interpretation contextual so that "contextual" interpretation is not a code-word for non-European or non-American interpretation, but, rather, that every and any interpretation is always and already traditioned and contextual. A second response has been in the form of a broader, ecumenically constructive Pentecostal theological hermeneutic, an ecumenical-Pentecostal hermeneutic that has engaged in theological interpretive work by drawing on multiple sources from the wider Christian tradition and has integrated multiple biblical theologies in constructing Pentecostal theology.[14]

Constructing Pneumatological Pentecostal Hermeneutics

This volume [*Constructive Pneumatological Hermeneutics in Pentecostal Christianity*] is a constructive effort that is demonstrative that a new and broader stage for Pentecostal hermeneutics is underway in which new constituents are providing more diverse approaches—in terms of disciplines,

11. See Anderson, "Pentecostal Hermeneutics: Part I"; Anderson, "Pentecostal Hermeneutics: Part II"; Menzies, "The Methodology of Pentecostal Theology."

12. While the Fall 1993 and Spring 1994 issues of *Pneuma* initiated important discussions, I have argued that this initial debate was largely unhelpful as it focused hermeneutical discussions among Pentecostals into unhelpful categories in which participants talked past one another. See my *Theological Hermeneutics*, 190–202.

13. See Archer, *A Pentecostal Hermeneutic*; Archer, "A Pentecostal Way of Doing Theology"; Archer, "Pentecostal Story"; Thomas, "Women, Pentecostals, and the Bible,"; Yong, *Spirit-Word-Community*.

14. This has largely been the tendency of certain Pentecostal systematic theologians. More historically, see Williams, *Systematic Theology*. Exemplars of contemporary ecumenical-Pentecostal theologians would include Simon Chan, Chris E. W. Green, Cheryl Bridges Johns, Frank Macchia, Tony Richie, Christopher A. Stephenson, and Wolfgang Vondey. I see Amos Yong as combining contextual-Pentecostal and ecumenical-Pentecostal approaches.

contexts, and approaches—which are nevertheless pneumatologically oriented and hold to Pentecostal identities. Most of the chapters in this volume stand in continuity with the emergence of the contextual-Pentecostal hermeneutic, though several stand in some level of dissent to it, and others still might be well understood as primarily in continuity with the ecumenical-Pentecostal hermeneutic. Nevertheless, this volume represents a broadening that is primarily twofold.

The first area of broadening is in the multitudinous constitution of the global charismatic-Pentecostal or renewal tradition. Over the course of the past century, Pentecostalism has become a major religious tradition within the wider Christian tradition to be accounted for along with Catholic, Orthodox, and Protestant traditions.[15] While Classical Pentecostals make up a sizable portion of this tradition, a majority of charismatic-Pentecostal or renewal Christians are part of the larger and more fluid set of movements which constitute the majority in this emerging tradition.[16] While our collection still operates with an acknowledgment of the terms of the hermeneutical discussion set by Classical Pentecostalism and its theological agenda, it also lowers the boundaries of the distinctions among Pentecostals to move into the wider world of the larger charismatic-Pentecostal or renewal tradition. It is also demonstrative of the manner in which contemporary Pentecostalism, while still closely related to contemporary Evangelicalism and its Protestant heritage, is no longer reliant upon Evangelical and even Protestant Christianity as it was through much of the twentieth century. The greater Pentecostal tradition now stands on its own resources. To pick up on D. Lyle Dabney's admonition that Pentecostals set aside Saul's armor and take up David's sling by "starting with the Spirit," perhaps this volume may include a number of those slings.[17]

The second area of broadening for Pentecostal hermeneutics which this volume represents is the widened scope of inquiry that involves inter disciplinary endeavors into newer frontiers for charismatic-Pentecostal thought. As the CHARIS Series itself represents, multidisciplinary, interdisciplinary, and transdisciplinary efforts in charismatic-Pentecostal and renewal studies have been underway for some time now, even as it is reasonable to say that the jury is still out on what has been accomplished thus far through CHARIS and other like work.[18] Thus, this project is made up of a series of

15. For example, see the Pentecostal tradition identified as one of the four major Christian traditions in Jacobsen, *Global Gospel*.

16. See Anderson, *An Introduction to Pentecostalism*; Anderson, *To the Ends of the Earth*; Miller and Yamamori, *Global Pentecostalism*.

17. Dabney, "Saul's Armor."

18. See Vondey, "Introduction."

forays into new areas opened up by interdisciplinary engagement, whether that interdisciplinarity functions as just an initial effort to utilize multiple disciplines side by side in a manner that allows for two or more disciplines to illuminate a subject matter, or if they are able to go further toward more integrative approaches that move easily between approaches usually seen as domains of certain disciplines in order to provide new understanding of their subject.

Hermeneutics is suited for this task as an umbrella for interdisciplinary work as it is well understood as a broad and interdisciplinary domain that integrates many of the matters traditionally covered by philosophy, which is an important reason why philosophical approaches open this collection. As the field of hermeneutics is about human understanding, particular hermeneutics function as full orbed paradigms of understanding, with deep faith commitments about reality operating in the core of each paradigm which include multitudinous layers of the ways in which humans and human communities know, feel, and altogether experience their worlds, deep into what the eminent philosopher Charles Taylor has called the "unthought," our deepest tacit assumptions through which we operate. Deep affirmations form hermeneutical paradigms, including anthropological, epistemological, ontological, empirical, and linguistic assumptions.[19] Further, hermeneutical development happens because of the dynamic nature of humanity, human understanding, and language. Taylor explains this dynamic becoming well, especially as it pertains to the affective aspects of human experience, which have often been emphasized in Pentecostal studies:

> If language serves to express/realize a new kind of awareness; then it may not only make possible a new awareness of things, an ability to describe them; but also new ways of feeling, of responding to things. If in expressing our thoughts about things, we can come to have new thoughts; then in expressing our feelings, we can come to have transformed feelings.[20]

Like all other language, Pentecostal understanding is becoming, and that is evidenced by the collection here in this volume. There is new awareness and description for Pentecostal hermeneutics. But not only that, there are new ways of feeling and being as Pentecostals; new expression of thoughts and new thoughts, with transformed understanding and feelings.[21]

19. For further explanation of my understanding of hermeneutics as paradigms, see Oliverio, *Theological Hermeneutics*, 327–42.

20. Taylor, *Human Agency and Language*, 232–33.

21. Since the early 1990s at least, Pentecostal scholars have been quite conscious of the interrelations between right belief and worship (orthodoxy), right affections

And scholars from within the charismatic-Pentecostal or renewal tradition have now developed a generation that is making forays beyond the domains of just biblical and theological hermeneutics. Though, because of the complexities inherent to addressing hermeneutical issues, the chapters found in this volume can only offer an account of, or a program for, or an evaluation of some layer of the complex paradigms that are the hermeneutics which constitute such a broad tradition.

(orthopathy), and right practices (orthopraxy). Land's *Pentecostal Spirituality* is the landmark work identifying orthopathy as central to Pentecostal spirituality and theology, in concert with orthodoxy and orthopraxy.

3

Pentecostal Theological Hermeneutics

Theological hermeneutics is an approach to theology and a way of human understanding concerning life in general. It considers the world in relationship to God as well as human selves and communities in relationship to God together with the affirmation that all human knowledge is a matter of interpretation formed by cultural-linguistically situated persons in communities who interpret what is and what ought to be. Such inquiry can occur, as has almost always been the case among Pentecostals, with a strong affirmation of divine revelation as well as ontological-metaphysical, moral, and even aesthetic realism; that is, with an affirmation of the reality of what is other and beyond, in each of these categories, the interpreter and the interpretive communities' own interpretive constructions. This chapter details the Pentecostal turn to theological hermeneutics and approaches to understanding, noting the recent development of explicit Pentecostal theological hermeneutics, before moving through implicit historical developments and on to contemporary approaches among Pentecostal theological hermeneutics in global contexts. Considering Pentecostal theologies as theological hermeneutics produces insightful understanding for considering and constructing these interpretive approaches since the category addresses powerful underlying considerations for interpretation of God, human selves, and the world.

The Turn to Theological Hermeneutics

Pentecostals have recently begun considering theological hermeneutics as an appropriate and comprehensive approach toward theological knowledge, explicitly reflecting on and developing Pentecostal theological hermeneutics.[1] Considered as such, Pentecostalism has itself been a family of implicit theological hermeneutics of life since its origins, and the Pentecostal traditions have embodied theological hermeneutics in different types among various movements.[2]

Theological hermeneutics affirms the late modern sensibility that culture and the particularities of human development have led to interpretive contexts which form various types of rationalities, in which various commitments about what is true or held to be true are embedded. Such rationalities are linguistic in that language carries constructions of reality within it and thus shapes human experience and understanding from the outset, while, in turn, human experiences shape language, so that this dialectic altogether forms hermeneutical paradigms. As a description of the theological task, theological hermeneutics is then a way of accounting for the manner in which theological understanding emerges from various sources in communities and persons in dialogue with transcendent, spiritual, and theological matters. As a prescription for the task of theology, theological hermeneutics holds that the recognition of the contextual and situated awareness of one's theological understanding is a basic affirmation necessary for the hermeneutical task, and that such contextual self-awareness manifests a responsible and truthful approach to forming theological interpretations.[3]

The turn to theological hermeneutics has followed the hermeneutical turn in philosophy where epistemology has been superseded by hermeneutics and where a return to ontology has taken primacy.[4] The hermeneutical turn in philosophy is an outworking of the "linguistic turn," the movement in twentieth-century philosophy which worked with the insight that ordinary human language development embeds culturally constructed understanding into the ways all persons understand life, and that all human knowledge must be understood in light of this insight.[5] This turn was anticipated by the Romantic philosophers of language, though the turn itself was initiated by Martin Heidegger and Ludwig Wittgenstein, and its hermeneutical philosophy by Hans-Georg Gadamer;[6] all of this was paralleled, at least in some regards, by developments in Anglo-American

---

1. Yong, *Spirit-Word-Community*; Oliverio, *Theological Hermeneutics*.

2. Archer, *A Pentecostal Hermeneutic*; Oliverio, *Theological Hermeneutics*.

3. Vanhoozer, *Is There a Meaning in This Text?*; Smith, *The Fall of Interpretation*.

4. Taylor, *Philosophical Arguments*; Westphal, *Overcoming Onto-theology*; Archer and Oliverio, *Constructive Pneumatological Hermeneutics*.

5. Rorty, *The Linguistic Turn*, 1–39.

6. Gadamer, *Truth and Method*.

"ordinary language philosophy," including that of John Austin and John Searle, but also that of Anglo-postmodernisms as found in philosophers such as Richard Rorty and Willard Quine. Yet it has gone in still more directions, from poststructuralism to postcolonialism and to varieties of postmodern Christian thought in late modern contexts.[7] The hermeneutical approach to knowledge is also found in a large stream of philosophy of science which has considered scientific inquiry as a series of human noetic paradigms and research programs.[8] Apart from its modern rationalist as well as fideist forms, late modern Christian thought has often turned toward hermeneutics as a way of knowing, and theological hermeneutics as a way of best accounting for the breadth of the theological task.[9]

Working in a dialectic with the contemporary tradition of philosophical hermeneutics as its companion, theological hermeneutics focuses on the theological level of a person or community's understanding and practices. Pentecostal theological hermeneutics thus includes particularities from Pentecostal affirmations as embedded in its own "Pentecostal" paradigm. The formative level of embedded theological affirmations, at various levels of development and sophistication, and as also formed by embedded cultural-linguistic understanding in dialectic, forms interpretive grids for understanding the objects of interpretation as an interpretive lens, a way of sensing, and as an affectivity. The objects of theological interpretation for Pentecostals have often included Scripture, reason, life experiences, religious and charismatic experiences, tradition, symbols of charismatic life, and many other interpretive loci.[10]

Theological hermeneutics, while able to affirm the authority of Scripture in Christian revelation, contests the concept that one reads the Scriptures without theological or cultural presuppositions, holding that it is naïve and is a way of implicitly begging the question of cultural and theological claims embedded in any hermeneutic. Rather, Pentecostal theological hermeneutics informed by the hermeneutical tradition usually claim that their theological assumptions form a theological hermeneutic which are

7. Thiselton, *The Two Horizons*; Thiselton, *Hermeneutics*; Taylor, *The Language Animal*.

8. Polanyi, *Personal Knowledge*; Lakatos, *The Methodology of Scientific Research Programmes*; Kuhn, *The Structure of Scientific Revolutions*.

9. Vanhoozer, *Is There a Meaning in This Text?*; Zimmerman, *Recovering Theological Hermeneutics*.

10. The six chapters in the second section on "Sources," [Moore, "Revelation," 53–62; Ellington, "Scripture," 63–72; Kay, "Reason," 73–83; Neumann, "Experience," 84–94; Chan, "Tradition," 95–105; Medina, "Culture," 106–16; Wilkinson, "Worship," 117–26] in Vondey, *The Routledge Handbook of Pentecostal Theology*, exposit these.

faithful to the Scriptures, to Pentecost, and to the continuing charismatic and missional work of the church.[11] Additionally, advocates of Pentecostal theological hermeneutics almost always consider multiple theological approaches as at least potentially illuminating rather than a single doctrinal perspective, while nevertheless maintaining orthodoxy. Ontologies of both the transcendent and the immanent are considered realities to be interpreted, with multiple vantage points considered advantageous as opposed to a single interpretive standpoint as superior to others, even as these almost always differentiate some theological accounts as truthful and faithful and others as false or inadequate, or at least as more or less so.

Explicit Pentecostal Theological Hermeneutics

The first full-fledged development of an explicit Pentecostal theological hermeneutics was not until the turn of the twenty-first century, when the Pentecostal theologian Amos Yong published his second major work, *Spirit-Word-Community: Theological Hermeneutics in Trinitarian Perspective.* Yong recognized the formative importance of ontology and metaphysics upon a hermeneutic so that, in developing a religious epistemology as well as an approach to interpretation of Scripture and discernment of the spiritual, certain assumptions powerfully inform the formation of one's hermeneutic. Thus, theological tenets and emphases, philosophical assumptions-especially ontological and metaphysical assumptions, and an understanding of the human knowing process all work together to form a theological hermeneutic.

Yong has constructed a theological hermeneutic which correlates and integrates a large set of particular philosophical and theological concepts into a hermeneutic, putting forth a theological paradigm which correlates a "pneumatological imagination" with the epistemic-metaphysical pragmatism of Charles Sanders Peirce, and integrates these and other concepts of his philosophical hermeneutic into a trinitarian theology that itself draws from both Western and Eastern trinitarian sources. The result is a "trialectic" of Spirit-Word-Community for contemporary Christian and Pentecostal theological hermeneutics.[12] In recent years, other works have either begun to explicitly address and employ the concept of theological hermeneutics for Pentecostal theology or to basically employ the approach so that

11. Archer, *A Pentecostal Hermeneutic*; Archer and Oliverio, *Constructive Pneumatological Hermeneutics*; Oliverio, *Theological Hermeneutics*; Keener, *Spirit Hermeneutics*; Yong, *The Dialogical Spirit*; Yong, *The Hermeneutical Spirit*.

12. Oliverio, "Amos Yong's *Spirit-Word-Community*."

they might be considered within this hermeneutical school of thought in Pentecostal theology.[13]

The explicit development of theological hermeneutics among Pentecostals began almost a century after the origination of Pentecostalism at the turn of the twentieth century. As classical Pentecostals and Pentecostal theology have largely employed practical and informal theological approaches to interpreting God, humanity, and the world, rather than the philosophical and theological categories employed more recently among some Pentecostal systematic and philosophical theologians, Pentecostal theology through its first hundred years has primarily been embedded in Pentecostal spirituality; that is, Pentecostal theology has primarily occurred through spiritual practices which carry theologies, such as song, story, testimony, prophetic utterance, and interpreted spiritual and general experiences.[14] As a result, Pentecostal theological hermeneutics may well be considered as an implicit yet important category for considering the first century of Pentecostal theology, functioning within types of interpretive approaches in many movements within the formation of the wider Pentecostal tradition.

Development and Types of Classical Pentecostal Theological Hermeneutics

Classical Pentecostalism, which represents many of the core and originating elements of the wider Pentecostal tradition, if now a minority within it, emerged at the turn of the twentieth century with a hermeneutic born amidst holiness, revivalist, premillennial, and (anti-)modernist influences, though with wider cultural worlds, so that the interaction be tween the classical and global Pentecostal traditions is dynamic and interrelated yet distinguishable.[15]

Classical Pentecostal theological hermeneutics may be considered in four basic types. The first is an original classical Pentecostal hermeneutic which was the hermeneutic of origination and birthed classical Pentecostalism. While the original form of this hermeneutic of origination cannot be replicated, since it is not possible to reproduce the cultural conditions and personal agencies from which this hermeneutic arose, this hermeneutic

13. These include Smith, *Thinking in Tongues*; Studebaker, *From Pentecost to the Triune God*; Archer and Oliverio, *Constructive Pneumatological Hermeneutics*; Vondey, *Pentecostal Theology*; Yong, *Learning Theology*.

14. Land, *Pentecostal Spirituality*.

15. Hollenweger, *Pentecostalism*; Oliverio, *Theological Hermeneutics*; Vondey, *Pentecostalism*.

represents an essence or core within Pentecostalism—much of which continues in subsequent Pentecostal hermeneutics. In its historical original form, and subsequently in its hybridization with continuing Pentecostal hermeneutics, it is a hermeneutic of origination: the idea and force of agency within Pentecostal communities produces and originates new Pentecostal understanding and experiences.

Original Theological Hermeneutics

The original classical Pentecostal hermeneutic is a hermeneutic of revelation and origination. It began with the founding fathers and mothers of the tradition-from William Seymour and the Azusa Street leadership to the breadth of the first generation of early twentieth-century North American Pentecostalism to the varied and multi-centered global locations of Pentecostal origins.[16] As a theological hermeneutic, it explicitly elevated the Protestant canon as authority in a dialogical relationship with Pentecostal experiences, producing new readings and new experiences of the text. Such was met by the restorationist ethos in the original classical Pentecostal hermeneutic, where the restoration of the faith of the early church was seen as the precursor to the end times missionary movement which would precipitate the eschatological millennium.[17] These elements met the "full gospel" theology that read Scripture and Christian life through the lens of Jesus as savior, sanctifier, Spirit baptizer, divine healer and soon-coming King, providing further interpretive structure for the early Pentecostal paradigm. This theological narrative has been described as a dynamic that emerges in Pentecostal spirituality where the prophetic in Scripture is fulfilled by present experiences, so that the experiences at the Pentecost event in Acts 2 were identified as fulfilling Joel 2 and other prophecies.[18] This theological hermeneutic of origination is thus productive of theological interpretations of both the present experience and past revelation, even as they usually blend together as these Pentecostal theologies are produced. Nevertheless, at least in principle, at the essence of Pentecostal hermeneutics there has remained the principle that Scripture should be interpreting us, and only, in turn, does the believer interpret Scripture; Pentecostal hermeneutics is a hermeneutic of encounter.[19]

16. Anderson, *To the Ends of the Earth.*

17. Blumhofer, *Restoring the Faith.*

18. Vondey, *Pentecostal Theology,* 16–17.

19. Davies, "What Does It Mean?"

A hermeneutic of origination cannot simply continue unabated, and thus requires stabilization. The three other types of Pentecostal theological hermeneutics that have emerged primarily through classical Pentecostals have each stabilized Pentecostal interpretive approaches in a general area: the Evangelical-Pentecostal in the relationship between the dynamics of revelation and textual-scriptural authority; the contextual Pentecostal with the cultural-linguistic and philosophical underpinnings of spiritual-theological understanding; and the ecumenical-Pentecostal with the larger Christian tradition and the development of systematic theology.

The outgrowth of the original theological hermeneutic in relationship to this quest for stabilization first occurred early in classical Pentecostal history, within a decade of the Azusa Street revival, as the early Pentecostal movement turned toward the older American Evangelical tradition to stabilize its approach to theological development, even as the latter was engaging in the fundamentalist-modernist controversy. This development occurred early on in Pentecostal history in the later stages of the ministry careers of Pentecostal pioneers and during the stage of formulation of early Pentecostal doctrines, developing a hermeneutical appeal to the authority of Scripture which operated in the longer Evangelical Protestant traditions,[20] and which then continued throughout the twentieth century and into the twenty-first century. The earlier versions of the Evangelical-Pentecostal hermeneutic regulated Pentecostal theological understanding through "Bible doctrines," justified by interpretations of Scripture through older Evangelical literary hermeneutics while still retaining the dynamic of newness and revision from the original and originating hermeneutic, creating a new hybrid.

Evangelical-Pentecostal theological hermeneutics emerged during the mid-twentieth century as a quest for a theology based upon a hermeneutic of Scripture that is both a "believing hermeneutic" that engages historical-critical biblical scholarship and a hermeneutic for Pentecostal praxis. Evangelical-Pentecostal hermeneuts considered variations on the inerrancy and infallibility of Scripture and author-centered literary hermeneutics, most often drawing from E. D. Hirsch Jr., the leading author-centered hermeneutic theorist of the twentieth century.[21] They also tended to explore a pneumatic element in hermeneutics. Sometimes this pneumatic element seemed more like an add-on to Evangelical hermeneutics, but more often there was an attempt to integrate this hermeneutic into the whole of Pentecostal approaches

---

20. Jacobsen, *Thinking in the Spirit*; Oliverio, *Theological Hermeneutics*, 83–184; Stephenson, *Types of Pentecostal Theology*, 11–27.

21. Hirsch, *Validity in Interpretation*; Anderson, "Pentecostal Hermeneutics: Part I."

to biblical and experiential interpretations.[22] This hermeneutic worked well to establish official doctrinal theologies for Pentecostal fellowships, as these doctrines found biblical justifications on more sophisticated base than did the earlier Evangelical-Pentecostal theological hermeneutic, yet its philosophical and hermeneutical development often remained underdeveloped in relation to theological hermeneutics across the Christian tradition.

Contextual Pentecostal Hermeneutics

The contextual Pentecostal hermeneutic began in the 1990s from resources latent within the Pentecostal tradition, from the kind of sources that Walter Hollenweger considered the "critical root" within Pentecostalism,[23] which drew on the modern tradition of critical analysis in the quest for truth and knowledge. Yet the move toward philosophical approaches for Pentecostal hermeneutics came at a time when the modern critical project was being deeply questioned, both from within and by its longstanding critics. A 1993 issue of *Pneuma: Journal of the Society for Pentecostal Studies* featured four articles and an editorial, each of which sought to find new approaches for Pentecostal hermeneutics in line with some version of postmodern or Romantic hermeneutics,[24] which initially generated debate with proponents of Evangelical-Pentecostal hermeneutics.

Contextual Pentecostal theological hermeneutics constructed fuller and more thorough going articulations in the early 2000s, with the work of Amos Yong and James K. A. Smith, as well as John Christopher Thomas, Kenneth Archer and the others from the so-called "Cleveland (TN) School." Yong's *Spirit-Word-Community* put forth the theological paradigm of one of the leading Pentecostal theologians as a thickly articulated theological hermeneutic which affirms the contextuality of all human understanding. The work of the early James K. A. Smith provided articulation of a philosophical theology of the limitations, situatedness, and embodied nature of human understanding, along with the ubiquity of interpretation, in his *The Fall of Interpretation*.[25] Yong and Smith, and their contextual Pentecostal hermeneutics, recognized the need for Pentecostal theological interpretation to

22. Horton, *What the Bible Says about the Holy Spirit*; Ervin, "Hermeneutics"; Stronstad, "Pentecostal Experience and Hermeneutics."

23. Hollenweger, *Pentecostalism*, 307–25.

24. Byrd, "Paul Ricoeur's Hermeneutic Theory"; Cargal, "Beyond the Fundamentalist-Modernist Controversy"; Dempster, "Paradigm Shifts and Hermeneutics"; Israel et al., "Pentecostals and Hermeneutics"; Plüss, "Azusa and Other Myths."

25. Smith, *The Fall of Interpretation*.

incorporate philosophical understanding of the cultural-linguistic layers involved in biblical and theological interpretation of Scripture and life.

The Cleveland School has represented a particular development of this hermeneutic, one which arose among American Pentecostal theologians, but which has had broader influence for classical and global Pentecostal hermeneutics, producing a narratival hermeneutic which emphasizes their own contexts. Among these theologians, Kenneth Archer has emphasized how modern Pentecostal narratives produced meaning for modern Pentecostal interpreters as they formed theologies from their readings of the biblical texts.[26] Lee Roy Martin has focused on the affective hearing of biblical texts as a more appropriate approach to Scripture, while still employing critical scholarly methods.[27] John Christopher Thomas had already developed a biblical hermeneutic modeled on Acts 15, where the community's discernment concerning their experiences and biblical texts led them to practical theological conclusions concerning the Christian life.[28] Both Archer and Thomas operate in a school of thought, largely generated by Church of God (Cleveland, TN) theologians, in which Pentecostals draw from their own spiritual and theological wells while retaining an ecumenical spirit. The Cleveland School has also followed the proposal of Steven Land,[29] in which Pentecostal theology is its spirituality, found primarily amidst songs, prayers, wisdom, and practices, and which is centered not just on its orthodoxy but also on its orthopraxy and orthopathy, bringing together right belief and worship with right actions and practices, and with rightfully disciplined affections that drive and motivate Pentecostal living. The Cleveland School thus has continued to produce a theological hermeneutic that involves distinctly Pentecostal approaches to interpretation with an emphasis on the affections which are nevertheless ecumenical.[30]

Ecumenical-Pentecostal Hermeneutics

While other forms of contextual Pentecostal hermeneutics have been arising, ecumenical-Pentecostal hermeneutics has emerged gradually alongside.[31] The relationship between the contextual Pentecostal and the

26. Archer, *A Pentecostal Hermeneutic*; Archer, "Pentecostal Story."

27. Martin, "Longing for God."

28. Thomas, "Women, Pentecostals, and the Bible."

29. Land, *Pentecostal Spirituality*.

30. Green, *Sanctifying Interpretation*.

31. Noel, *Pentecostal and Postmodern Hermeneutics*; Archer and Oliverio, *Constructive Pneumatological Hermeneutics*.

ecumenical-Pentecostal may be understood in line with dynamics of the
particular and the whole, or the one and the many, or the local and the
global as these arise in Pentecostal studies.[32] The ecumenical-Pentecostal
hermeneutic is a theological hermeneutic of (re)integration of Pentecostal
theology and hermeneutics with that of the wider Christian traditions.

The ecumenical-Pentecostal theological hermeneutic has deep roots
in the ethos of the Pentecostal tradition, drawing on the original drive of
Pentecostalism as an ecumenical revival movement, before its early splin-
tering into factions. Thus, the ecumenical-Pentecostal hermeneutic is a (re)
activation of this interpretive movement, to find Pentecostal theology as
both a contribution to and participation in the theological interpretations
of the greater household of Christian faith. As this approach would necessarily generate dialogue with other interpretations of Scripture from other
theological traditions, the dialogical task of systematic theology is most
often employed here.

Development toward this hermeneutic is seen in the systematic theology of Ernest Swing Williams, General Superintendent of the Assemblies
of God from 1929–49. Williams engaged the complexities inherent in the
issues addressed by Christian systematic theology with an irenic tone which
dialectically moved between Pentecostal and other Christian understandings.[33] The approach also functioned as a living theological hermeneutic
among pioneering Pentecostal ecumenists, including David du Plessis and
Cecil M. Robeck Jr. Yet it has been most developed by contemporary Pentecostal systematic theologians.

The ecumenical-Pentecostal hermeneutic is a theological hermeneutic
which draws on the spiritual resources of the Pentecostal tradition and dialogically engages other Christian theological traditions in order to produce
a Pentecostal theology that is also a faithful rendition of the wider Christian
tradition. The contemporary version of this hermeneutic is exemplified by
Pentecostal theologians Simon Chan, Frank Macchia, Steven Studebaker,
and Wolfgang Vondey, among others who have developed this hermeneutic,
including Daniel Castelo, Dale Coulter, Chris E. W. Green, Cheryl Bridges
Johns, Veli-Matti Kärkkäinen, Edmund Rybarczyk, Christopher A. Stephenson, Lisa Stephenson, and Koo Dong Yun.

This hermeneutic represents an important development that moves
away from Pentecostal attempts to stand in contrast to or overcome other
Christian traditions and stabilizes the original Pentecostal hermeneutic's
penchant for newness by countering with the resources of these theological,

32. Oliverio, "The One and the Many"; Vondey, *Pentecostalism*, esp. 9–27, 69–88.

33. Williams, *Systematic Theology*.

and their attendant cultural, traditions. It thus concurs with the contextual Pentecostal hermeneutic, at least basically, on the conditions of human knowledge, while focusing on bringing about a Pentecostal *ressourcement* with the older Christian traditions, while retaining the hermeneutical and theological tenet that all traditions must recognize the authority of Scripture. Thus, its current representatives tend toward an incarnational hermeneutic that, like Smith's approach, finds divine revelation and presence within the created or der, drawing Pentecostalism away from more gnostic tendencies, so that the Spirit is found in the church, past and present, as the church develops its understanding of God and God's ways.

While also drawing on the affections, in line with Land's theological hermeneutic, Simon Chan seeks to draw Pentecostal theology back into the larger Christian tradition through spiritual practices in a process of "traditioning" that forms the theological interpreter, so that Pentecostal Christian spiritual formation becomes central to biblical and theological interpretation.[34] Frank Macchia's use of the dialectical approach to theology, in line with Karl Barth, opened space for his development of an ecumenical-Pentecostal theological hermeneutics. Such can be seen across his works, but perhaps most so in his development of an ecumenical-Pentecostal theology of Spirit Baptism, the "crown jewel" of Pentecostal theology. Rather than to defend Pentecostal doctrine through claiming the superiority of Luke's corpus over other New Testament passages, Macchia broadens the Pentecostal metaphor of Spirit Baptism by drawing from the breadth of the New Testament as well as Reformed and Catholic theological sources in order to construct a theological understanding of Spirit Baptism representative of Pentecostal empowerment in love as well as aspects of the scriptural image as understood in other Christian theologies. In doing so, Macchia has deepened, rather than watered down, the Pentecostal doctrine, through his construction and employment of his version of an ecumenical-Pentecostal hermeneutic.[35] Vondey's dialectical approach can be seen in his drawing on the tensions inherent in the coexistence of Pentecostal polarities: local identity and global pluralism, holism and extremisms in spirituality, ecumenicism and separatism, orthodoxy and sectarianism, social engagement and triumphalism, egalitarianism and authoritarian institutionalism, and scholarly development and anti-intellectualism.[36] Still, he finds the "full gospel" as the centering narrative underlying Pentecostal theology with its inherent

---

34. Chan, *Spiritual Theology*; Chan, *Pentecostal Theology*.
35. Macchia, *Baptized in the Spirit*.
36. Vondey, *Pentecostalism*.

tensions.[37] Studebaker has developed a Pentecostal trinitarian theology which also stands as an exemplar of this ecumenical-Pentecostal approach, identifying a "nexus of experience, practices, doctrine, and tradition" in Pentecostal theology as a dialectic between theology and experience takes place for Pentecostals.[38] Studebaker develops his Pentecostal trinitarian theology in dialogue with the trinitarian theologies of other Christian traditions, resourcing the Greek Fathers, Augustine, and Jonathan Edwards, as well as contemporary theologians such as Catholic theologians David Coffey and Thomas Weinandy and the Orthodox theologian John Zizioulas, in addition to a number of contemporary Evangelical Reformed theologians.

Contemporary Pentecostal theological hermeneutics is thus moving in more integrative directions. Pentecostal theologians have been addressing the need for coherence and continuity while desiring to retain the original impulse and its power. The original impulse to experience the newness and renewal of God in power and love, at the essence of the original classical Pentecostal hermeneutic, gave birth to a series of movements which emerged into a theological tradition, albeit a very decentered tradition, a tradition amidst late modern cultures that serves as a center of continuity for many movements and Christian fellowships. The work of Evangelical-Pentecostal hermeneutics continues in its work of connecting a hermeneutic of revelation with a hermeneutic of biblical authority and textual hermeneutics. That of the contextual Pentecostal continues in connecting the hermeneutic of revelation with a hermeneutic of general knowledge and cultural understanding amidst a plurality of global cultural, philosophical and religious traditions in late modernity. The ecumenical-Pentecostal hermeneutic leads the way in connecting the hermeneutic of revelation with a hermeneutic of tradition and the broader church, incorporating and carrying the Christian tradition in the particularities of the Pentecostal tradition.

Developing Global Pentecostal Hermeneutics

Some recent work by leading Pentecostal scholars has not only sought to integrate the existing Pentecostal hermeneutical impulses but to draw them toward more thoroughgoing engagement with the wider global Pentecostal world, a project that is in an early stage. Nevertheless, this tendency can be seen in the work of Craig Keener, Nimi Wariboko, and Amos Yong, and the typology set forth by Donald E. Miller and Tetsunao Yamamori[39] offers

37. Vondey., *Pentecostal Theology.*

38. Studebaker, *From Pentecost to the Triune God,* esp. 14–26.

39. Miller and Yamamori, *Global Pentecostalism.*

an entry point not merely to Pentecostal socio-religious types but to the theological hermeneutics productive of and resulting from them. Further, local Pentecostal theologies are emerging, and while current trajectories may be tracked, perhaps all that can be well anticipated is that they will likely grow in influence in the twenty-first century.

Keener's *Spirit Hermeneutics* is the most comprehensive proposal for a Pentecostal biblical-theological hermeneutic to date, as it integrates the concerns of Evangelical Pentecostal hermeneutics with the concerns and philosophical resourcing of contextual Pentecostal hermeneutics in the irenic spirit of the ecumenical-Pentecostal hermeneutic.[40] Notable for its resourcing of the internal resources of the New Testament texts themselves, coming as it does from one of the current era's leading scholars and commentators on them, Keener's *Spirit Hermeneutics* provides sympathetic resourcing for the formation of interpretive habits and spiritual-theological convictions from global Pentecostal communities, what he refers to as "'majority world insights.'" Keener brings together Western historiography and global Pentecostal spiritual convictions concerning the reality of the spiritual world and the miraculous, in a move to resource and respect Pentecostal and charismatic Christianity and its local insights for global Pentecostal hermeneutics.

Amos Yong's recent work also represents an integration of the concerns of the four classical Pentecostal hermeneutical types while moving attention more into global Christian and Pentecostal concerns.[41] In *Renewing Christian Theology*, Yong uses the World Assemblies of God's Statement of Faith and draws on global sources in developing a one-volume Pentecostal systematic theology. *Learning Theology* returns to the Wesleyan quadrilateral for resourcing a pneumatically driven theology, while advocating affective spiritual practices for those who practice theological inquiry and reflection. Further, Yong's "many tongues" principle, which has been developed throughout his works, theologically considers tongues as a symbol not just of a personal reception of Spirit baptism but also as the multiplicity of voices, interpretations, gifts, skills, disciplines, and insights coming from all of those who have received and are led by, or even temporarily responsive to, the Spirit.[42] In his total set of works, Yong has put forth the most comprehensive theological hermeneutic from any Pentecostal theologian to date.

If Keener has produced the most comprehensive biblical-theological hermeneutic, with attendant global concern, and Yong has developed the

40. Keener, *Spirit Hermeneutics*.

41. Yong, *Renewing Christian Theology*; Yong, *Learning Theology*.

42. Yong, *The Spirit Poured Out on All Flesh*.

most comprehensive theological paradigm to date, Nimi Wariboko has perhaps put forth the most stretching and groundbreaking philosophical-theological interpretations of Pentecostalism. In a series of writings, Wariboko reflects upon continental philosophy and the implicit theological and philosophical affirmations found in Pentecostal practices in order to find insights into what underlays the many localities of global Pentecostalism, producing new interpretive lenses for Pentecostal studies. In *The Pentecostal Principle*, he proposes that Pentecostalism embodies the "pentecostal principle" as a dynamic principle of life, of God-given energy for existence, which interacts with, following Paul Tillich, Catholic substance and the Protestant principle, respectively substance and reform. He has considered new urbanization in terms of the "charismatic city" where networks of spiritual energy dynamically manifest,[43] and that in Pentecostal practices God's attributes are commonly split from the unity of God's being for their functions apart from the whole.[44] Currently emerging, Wariboko is putting forth an understanding of Pentecostalism as archetypical for the spiritual life of the late modern world and is providing a significant new lens for understanding global pentecostalism that has the potential of bringing together African and Western interpretations of Pentecostal realities.[45]

Conclusion

Theological hermeneutics has emerged in the twentieth century from classical Pentecostal origins through the formation of Evangelical-Pentecostal relationships, a contextual appropriation of cultural-linguistic and spiritual-theological approaches, and an ecumenical perspective formed by larger concerns for the Christian tradition and the development of constructive and systematic Pentecostal theology. Global Pentecostal theological hermeneutics are still emerging, with a myriad of local and regional forms of expression. At this historical point, there does not exist a single Pentecostal theological hermeneutic worldwide. The trajectory of the different hermeneutical types can perhaps be best understood through practical, socio-ethical, and theological lenses found in the structures of global Pentecostal communities themselves and the emphases of different scholars. A classical Pentecostal hermeneutic interprets the Christian life in biblical and otherworldly terms, carrying on traditions of prohibitions in a sectarian approach to theological understanding. Other groups propose

43. Wariboko, *The Charismatic City*.
44. Wariboko, *The Split God*.
45. Wariboko, *Nigerian Pentecostalism*.

a variety of metaphysical and interpretive assumptions concerning the spiritual world through which Scripture and human experiences are read. Holistic or progressive Pentecostals consider living theology to be interpretations of missional action aimed at spiritual salvation, together with social and personal identity and well-being, while again, others react within Pentecostalism against sectarianism and propose reconciliation with broader cultural norms, producing a hermeneutic of accommodation with culture. Local and unanticipated developments are likely to continue to transform the development of theological hermeneutics as the Pentecostal theological tradition moves into the middle decades of the twenty-first century.

4

Contours of a Constructive
Hermeneutic

But hermeneutics, so conceived, is a reflection on the nature
and limits of human knowledge; for it is no longer limited to
the interpretation of texts but interprets all cognition as interpretation. In terms of the nature of knowledge, it emphasizes
the embeddedness of knowledge in historically particular and
contingent vocabularies . . . in terms of the limits of knowledge,
it emphasizes our inability to transcend that embeddedness in
order to become pure reason or absolute knowledge or rigorous
science. In other words, hermeneutics is epistemology, generi-
cally construed.[1]

1. This is from Merold Westphal's essay "Hermeneutics as Epistemology," in
Westphal, *Overcoming Onto-theology*, 49. Similarly, Kevin Vanhoozer explains that
"Traditionally, hermeneutics—the reflection on the principles that undergird correct
textual interpretation—was a matter for exegetes and philologists. More recently, however, hermeneutics has become the concern of philosophers, who wish to know not what
such and such a text means, but what it means to understand" (Vanhoozer, *Is There a
Meaning in This Text?*, 19). Concerning the hermeneutical approach to human rationality, Anthony Thiselton considers that "Exponents of hermeneutics distance themselves,
then, on one side from the naive overconfidence in human reason adopted by those who
fail to recognize the influence of historical and social factors in shaping how we reason.
On the other side they distance themselves from the pessimistic retreat from reason and
rationality adopted by those who ascribe everything to social, historical, and economic
factors" (Thiselton, *Hermeneutics*, 18). For further explication of my accounting for the
hermeneutical approach in relation to Pentecostal hermeneutics, see "Introduction," in
Archer and Oliverio, *Constructive Pneumatological Hermeneutics*, 1–14.

In earlier work, I have accounted for Pentecostal hermeneutics on the levels of general-philosophical, theological, and biblical hermeneutics by attending to the hermeneutical approaches of key pioneers who developed Classical Pentecostal theologies, providing a typology of Pentecostal theological hermeneutics, at least those developed by Classical Pentecostals. Chronicling these up to recent years, I found four major types: an original and originating type which has been productive of a major Christian tradition, an evangelical-Pentecostal type which has fused that original type to evangelical Protestant theological convictions and hermeneutical habits, a contextual-Pentecostal type which has emphasized the human contingencies and communities involved in interpretation, and an ecumenical-Pentecostal type which has deepened Pentecostal approaches by engaging in a theological dialectic with other Christian traditions and their theologies in order to integrate their wisdom into Pentecostal theological interpretations.[2] Of course, by the time these have been accounted for with any adequacy new trajectories are in development, and I have made subsequent efforts at further accounting for Pentecostal hermeneutics.[3] But in the final chapter of *Theological Hermeneutics*, and after accounting for these four major types of Pentecostal theological hermeneutics, I put forth a constructive philosophical-theological approach to Pentecostal hermeneutics entitled "Toward a Hermeneutical Realism for Pentecostal Theological Hermeneutics," and elsewhere have accounted for the role of theological affirmations in producing a Pentecostal hermeneutic.[4]

In approaching the task of constructing Pentecostal hermeneutics, I have focused away from the important discussions of biblical hermeneutics, which fill the pages of Pentecostal journals and the programs of our scholarly conferences, to the structural conditions formed by a variety of sources— from cultural assumptions to anthropological-ontological presuppositions to linguistic habits as well as theological affirmations—which produce a dialectic between the interpreter(s) and Scripture. My perlocutionary point has been that these presuppositions have too often been taken for granted, or at least underappreciated, in accounting for Pentecostal hermeneutics and in debates concerning them, and that a certain focus on these factors is productive of insight for better developing Pentecostal hermeneutics as a needed correction in the agenda of constructing hermeneutical approaches among

2. This accounting for can be found in my *Theological Hermeneutics*.

3. Oliverio, "Theological Hermeneutics"; Oliverio, "The Nature of Theology and Pentecostal Hermeneutics"; Oliverio, "Reading Craig Keener"; Oliverio, "True Religion."

4. This can be found in Oliverio, "Spirit Baptism in the Late Modern World"; Oliverio, "The One and the Many."

Pentecostals. For in reality, my claim is that these presuppositions are often the tacit locations of disagreement in Pentecostal hermeneutical debates, even as the arguments involved in these have at times tended to merely talk past one another or address key points of disagreements rather than engage in more productive discussions concerning their underlying paradigms. What I have tried to contribute constructively is *philosophical-theological reflection on the task of interpretation for Pentecostal hermeneutics.*

The contours of the approach which I have been advocating for concerning Pentecostal hermeneutics identifies with the Abrahamic journey of the hermeneutical realist who *affirms the voice of God and walks in trust with God*, yet also recognizes the human frailties and failures involved in what it means *to interpret and understand what is as a mere human.* That is, a hermeneutical realist approaches the epistemic task through holding two seemingly contradictory affirmations as a necessary dialectic for the interpretive task of forming human understanding:[5]

1. Humans are always and inevitably limited, contingent, contextualized, aspectival-partial, and otherwise situated in all ways in which we seek to know. Thus, the very mode of human knowing at any level of complexity concerning the interpretation of language and all that is culturally formed as symbols and signs inevitably partakes in this. Charles Taylor has well named this initial naming and interpreting of the world the 'constitutive-expressive' role of language as situated persons in cultures understand the world through our inherited languages of understanding and continue to contribute to its construction through new linguistic-symbolic expression.

2. There is actual ontological reality there, that is, 'there is a there there,' not of necessity dependent on human conceptual imaginations. The congruence and resistance of what is there to symbolic-linguistic conceptions pushes back against all deceits and works in covenantal trust with all truth-speech, even as so much of what is there is cultural (in so far is we might distinguish such from the natural) and constructed by we human-hermeneutical social agents. The ontic is manifold, complex, layered, and, in the end, beyond our conceptual grasp—yet truly there.

That is, there is truth to be known among the kinds and types of realities humans know and experience, though we always only know realities aspectivally-partially, notwithstanding the actuality that human communities

---

5. The approach I am referring to here especially draws on the philosophical work of Charles Taylor as developed in his *Human Agency and Language*, 215–47; Taylor, *The Language Animal*; Dreyfus and Taylor, *Retrieving Realism*.

participate in its production. Such a hermeneutical realism affirms a given-ness (a giftedness in its otherness to the interpreter) to what is, a givenness to human understanding which decenters the human from solely providing meaning to all things (refusing the primacy of an anthropocentric ideal-ism), while simultaneously (the hermeneutical side here) recognizing that the only way for humans to understand is as humans whose neurological-epistemic, physically embodied faculties organize what is given to be known (recognizing the insight that is especially linked with Kant's 'Copernican revolution' in epistemology, yet moving beyond it with 'the linguistic turn' in philosophy). Yet we can and must, with all proper epistemic-hermeneu-tical humility, name what is there. This is precisely what many contextual-Pentecostal and some ecumenical-Pentecostal hermeneutics have begun to do well, in more or less sophisticated ways.

There is thus both connectedness and otherness in the human dialectic of understanding which refuses to conflate the 'both-and' of finite-situated interpretation of the ontic into a singularity, or to synthesize and subsume one under the other in a hermeneutical Hegelianism. It respects 'otherness,' and so is unafraid to live in the tension of faithful confidence and epistemic humility, the wonder in a marriage of the kataphatic and the apophatic; it lives in this dialectic and embraces the Abrahamic journey of faith in a sub-lime aesthetic which recognizes interpretive beauty and pain as both found in the human epistemic journey. None of the above here is, of course, novel information or the basis for a revolutionary paradigm; however, acknowl-edging a basic structure such as this one for Pentecostal or any Christian hermeneutics is nevertheless critical for understanding approaches to any sector of it, and here I am ambitiously sketching out broad contours for Pentecostal theological hermeneutics to further develop this paradigm.

The purpose here is thus to further envision the contours of a Pen-tecostal philosophical-theological hermeneutic as I have argued that this is a necessary complement to Pentecostal biblical hermeneutics.[6] Such a philosophical-theological hermeneutic requires, as pointed to in the basic structure above, an affirmation of the 'otherness' of the text—in an ontic status of original and continuing inspiration in a divine-human dialectic, which has led, for example, to proposals among Pentecostal theologians of a trialectic, most notably that of Spirit-Word-community.[7] This proposed tri-

6. As in Oliverio, "Reading Craig Keener."

7. Yong, *Spirit-Word-Community*; Archer, *A Pentecostal Hermeneutic*. The degree to which this trialectic may be present in the hermeneutical approaches of other Pen-tecostal systematic and biblical theologians as well as biblical scholars is an interesting topic for further investigation. The divine-human dialectic is considered, for example, in Westphal, "Spirit and Prejudice."

alectic implies an inherent excess such that there is a Pentecostal plentitude in the text itself, both bounded and also layered and dynamic in its revelatory essence—because Pentecostals interpret the Word 'after Pentecost' in the living Spirit who inspired it.[8] The biblical text thus relates to interpreters situated in formative communities of interpretation and their life experiences, including the experiences of philosophical-theological formation. Because human interpretive formation always occurs over the course of time with the desire to understand diachronic realities, interpreters string together stories, that is, as storied people who interpret and construct stories.[9]

The Story: In Which We Interpret

Pentecostal Christian faith affirms that at the center of what is to be known for humanity is revelation from God, through God's Word and Spirit, especially involving Scripture and the experience of the Spirit in the lives of Christians. Special revelation and contemporary experience of the Spirit integrate with interpreters' conceptual understandings and affirmations of what is concerning the world in general, with these conceptual approaches formed in the cultural and epistemic milieu in the languages (the "many tongues") of those who have filled the earth and multiplied.[10] Pentecostals have especially emphasized the affective and experiential dimensions of theological hermeneutics of Scripture, hearing the Word of God in the expressions of ancient near eastern Israelites and first century apostles as divine discourse with the power to transform contemporary hearers in a continuationist hermeneutic.

In a comparative essay, the Dutch Reformed theologian Dean Deppe set together some gleanings concerning Classical Pentecostal hermeneutics with the particular charismatic-Pentecostal strategy for biblical hermeneutics found in Craig Keener's "Spirit hermeneutics." In doing so, Deppe provided a modestly critical assessment of Keener's reading of Scripture "in light of Pentecost," coming from the former's place in the historic Reformed tradition.[11] In his *Spirit Hermeneutics: Reading Scripture in Light of Pentecost*, Keener detailed out numerous areas of a continuationist Pentecostal biblical hermeneutics, perhaps especially contrasting an eschatological

8. This theme of interpretation after Pentecost can be seen in Keener, *Spirit Hermeneutics*, and is also a theme developed by Yong, as in his *Mission after Pentecost*.

9. How this has functioned is demonstrated in Archer, *A Pentecostal Hermeneutic*.

10. The "many tongues" reference here points to the principle as developed as a major motif throughout the theology of Amos Yong.

11. Deppe, "Comparing *Spirit Hermeneutics*."

hermeneutic of the "already but not yet" in contrast to dualistic and dispensationalist tendencies among Pentecostals. Albeit a polymath regarding the Scriptures and their attendant historical contexts himself, Keener eschewed the tendency to overestimate the noetic abilities and sanctification of Pentecostal interpreters while still emphasizing holiness and the power of interpreting in the Spirit and from within Pentecostal experiential realities. Such an approach, Deppe suggested as a key point of his critique, actually requires greater emphasis on the larger narrative of Scripture. Rather than simply reading Scripture "in light of Pentecost," Deppe recommended that the Christian ought to read "Scripture in light of the cross, resurrection, ascension and Pentecost."[12] Deppe admits that Keener would likely agree that something like this is not only needed for Christian hermeneutics, but that Keener in fact at least implicitly employs such both in his greater corpus and in *Spirit Hermeneutics*, yet he still critiques the focus here on human action among Pentecostals. Deppe believes such an emphasis is the result of reading Scripture in light of the mission of the Church and centering biblical hermeneutics on Luke-Acts rather than the Reformed emphasis on God's grace, and he suggests both a broadening of the biblical sources of formation for Pentecostals as well as a general theological reaffirmation of the doctrine of grace.

Deppe's critique is notable and helpful here for Pentecostal hermeneutics, not because I find a Reformed-Calvinistic critique of Pentecostal theology is needed to refine Pentecostal theology or biblical hermeneutics (we Pentecostals are, in fact, perhaps a little weary in this regard), even if points such as Deppe's critique of the overemphasis on human action towards a more robust theology of grace may be helpful accountability for Pentecostal theologies which sometimes become forgetful on this essential topic. Rather, Deppe's critique illustrates the need for Pentecostal theology to broaden the story it tells to *regularly* include the other key moments of the story of Scripture in its theological hermeneutic of Scripture, in the story Pentecostals tell and read Scripture from—which itself, Pentecostal theologians usually contend, has emerged from Scripture—even as it also is always already informed by the cultural-linguistic formation of its interpreters and interpretive communities, which are typically founded on a certain focus on Acts and the Pentecost event. Broadening our narrative here, I would like to suggest, is a matter of theological maturation for the Pentecostal tradition, of a moving into a theological adulthood where Pentecostal theology can begin to take responsibility for passing on the whole of the Christian faith.[13]

12. Deppe, "Comparing *Spirit Hermeneutics*," 276.

13. In this statement I am thinking, a quarter century later, of Johns, "The Adolescence

Such a broadening story of Pentecostal Christian faith, of course, risks and will lose its identity unless it retains the emphasis on Pentecostal hermeneutics interpreting "in light of Pentecost" (as with Keener) or "after Pentecost" (with Amos Yong) or conscientiously from within the Pentecostal tradition (as developed by 'Cleveland School' approaches) for Pentecostal hermeneutics. That is, Pentecostals might just be able to pull this off so that we could *both* deepen our affirmation of Pentecost *and* draw more broadly from Scripture at the same time. This is the very theological hermeneutic employed by ecumenical-Pentecostal theological hermeneutics already, perhaps most thoroughly modeled by the theological work of Frank Macchia, Wolfgang Vondey, and Amos Yong, leading a score or two of others in the Pentecostal theological guild.[14]

What I propose below concerning the theological contours of Pentecostal hermeneutics considers a response to the need above that elevates other epochal themes which emerge from Scripture's overall narration of the story of humanity with God while considering Pentecost in its place of hermeneutical primacy for the people of God today. The motto of our hermeneutical confession of faith is: *We are the post-Pentecost people of God.*[15] Thus, Pentecost might retain a certain primacy as it is considered in its relationality to these other epochal themes which provide the contours for theological understanding of our communities in mission together today. For this is not a zero-sum game where emphasis on another theme necessitates detraction from Pentecost; rather, Pentecost presupposes and anticipates other themes in the narrative of salvation history. Further, with the ecumenical-Pentecostal theologians, we enrich our theology and Christian traditions through a deepening engagement that broadens and integrates other Christian theological understanding. This means a broadening and deepening of the story in which Pentecostals interpret, drawing from both Scriptural sources and varieties of Christian theological witness.

That Pentecostals interpret in light of story, guided by central narrative convictions, has been especially developed by Kenneth Archer. The particular stories that guide interpretation are inevitably and deeply influenced by our social locations and our attendant points of entry to that which we interpret. Here influenced by Alasdair MacIntyre, Archer has understood all human reasoning to take place in the stories formed by the communities which form persons, and so theological, moral, and spiritual reasoning

---

of Pentecostalism."

14. See Oliverio, *Theological Hermeneutics*, 253–314. Frank Macchia's *Baptized in the Spirit* is a prime exemplar of this approach.

15. As exemplified in (especially the more recent) hermeneutics of Yong, as in *Mission after Pentecost*.

occurs within narrative traditions.[16] While Archer and my accounts of the development of Pentecostal hermeneutics have taken different approaches and have had some divergent emphases and conclusions, one important commonality between us—among many other points of commonality— is in our agreement that the early Classical Pentecostal hermeneutic was necessary for originating Pentecostalism. Pentecostalism does not originate without its hermeneutic, and its hermeneutic centers around a narrative, "'a distinct narrative' which held the similar methods together in a coherent and cohesive interpretive manner . . . [in] continuation of Holiness praxis in confrontation with cessationist Fundamentalism and liberalism," as he puts it.[17] That is, Pentecostalism is a major interpretive development of the Christian tradition, not merely a sociological or ecclesiological development or offshoot of another tradition which requires only minor hermeneutical changes. Pentecostal hermeneutics has been a major paradigm shift attendant with a living faith among the people of God.

The theme of the people of God in a living dramatization of faith—we might say a 'narrative tradition' here—has been notably furthered by Kevin Vanhoozer in his *Drama of Doctrine*, in a canonical-linguistic approach towards a theological interpretation of Scripture and life. Vanhoozer finds that the doctrinal lack in contemporary Christian communities, where feeling guides beliefs (Schleiermacher has triumphed, on some important levels, Vanhoozer seems to concede), needs a correction. This correction comes through the rightful place of doctrines through which Christian communities perform the truth of their faith.[18] Vanhoozer's approach to theological interpretation—of Scripture and life—seems to stand, then, in contrast with that of the Cleveland School of Pentecostal theology and hermeneutics for whom spirituality holds a primacy in relation to the doctrinal.[19]

Yet Vanhoozer and the Cleveland School have much else in common. Central to both Vanhoozer's Evangelical hermeneutics and the Cleveland School's Pentecostal hermeneutics is the quest to retrieve the living embodiment of theological articulation in the life of the Church over and against rationalisms which create a disjunct between faithful theology and the life of the Church. These disjuncts, in actuality, create an opening for the dominance of cultural norms over the people of God, whether the dominance

16. Archer, *A Pentecostal Hermeneutic*, 128–34.

17. Archer, *A Pentecostal Hermeneutic*, 128.

18. Vanhoozer, *The Drama of Doctrine*.

19. The Cleveland School especially includes the work of Steven Land, John Christopher Thomas, Lee Roy Martin, and subsequently Kenneth Archer, Robby Waddell, and Chris E. W. Green, among a number of other established and emerging Pentecostal theologians and biblical scholars.

of known cultural powers or simple local folk theologies. Over and against these, Vanhoozer and the Cleveland School provide theological interpretations of Scripture in order to provide a way of living embodiment of faith for God's people.

As one of the founders of the Cleveland School, Steven Land's trilogy of orthodoxy, orthopraxis, and orthopathy in his landmark work *Pentecostal Spirituality* has provided this noted articulation of a living Pentecostal theological hermeneutic, one where orthopathy, the formation of righteous affections in the believer, plays a critical role in the agency of Pentecostal spirituality, which is its theology embedded in Pentecostal living.[20] Albeit this is true only insofar as a Pentecostal or Pentecostal community is a spiritual-theological community over and above a mere cultural manifestation. Orthopathy means that not just mere feeling but right affections are productive and motivating towards Pentecostal Christian living. Such an affirmation stands in a long line of Christian tradition concerning the power of the affections in forming the self and communities, in many renditions from Augustine's inward sense of desire to Aquinas' Christian virtues to Edwards' religious affections. Affections form moral and spiritual life, and the connections between Pentecostal hermeneutics and the Romantic responses to Enlightenment rationalisms represent a broader cultural-philosophical tradition from which Land and other Pentecostal theologians here at least implicitly draw, abundantly resourced through the Wesleyan holiness side of Pentecostalism.

A Pentecostal philosophical-theological hermeneutic might thus have several key characteristics. One is that it recognizes itself as participating in a living and continuing story, and that the broad context which drives it are persons in communities who think of themselves in such stories. A second is that theological heremeneutics, as they interpret Scripture in a dialectical relationship with a theological interpretation of life, develop into a living dramatization of Christian understanding, insofar as they are not merely assent to beliefs or just cognitive considerations. Rather, as driven by the underlying habits and neurological patterning which guide human understanding and form the embodied gestalts of interpretation together in linguistic communities, theological hermeneutics are lived embodiments of understanding of God, self, and the world. Third, affections play a key role in agency, particularly for Pentecostal hermeneutics. Pentecostals have tended to be people of feeling and action. Attending to affections describes these as deeper moral and spiritual intuitions, while naming as such also prescribes a disciplined way of knowing through feeling, as Land's orthopathy has set out a principle here for Pentecostal theology.

---

20. Land, *Pentecostal Spirituality*.

Fourth, there is this clear need for broader theological narration that would provide a larger doctrinal-theological grid for Pentecostal hermeneutics. Such has already been accounted for and developed in a number of ways. The theological grid of the 'full gospel' has been developed implicitly throughout the history of Pentecostalism, but also recently and explicitly by Pentecostal theologians including Vondey and Yong. Macchia's theology has opened up Pentecostal theology to broader ecumenical sources in an integration with Pentecostal theology, enriching Pentecostal interpretation as a result. Yet there is still a frontier ahead for Pentecostal theology to mature in development of the back-and-forth between its theological understanding, contemporary issues for Pentecostal communities, underlying philosophical and rational development, the integration of other sources of knowledge—from the sciences to the humanities to the practical disciplines and phronesis of common life—and Scripture as the revelation of God in written Word. Still, recalling Deppe's critique here, such a grid should arise from the overall narrative of Scripture, and the proposal below provides an overarching framework for major Scriptural loci under which manifold portions of a Pentecostal theological hermeneutic might operate in a living dialectic between Scripture and life.

The proposal here is that, complementary to the 'full gospel' grid, another might develop that would narrate the epochal events of salvation history: Creation-Incarnation-Pentecost-Eschaton. This is not to claim that this is the Pentecostal theological hermeneutic of salvation history; rather, it is to claim that it represents *a legitimate, helpful, and nurturing Pentecostal theological hermeneutic* through which Pentecostal communities might mature as they come to dramatize and embody such a living hermeneutic. However, such a commonly shared narrative among Pentecostals might open up greater space for Pentecostal theology to engage the world in wider areas with greater shalomic potential, since it draws on a greater witness from Scripture. It may also allow more Pentecostals to find their places in Scriptural stories from epochs beyond, say, on the negative side of the focus on Pentecost and Luke-Acts, the too narrow readings which limit Christian life to a few scripts, forgetting manifold other ones, and (usually) unwittingly betraying the plurality of the tongues of Pentecost for a return to Babel.

Commonly shared narratives function to string together principles of understanding and what is considered the data of historical actualities—themselves interpretive constructions of what is. Put another way, governing hermeneutical narratives string together the *de jure* conditions of human understanding with the *de facto*. They further involve both communitarian-cultural understanding and the underlying proclivities of the persons involved in interpretations so that there is commonality and difference within each. Such narratives are found at the three locations commonly used to picture the hermeneutical task: the narrative world in-front-of-the-text, the interpreter's storied understanding producing understanding, *itself also potentially produced* by the text; the narrative world in-and-with-the-text, the internal sources of the historical transmission of the text in its grammatical and linguistic becoming from its origination through redactions, translations, and printings to its interpreters; and the narrative world behind-the-text, the storied background of the origination and authorship of the text in its enculturated (and for Scripture, inspired and revelatory) background.

My suggestion here, with my fourth point above, is that both descriptive recognition and prescriptive attentiveness to the broader theological narration involved in all interpretation provides a more productive way forward for Pentecostal theological hermeneutics. That is, with more sufficient attention to the ways in which theological understanding has been derived from the world in-and-with-the-text of the inspired Scriptures along with the varied influences of the worlds behind-and in-front-of-the-text, Pentecostal theological hermeneutics might better recognize and live as creative interpretive reconstructions of the embedded theological understandings which govern the narrations of the biblical texts. To this degree, Pentecostal hermeneutics might draw upon the 'theological interpretation of Scripture' movement which has developed in recent years, a movement which has recognized that any developed biblical hermeneutics involve some type of theological tradition which provides background presuppositions which inevitably organize interpretation of Scripture.[21]

Theological Contours of a Pentecostal Philosophical-Theological Hermeneutic

In this section, the purpose is to provide a summarizing sketch of the theological dimensions of this proposal for a philosophical-theological hermeneutic. The nexus of Creation-Incarnation-Pentecost-Eschaton provides the major acts through which the many stories of Scripture might emerge into an ephochal narrative for a Pentecostal theological hermeneutic. Creation places God and humanity in the God-world relation, and it provides an approach for the grammar of Scripture and human experience here that, along with Incarnation, can see a fabric in Scripture as that of a divine-human encounter in the inspiration of composition and the illumination of its interpretation, and in a more general way interpret human experience and general knowledge along these axes. This allows for an understanding of

---

21. As exemplified in Vanhoozer, *Dictionary for Theological Interpretation of the Bible.*

the grittiness of the Scriptural text as well as the world because Creation, in the Christian rendering of it, implies that finitude and fallenness (the latter fuses together with our experience of the goodness of creation in humanity's postlapsarian status) must also always be taken into account. Creation also notes the pregnancy of all things for Christian theological hermeneutics, in that the inherent goodness of God remains within God's creation with attendant potentialities, while the Incarnation marks the axis on which both revelation and the redemption of this creation takes place within the words of the Scriptural texts and in any other way we encounter the living Christ, God with us—Immanuel, the Word become flesh. Pentecost and Eschaton move this theological hermeneutic to the outworking of the redemption. Babel is reversed, and the plurality of tongues marks the outpouring of the Spirit of understanding. This is so that the Eschaton marks all things so that the vision of the new heaven and the new earth calls redeemed humanity and creation from ahead in order to participate in the work of the Spirit who is creating new realities in the present. Scripture and all of life might thus be read in light of this epochal narration.

Such an approach might also be met with the development of a spiritual-moral aspect of a Pentecostal theological hermeneutic, one with the overarching consideration of the wholeness and holiness of God, drawing on the holiness tradition's influence on Pentecostalism. Following William Seymour, Scripture might be read with the spiritual affirmation that God's love takes precedence over power, so that God's love rightly holds all secular and spiritual quests to account. Such would also entail the power of God's holiness, centered in the love of God, as standing in power to transform humanity out of sin and make a new creation out of persons and communities. It might also take seriously Nimi Wariboko's consideration of the pulling apart of the attributes of God in the practices of Pentecostals, for their utility.[22] Moving past this descriptive assessment, it would move towards the unity of God so that the Pentecostal practice of knowing God through Word and Spirit might do so authentically, looking to the Lord's wholeness and holiness rather than merely seeking the Lord's gifts and power. Such a turn takes the Pentecostal deeper into encountering the Triune God rather than seeking some kind of totality, of *Yahweh* worship rather than the attempt to build, grasp, and control a god (an idol).

This may then result in the continued advancement of the hermeneutic of Spirit-Word-community among Pentecostals. The Word is revelation for persons, in an I-Thou encounter with God. The Spirit, that is, the Spirit of Love, might be encountered and understood with a personalist ontology

22. Wariboko, *The Split God.*

as well, as the personal love of God made manifest to each and every situation. Following Clark Pinnock, Word and Spirit might be understood as the particular revelation of God for all humanity, in the Word, and the universal love of God made manifest amidst each and every situation for every human particularity.[23] The transcendence and immanence of God are here in dialectic, in both the real presence of the Lord within embodied, inconsistent, flawed persons, yet the otherness of God remains over and against us in a God who is for us. The Triune God is encountered as the three divine Persons in revelation to humanity, and as the one Communion in whom we live and move and have our being. Human experience of being drawn into life in God also returns from its moments of *theosis* into incarnational moments (in so far as these are matters of human recognition) so that what is good in each of the enculturated languages and rationalities of the world are considered in the gritty conceptualized and linguistic ways of interpreting the world, in the plentitude of legitimate hermeneutics. Such a theological hermeneutic integrates special and general revelation, knowledge from other disciplines provided through the God-given human noetic capabilities seen in the flourishing of human endeavors of inquiry upon the world, and thus such a hermeneutic would also necessarily, not just possibly, be interdisciplinary. Readings of Scripture and readings of the world inevitably draw together.

Such a theological hermeneutics looks to the biblical texts for what they mean for today, though always in accountable relation to the origination of Scripture and what the text has meant to God's people in history; the otherness of the text remains and calls interpretations into account, both as historical text and as living Word of God. In the end, as in the beginning, such a hermeneutic might recollect the shaping of epistemology by ontology; it might embark in a hermeneutical and plural realism amidst cultural-linguistic multiplicities in the late modern world; it might live in the continued covenantal relationship between God and His people who live as people amidst many living and enculturated traditions, rather than as situated (yet conceived as unsituated) modern observers dissecting texts; it might produce a people who might live as Christians in particular ways in a late modern glocalized world where certain enforcement of globalized cultures and pluralization of not just many righteous ways but many unrighteous ways are also found. In this way, we might have a vision of what it is to interpret Scripture and life theologically as Pentecostals.

These considerations push this accounting of the hermeneutical task back towards starting points. Hermeneutics always begin within situations

---

23. Pinnock, *Flame of Love.*

in which interpreters already find themselves amidst. A Pentecostal Christian theological hermeneutic best begins by acknowledging the dimensions of a theological understanding of an arc of the overall biblical narrative in which Pentecostals find themselves in; starting points are themselves traditioned understanding and locations into which persons are thrown (often not willed). Pentecostal hermeneutics are somehow located and start in relation to Pentecost, forming their identity so that Pentecostal hermeneutics are continuationist hermeneutics. To be a Pentecostal, then, is to see one's self not as a dispassionate high modern observer of Scripture, theology, Christian experience, and the world, but to see one's self as included amidst communities who are in continuity with the story of the people of God, formed by the particular epochal moment (and continued iterations) of the Pentecost event. So the reading of that Scriptural narrative, the understanding of an interpreter's communities as found in the story of God's people, the interpreter's cultural influences and personal proclivities, inherited theological traditions, epistemic and ontic affirmations, and more, all inform the structure of a theological hermeneutic.

In the face of all of these factors, some still continue the search for a 'right' or 'correct' hermeneutic, as if one particular set of human principles and conceptualities can properly account for general knowledge and divine revelation, rather than developing a theological hermeneutic that focuses its core affirmations on being faithful to what is given in revelation and developing an interdisciplinary integration with other forms of human knowing. Such attempts at 'correctness' mix up the interpreter's authority with the authority and givenness of God's Word and Spirit and embody modern overconfidence far more than Christian orthodoxy. On the other hand, affirmations of what is given lead to confidence in the realities of God's revelation, even as these are understood within given hermeneutics. I have thus contended that such contours for theological hermeneutics lead to a hermeneutical realism.

Here, I have briefly sketched out the basic hermeneutical implications of key theological affirmations from an interpretation of these four major epochs of revelation. What is central to each of these epochal events is the continuity they provide within Christian life. Creation-Incarnation-Pentecost-Eschaton are well understood as having the ontic status both of critical historical moments of instantiation and basic structures of continuity of being in God's world. Eschaton, of course, represents something special here. It is the power of God's future historical work, already in the now prior to the not yet, calling and drawing us from ahead. These affirmations form the core structure for a Pentecostal theological hermeneutic, as a paradigm for Pentecostal Christian life here and now.

Philosophical Contours of a Pentecostal Philosophical-Theological Hermeneutic

As I have stated and implied above, my sketch assumes and affirms that reve-latory and general knowing are embedded together. Therefore, philosophical contours of Pentecostal hermeneutics are either accounted for or naively (and thus quite often underdeveloped and problematically) assumed. Contrary to some popular teaching in evangelical circles, the cultural-linguistic structure of all interpretation does not entail what too often inarticulately and inaccurately goes by the boogey-man 'relativism' (rather than, I often suspect, as they mean to do, criticize a lack of moral ontology or a problem in a moral philosophy). I have contended what is implied is a hermeneutical realism. This is because language may be considered to actually or really point to what is, even without a full grasp or complete adequacy, as the latter would be a quest which itself is based only on naivete or hubris or some blending of the two. Rather, language might be considered to indicate what is with various measures of adequacy. A plurality of true words spoken of that which is interpreted commonly gives a greater richness towards true description. Language can rightly be used to speak an authoritative and defining word or pronouncement on what is or is to be (among its many functions), for example what might be conveyed in the following, "Jesus saves," "You are a child of God," "I now pronounce you husband and wife," "I forgive you," "Your creative work inspires me," "God bless you, friend." It can speak in such a way without confusing human con-fessions (even of great faith) with divine authority. While Pentecostal herme-neutics have needed to correct themselves from naïve forms of human noetic authoritarianism, Pentecostals have nearly universally stood in polar relations to rationalisms and scientisms which have attempted to assume governing authority over human knowledge. As I alluded to above, Pentecostalism might be understood in line with the Romantic rejoinder to Enlightenment ratio-nalism. So Pentecostal hermeneutics may just take for granted the primacy of the *Geisteswissenschaften* over the *Naturwissenschaften*, what in the field of philosophical hermeneutics has been commonly articulated as the firstness of the human languages emerging from the crafts of common existence and their attendant disciplines over the theoretical and technical disciplines which seek to categorize and master nature.[24] The insights of Hamaan, Herder, and Humboldt and other Romantic hermeneutic theorists and philosophers of lan-guage, and even Schleiermacher a little later on, in at least his hermeneutics, might be seen as not only latent sources (from the Romantics to Wesley and the pietists to modern Pentecostals) but as current resources.

24. That is, in line with Gadamer's, *Truth and Method*.

Yet the technical, modernist, and fundamentalist tendencies within Pentecostalisms have often driven Pentecostal hermeneutics towards the kinds of conceptual and linguistic habits concerning God and what God is doing that have often been subjected to the criticisms which find human conceptual languages engaging in the hubris of turning theology into a human *techne* that, wittingly or unwittingly, seeks to control knowledge of God. Some of this certainly came into Pentecostalism in its early decades through the unwitting resourcing of modern rationalisms smuggled in through the theological methods of what were considered to be fundamentalist allies. Problems with this have led to the critique of the project of onto-theology, as a smuggling in of philosophical notions of being, often even more powerful in their common sense varieties than the theoretical, as creating onto-theo-logics which seek to control the givenness of what is revealed, divine and otherwise, through metaphysics and ontologies which govern the givenness of revelation rather than those which (hermeneutically) receive such. Among Pentecostals, the prominence of the fundamentalist strand of evangelical-Pentecostal hermeneutics exemplifies this.[25]

Among Christian theologians who are both orthodox and postmodern, onto-theology is considered a pride concerning human understanding—not the glory of God. It is the pride of conceptualizing a Highest Being, made in the image of man (maleness intended here), producing a god of philosophy, often enough just the philosophy of common sense localities rather than that of a grand philosophical project, over The One Who Is and revealed, encountered not grasped (cf. Exod 3:14; John 1:5) as *Yahweh*, the One in whom we are baptized in the name of the Father, and the Son, and the Holy Spirit (Matt 28:19).

That is, there is both the content that is given and a necessary apophaticism to all human understanding of the divine, even as the Spirit is in our midst. There is a dialectic, then, of our human, "all too human" understanding that is always already prejudiced since it is traditioned, and yet it is the Spirit who guides us in all truth. This dialectic, this tension in which theology lives, is a necessary reality, a divine-human dialectic that is not overcome, at least not this side of the eschaton, as Merold Westphal

---

25. Both Archer and I have narrated this for Pentecostal hermeneutics in my *Theological Hermeneutics* and his *A Pentecostal Hermeneutic*. This is well accounted for in Marsden, *Fundamentalism and American Culture*. Steven Land's *Pentecostal Spirituality* might be well interpreted as addressing the manner in which Pentecostal affections have provided a rupture amidst the fundamentalist-modernist structures which attempted to frame Pentecostal spirituality in overly simplistic commonsensical yet unwitting modernist structures and leading towards the direction among 'Cleveland School' Pentecostal hermeneuts to drink from their own revelatory wells.

describes it.[26] Westphal puts this into a confession of faith away from interpretive hubris:

> In affirming God as Creator I am affirming that there is an explanation of the whole of being and I am pointing in the direction of that explanation; but I am not giving it, for I do not possess it. To do that I would have to know just *who* God is, and just *how* and *why* God brings being into being out of nothing. But both God's being and God's creative action remain deeply mysterious to me. They are answers that come loaded with new questions, reminding me in Heideggerian language that unconcealment is always shadowed by concealment, or in Pauline language that I only see "through a glass, darkly" (or "in a mirror, dimly," 1 Cor. 13:12). My affirmation of God as Creator is not onto-theological because it is not in the service of the philosophical project of rendering the whole of being intelligible to human understanding, a project I have ample religious reasons to repudiate.[27]

This is what the great thinkers of the Christian faith have all known:

> With or without help from Pseudo-Dionysius, theologians such as Augustine, Aquinas, Luther, Calvin, and Barth have spoken this way. All of them have insisted, with or without help from Rudolf Otto, that the God of the Bible and of their theologies is Wholly Other in an epistemic sense as being the *mysterium*.[28]

This is *Yahweh* we are worshipping—and of whom we are speaking. There is thus the continual tension between the kataphatic and the apophatic in genuine theological interpretation. This is not, as Westphal notes, to smuggle in the silencing of the witness of the divine which poses as silence before the Lord. Rather, it is to continue to refuse the interpretive temptation to turn the Lord into our mere idol. It is rather to sing our faith ("O Mary, don't you weep, don't you mourn. Pharaoh's army got drowned" is his example), itself "a performative refutation of Hume on miracles!"[29] rather than to create a god made by our own philosophical machinations (or imaginations) where:

> God is at the beck and call of human understanding, a means to an end of making the whole of being intelligible in keeping with the principle of reason. In order to place the world at the disposal of human theory (and practice), it becomes necessary

26. The theme of Merold Westphal's "Spirit and Prejudice."

27. Westphal, *Overcoming Onto-theology*, 7.

28. Westphal, *Overcoming Onto-theology*, 8.

29. Westphal, *Overcoming Onto-theology*, 2.

to place God at our disposal as well. But there is no awe, or sing-
ing, or dancing before such a factotum And if there is any clap-
ping, it will have the form of polite applause. "Please join me in
welcoming the Ultima Ratio."[30]

Westphalian critique of onto-theology encourages and prays for Pentecostal
hermeneutics to embrace its robust engagement and faith in the revelatory presence of God while simultaneously chastening us to put away our
hubristic categories and cheap metaphysics and point to the glory of God.
"This is that" in Pentecostal spiritual hermeneutics must be a pointing to
the work of God over the (often cheap, or unwitting) categories of human
understanding. For *the categories are not bad* in and of themselves—for they
are our humanity—*until they confuse themselves with the divine.* Pentecostal
hermeneutics is to live in that divine-human dialectic, not to "overcome"
it. God speaks to me. But I must own my understanding of it as human
interpretation, my understanding of a divine gift.

Still, we name it and say what it is, *with this chastened understanding.*
To speak of the ontic is to name what truly is but so as to refer to and enter
into relationship with. This is the task given in the Garden, where the tasks
of work, of naming and relating (Gen 2:15–20), are given to the human. It is
our task to use our constructive powers to form language to name, a work of
understanding what is, and to construct social relations, so that the power
of naming what is remains a key power endowed upon humans. This is intimately connected to the command not to bear false witness (Exod 20:16;
Deut 5:20) against neighbors. The affirmation of the ontic, to speak truth,
which can be spoken with many layers and significant multiplicity, is a task
whose end is the shalomic realities of God's teloi for all creatures.

Moving Ahead in Faith

Philosophical contours are much funded by theological affirmations.
Therefore, a Pentecostal philosophical-theological hermeneutic is full of
particularities even as these are shaped by plural realities and interpretations. Pentecostal hermeneutics are shaped by the covenant traditions in
Scripture, structured by the history of God's people, of Abraham, of Moses,
of David, in the prophetic traditions and the varieties of modes of expression found among the psalmists. Of the many traditions of many peoples,
the covenant people of God find their fulfilment among the peoples of the
earth (Isa 61–62).

30. Westphal, *Overcoming Onto-theology*, 12.

Pentecostal Christian interpretations of Scripture and life are exercises in particularities. They affirm embodiment and boundaries, limits amidst presence, encounters with transcendence among immanent realities. Pentecostal hermeneutics is to particularize into the explosion of plurality in unity that is the Pentecost event in its continuation, a continuation of the journey of God's covenant people, begun with Father Abram and his clan but pointing back to the origin of all things and God's purposes for humanity. Engaging in Pentecostal hermeneutics is to participate at the limited point of existence, in becoming, that is to be a broken-yet-reconciled person in whom the Spirit is present and bringing forth a new tongue. It is to be a person whose life and self is formed as a living interpretation of God's love in a particular time and place. Yet it is to be with and for the manifold people of God who are together a living witness of the Triune God in a particular time and place witnessing the narrative of salvation history: Creation-Incarnation-Pentecost-Eschaton.

PART TWO

Ecumenical Hermeneutics

5

Spirit Baptism in the Late Modern World

On the one hand, The Church: Towards a Common Vision seems kind enough to name Pentecostals—along with the Orthodox, Protestant, Anglican, Evangelical and Roman Catholic churches—as among the major contributors to the document and to the ecumenical table. Ecumenical representation and participation from Pentecostals has been on the lighter side, largely because Pentecostals have been reticent or even opposed to the call for visible unity between these Christian traditions. On the other hand, the document would have been remiss if Pentecostals were not included as important to ecumenism in the present. This is not just on account of Pentecostal ecumenists who have contributed to the WCC's Faith and Order Commission and the current state of ecumenical dialogue. Even more importantly, it is because Pentecostals represent a significant proportion of the world Christian population. Pentecostals are part of the body of Christ, and in the contemporary moment they are especially positioned at cultural strata where they are often at the vanguard of Christian mission.

Pentecostal Christianity has more to contribute to contemporary discussions of ecumenical renewal in the late modern world than is often assumed by insiders as well as outsiders. There is more implicit in Pentecostal experience—especially in experience of the Spirit—and Pentecostal theology than assumed by many who have too often only seen its broad yet still implicit theological and ontological vision reduced to ad hoc and borrowed forms. Yet the ontology implicit in Pentecostal pneumatology and experiential practices has funded a renewal of Christian life and experience across the globe. Implicit in Pentecostal spirituality is a naming of reality as spiritual life in relation to the Spirit of God. There ought to be significant interest in exploring the connection between this global renewal and this implicit ontology, and its ecumenical potential queried. Here, I want to claim that the ontology of Spirit baptism in Pentecostal theology and experience has ecumenical potential for the Church, and that an ecumenical-Pentecostal understanding of Spirit baptism helpfully frames Pentecostal response to this important document from the WCC.

Pentecostal theology has so far spent the first years of the twenty-first century explicating what is implicit in Pentecostal spirituality. For instance, of particular importance for understanding the variety of developments embedded in Pentecostal or 'renewal' Christianity has been the 'many tongues' principle which has been, thus far, most fully articulated by arguably the leading Pentecostal theologian in the world, the Asian-Amencan philosophical theologian Amos Yong. The principle holds that the many tongues of Pentecost (as in Acts 2) represent, beyond what else they signify, the varieties of local and particular expressions of Christianity.[1] This principle provides a way for legitimate differences in Christian theological understanding and life, just as God "poured out his Spirit upon *all flesh*" in all its multiplicity on the day of Pentecost in Acts 2. These 'many tongues' of Pentecost allow for legitimate differences playing out a Christian response to late modern pluralism and the threat of the dissolution of meaning, According to the 'many tongues' principle, truth and meaning continue to be found in a Christian understanding of life that accounts for difference and plurality yet speaks a common confession of faith.[2]

This principle is both expressive of the Pentecostal vision of diverse churches making up the body of Christ and, in light of Pentecostalism's history of sectarianism, a reason for making spiritual and a kind of visible unity within a plurality of Christian churches goals for Pentecostal ecumenism. As the ecumenical-Pentecostal theologian Wolfgang Vondey has put it, in response to the predecessor document to *The Church*, the WCC's *The Nature and Mission of the Church* (2005), "many Pentecostals suggest that there exists a plurality of ecclesial self-understandings and nuances that are theologically complementary and desirable since they are often born from and determined by a community's experience and praxis of faith rather than

---

1. This approach is seen throughout Yong's works, and can also be found as he uncovers justification for a plurality of methodological approaches, but especially theological ones, into areas of concern in the late modern world, such as politics and science: Yong, *In the Days of Caesar*, 109–11; Yong, *The Spirit of Creation*, 34–35.

2. Oliverio, "The One and the Many." Yong's 'many tongues' principle has a number of similarities to Balthasar, *Truth Is Symphonic*.

a division of doctrine."[3] Or, as the Final Report of the Third Quinquennium of the Roman Catholic-Pentecostal Dialogue (1985–89), *Perspectives on Koinonia*, stated concerning the Pentecostal position on ecumenism, "Pentecostals tend to view denominations as more or less legitimate manifestations of the one, universal Church. Their legitimacy depends on the degree of their faithfulness to the fundamental doctrines of the Scripture."[4] For Pentecostals, an important motivation for ecumenism has been greater faithfulness to Scripture and to the mission of the Church. Visible unity has tended to be seen as secondary to that goal. Yet at least a measure of visible unity may in fact be necessary to be faithful to Scripture and the mission of the Church in the first place.

The style of this chapter will differ in certain ways from some other ecumenical discussions. It will highlight themes and practices and ways of approaching the Church and its mission that reflect particularly Pentecostal realities. Nevertheless, this chapter will also evaluate and criticize Pentecostal movements and the tradition itself. As the Singaporean Pentecostal theologian Simon Chan has rightly pressed the point in the community of Pentecostal theologians, Pentecostals have struggled to properly appreciate tradition and its roles.[5] Pentecostals operate with an underdeveloped ecclesiology. Because of this underdevelopment, in part the result of Pentecostal urgency and impatience in mission, Pentecostals have often produced church structures which sometimes fail to draw on even basic Christian ecclesiological affirmations. There is a lot of work to be done in Pentecostal ecclesiology for Pentecostals to better engage in ecumenical discussions. Yet there is also a great deal that is implicit in the tradition and its spirituality. I will thus focus my response to *The Church* around the ecumenical potential of the central and distinctive Pentecostal doctrine, that of baptism in the Holy Spirit.

This chapter will proceed by, first, addressing the not so easily answered question about what constitutes Pentecostalism. Second, it will recount some relevant developments in Pentecostal ecclesiology in order to frame the discussion. Third, it will address the critical issue of Pentecostal ecclesial engagement with culture. Fourth, the Pentecostal doctrine of Spirit baptism will be explored for its ecumenical implications. Fifth, in light of the preceding understanding of Pentecostal ecclesiology, *The Church: Towards a Common Vision* will be engaged from a Pentecostal perspective, with special attention to Pentecostal understanding of the Church's oneness,

3. Vondey, "Pentecostal Perspectives," 57.

4. International Roman Catholic-Pentecostal Dialogue, "Final Report," n34.

5. Chan, *Pentecostal Theology*.

holiness, catholicity, and apostolicity. Finally, several pastoral and practical implications of such a Pentecostal engagement will be teased out in the concluding section.

Identifying Pentecostals

Discussions of Pentecostal Christianity are often forced to begin with a review of just what is being referred to by 'Pentecostals' or 'pentecostals' or 'charismatics' or 'charismatic-pentecostals' or, more recently, 'renewal Christianity.' There are several reasons for this, but the primary one is that the boundaries among Christian churches and movements associated with Pentecostalism are porous and thus confusing to those inside, let alone those outside, of Pentecostal and charismatic studies. Surveys have chronicled the emergence of many varieties of charismatic and Pentecostal forms of Christianity as they have developed in manifold theological and cultural contexts.[6] Sociologists and demographers struggle to keep up with the developments, just as they do the categories. Identifying someone as a Pentecostal or charismatic, or any of the other possibilities in nomenclature, is difficult, even before a topic like Pentecostal ecclesiologies can be addressed. Offering a Pentecostal response to *The Church* requires accounting for chose on whose behalf I am offering a response.

To even the best historians tracking the emergence of Pentecostal and charismatic Christianity, like Allan Heaton Anderson and Douglas Jacobsen,[7] or those tracking its demographics, like the Pew Forum or the *World Christian Encyclopedia*, this is a daunting task since the ground is moving so fast underneath our feet.[8] Recent estimates are that there are about five-to-six hundred million Pentecostal-charismatics worldwide, or roughly between a fifth (Jacobsen) or even a fourth (Anderson) of the world Christian population, and somewhere around 7–8 percent of the world population altogether. It is not just the sheer size of these emerging movements and our inability to track them all that make this tradition so difficult to account for. Jacobsen, for example, has ended up speaking of 'pentecostals' (with a small 'p') because their theologies differed so much that he felt he could not label them with one proper (big 'P') heading.[9] According to

6. For example, Anderson, *An Introduction to Pentecostalism*; Miller and Yamamori, *Global Pentecostalism*; Wilkinson, *Global Pentecostal Movements*.

7. See Anderson, *Introduction to Pentecostalism*; Anderson, *To the Ends of the Earth*; Jacobsen, *The World's Christians*.

8. See Jacobsen's video introduction: "Global Christianity."

9. Jacobsen, *Thinking in the Spirit*.

Jacobsen, the main continuities among early 'pentecostal' theologians came in the form of interpreting Scripture and experience "in a pentecostal way," and an openness to God doing new things in their midst.[10] There are questions as to whether there is even enough continuity, theologically or on the ecclesial level or even practically-experientially, to speak of a tradition.

Though there is dissent concerning this, many Pentecostal theologians and other scholars, including the present author, have concluded that we are really dealing with a tradition here—in the sense that there are beliefs, practices, ways of life, understanding, and the like being passed down, in ways that are at least somewhat traceable, at least if we have the interest and resources to do so—and even if this is a very diverse and challenging one to track. It is a tradition at least in the sense Alasdair MacIntyre has described as a historically extended, socially embodied argument.[11] The guild that gathers around the Society for Pentecostal Studies, the leading international society, tends to use the following nomenclature:

- Pentecostalism: the Classical Pentecostal tradition that emerged primarily in North America, but also in Wales, India, Sweden and a few other movements, at the turn of the twentieth century. Its key theological contribution came in a rereading of the Acts of the Apostles in relation to other scriptural passages to develop a theological basis for believing in an experience of baptism in the Spirit as an event subsequent to salvation and sanctification in the life of a Christian. The doctrine that developed affirmed the 'Bible sign' of Spirit baptism as *glossolalia* ('speaking in tongues'). Classical Pentecostalism can also be identified by its proclamation of the 'Full Gospel' where Jesus is proclaimed as savior, sanctifier, divine healer, Spirit baptizer, and soon coming king.

- Charismatic or charismatic: Protestant, Catholic and Orthodox Christians who experienced a renewal of charismatic Christian experience either through encounter with Pentecostalism or because of the renewal in Christian pneumatology. Originally emerging in the 1960s, the variety of movements in North America and globally has been significant but is, in North American and European contexts, perhaps "on pause."[12] On the other hand, in the global south it is these charismatics who are at the vanguard of much of the growth of

10. Jacobsen, *Thinking in the Spirit*, x–xi, 3–12.

11. MacIntyre, *After Virtue*, 222.

12. The phrase of Monsignor Juan Usma Gomez of the Pontifical Council for Promoting Christian Unity, in a meeting with Assemblies of God pastors and missionaries in Rome, May 2012.

Christianity worldwide. Further, many 'non-denominational' Christians in the Evangelical vein are often charismatic. Much of global Christianity, as far as it can be tracked, includes hybrid forms from various Christian traditions that can often be characterized as charismatic Christianity.

- (Small 'p') pentecostal: a catch-all category that includes Classical Pentecostals, charismatic Christians whose affiliation is primarily with another Christian tradition but whose practices and worship include charismatic aspects, and the vast array of indigenous churches who have sometimes been labeled 'neo-pentecostal' since their practices resemble that of Classical Pentecostals but their doctrines can vary and differ. It is these 'pentecostal' Christians who constitute much of the growth of global Christianity in the past century. They are found in African Indigenous Churches, independent churches in North America and Europe, as well as small and regional Christian denominations across the globe. Nevertheless, some use (big 'P') 'Pentecostal' to refer to this larger category rather than just Classical Pentecostals, as I do in this chapter.

- Charismatic-pentecostal: a hybrid catch-all also used to refer to the larger tradition as it uses both terms in the lower case, and expresses the sense in which this is a large and varied tradition in mixed forms, emphasizing the overlap between Christian traditions that comes with the term charismatic.

- Renewal Christianity: a more recent alternative used to account for the essence of charismatic-pentecostal Christianity as renewal. Several leading sources have begun using this term as a way forward for understanding the breadth of this Christian tradition, including the Pew Forum on Religion and Public Life. Speaking of renewal Christianity has tended to indicate an emphasis on pneumatology and experience of the Spirit in a variety of Christian movements and traditions that have seen a revival of Christian faith across the globe, and who represent hope for the growth of Christianity in the current era.

This chapter seeks to present a response to *The Church: Towards a Common Vision* from these movements and traditions to the larger household of Christian faith. Since this larger *oikumene* of Christian faith tends to think of the complex situation above as 'Pentecostals,' and that is a reasonable enough reference, this chapter will speak of Pentecostals and Pentecostalism and Pentecostal ecclesiology below. This reference includes a conviction that Classical Pentecostals embody a certain core in the appearance of the wider renewal Christianity that has emerged in the late modern world. This leads to the question, what is the essence of Pentecostalism?

For the Pentecostal systematic theologian Steven Studebaker, Pentecostalism is not reducible to a vague experience of a universal spirit. Rather, the essence of Pentecostalism is experience of the Spirit *in which* knowledge and understanding of the Triune God is embedded.[13] Spirit baptism represents not merely a doctrinal distinctive of Pentecostal denominations but "an orienting source and category for Pentecostal theology—as well as other traditions."[14] Or as Frank Macchia has claimed, "Spirit baptism as an eschatological gift . . . that functions as an out pouring of divine love . . . [is] an organizing principle of a Pentecostal theology."[15] Pentecostal identity is as the Spirit-baptized people of God. Thus, a number of contemporary ecumenical-Pentecostal theologians see Spirit baptism not as a dividing distinctive of Pentecostal faith but, as the Eucharist has become in other ecumenical discussions, a place for Christians to come together in our common experience, here of the Spirit.

Affirming Studebaker's and Macchia's thematic understanding of the essence of Pentecostalism does not rule out unthematic interpretations as complementary, even if incomplete without the thematic. Implicit as well in the essence of Pentecostalism is the kairotic and the primal. Regarding the latter, Harvey Cox has suggested that Pentecostalism represents a recovery of a primal spirituality at this moment in history, and its "meaning transcends all merely social or psychological explanations" so that "what began as a despised and a ridiculed sect is quickly becoming both the preferred religion of the urban poor and the powerful bearer of a radically alternative vision of what the human world might one day become."[16] Nimi Wariboko has spoken of this similarly, as the kairotic, or 'the pentecostal principle.' Adapting Tillich's Protestant Principle, Wariboko speaks of 'the pentecostal principle' as the creative and transformative energy within human existence. The 'pentecostal' kairotic energy plays off of the 'Catholic' substance and the 'Protestant' reform as the power of newness and grace.[17] While Wariboko has made this claim with a more avant-garde thesis, Jacobsen's careful historical study of the theology of early Pentecostals came to a very similar conclusion—that at the essence of Pentecostalism is the conviction that God is doing new things, offering new charisms, beyond

---

13. Studebaker, *From Pentecost to the Triune God*, 11–26.

14. Studebaker, *From Pentecost to the Triune God*, 46.

15. Macchia, *Baptized in the Spirit*, 17.

16. Cox, *Fire from Heaven*, 83.

17. Wariboko, *The Pentecostal Principle*, 42–70.

what has been conceived.[18] Pentecostalism is associated with a primal, dignifying and gifting grace, which comes into fulfillment in the here and now in Spirit baptism.

As Pentecostalism emerged and broadened into the wider Pentecostal, charismatic, and renewal movements which have blossomed around the globe over the past century, there have been varying degrees of ecclesial and ecclesiological developments. Popular and even some scholarly discussions of Pentecostal Christianity are reminiscent of the famous Indian parable of the six blind men of Hindustan where each blind man describes a part of the elephant as if it were the whole. Some rub against fundamentalist-leaning parts of the tradition and take Pentecostals to be simply "fundamentalists with a difference."[19] Others know mostly of the varieties of charismatic worship, others the success of Christian renewal among the poor and oppressed. Then there are those who know primarily the historical and ecclesial connections between Pentecostal churches and other Christian traditions. Still others touch the portions of the tradition that have quickly enculturated and taken on indigenous ways. And yet others have felt the strong emphasis on mission work and manifold forms of evangelism. Of course, that Hindu parable is about the limitations of human knowledge, but it also might represent inadequate perspectives on Pentecostal Christianity. Yet it also induces humility here. This discussion of Pentecostal ecclesiology responds to a particular ecumenical document. Despite trying to be broadly representative this chapter represents only a particular take from a Pentecostal theologian on a broad tradition with a contested and complex identity yet also seeks to be attentive to certain significant issues for the unity of the Christian Church.

In my estimation, then, Pentecostalism *is* a tradition, evidenced by the complexity and continuity noted above, and thus not merely a movement within or a denomination of Christianity. The Pentecostal elephant in the religious room is also an oft-ignored elephant, and this neglect is very present in the halls of academic theology and religious studies.[20] There is much

18. Jacobsen, *Thinking in the Spirit*.

19. This phrase arose as a Pentecostal self-identification in the 1920–30s in North America when Pentecostals were seeking affirmation from Fundamentalists who, in turn, were rejecting them.

20. There are very few institutions of higher education besides those within the Pentecostal tradition that hire tenure-track scholars to teach and study the charismatic-Pentecostal tradition; the University of Birmingham (UK) is a notable exception. While the Society for Pentecostal Studies, the tradition's primary and largest international scholarly organization, functions as a scholarly home for scholars from a variety of institutions outside of charismatic-Pentecostal circles, most of these scholars have forged a theological or scholarly career in spite of indifference toward or prejudice against

work to do on Pentecostalism, Pentecostal theology, and, in particular, Pentecostal ecclesiology. There is a lack of development and, compared to other Christian traditions, a paucity of resources.

Ecclesiology and the Pentecostal Tradition

When in 2012 the WCC put forth *The Church: Towards a Common Vision*, the document addressed the mission and unity of the Church, the nature of the Church in relationship to the Trinity, as well as sacraments, ordination, authority and over sight, and the Church's relationship to the world. Visit, however, a Pentecostal congregation—from an urban storefront in North America to a West African megachurch—to a rural Latin American assembly to an Asian house church—and you will most likely hear little of the ecclesiological language found in this document. Instead, you will discover various indigenous expressions of Christianity and a common belief that it is the presence of the Spirit moving among them that is driving Pentecostal ecclesiological understanding.[21] While the roots of Classical Pentecostalism in North America are more clearly traceable, the blending of elements from various Christian traditions and movements with local and global cultural traditions and movements has produced a tradition that has roots in a wide variety of theological and cultural sources.[22] As Vondey has put it, "The Pentecostal movement is an ecumenical melting pot."[23]

Still, as the Finnish Pentecostal ecclesiologist Veli-Matti Kärkkäinen has concluded, "Pentecostals have written surprisingly little on ecclesiology." There is not yet a clearly defined Pentecostal view of the Church. "Pentecostal ecclesiology is of an ad hoc nature which leaves much room for improvization."[24] Like much else with Pentecostals, the lack of explicit reflec-

---

academic recognition of charismatic-Pentecostal Christianity. Charismatic-Pentecostal scholars regularly testify to a 'double marginalization' from, on the one side, the academy, which finds their work marginal, and, on the other, the church institutions of their own tradition, which find their work of small importance. The latter, however, seems to be in a time of transformation, though institutional development to support charismatic-Pentecostal scholars will take time.

21. Mark Cartledge approaches Pentecostal theology through the empirical theology school, where theology begins with studies of what is actually believed and practiced in the churches. See, for example, Cartledge, "Renewal Ecclesiology in Empirical Perspective."

22. Hollenweger's *Pentecostalism* is structured around his account of five primary roots of global Pentecostalism: the black oral, the Catholic (via Wesley), the Evangelical, the critical, and the ecumenical.

23. Vondey, *Pentecostalism*, 49.

24. Kärkkäinen, *An Introduction to Ecclesiology*, 73.

tion does not imply a lack of practical and implicit development, nor does it imply a lack of meaning from within the tradition. Nevertheless, Pentecostal ecclesiology as explicit theological articulation is in need of development.

Despite the ad hoc nature of much of Pentecostal ecclesiology, and the many local varieties of it, Yong has seen a resource and a commonality within the Pentecostal tradition in the five-fold 'full gospel' that finds its roots in Pentecostal beginnings. From its turn-of-the-twentieth-century origins, Pentecostals proclaimed that Jesus is savior, sanctifier, baptizer in the Spirit, divine healer, and soon coming King. This rubric has functioned to organize much of Pentecostal theology, including Pentecostal ecclesiology, and this shows potential for a way forward.[25] This core to Pentecostal theology has functioned as a doctrinal grid for interpreting Scripture and experience.[26] Some who are seeking to develop an authentic Pentecostal ecclesiology are exploring the thesis that Pentecostal ecclesiology has developed in relation to Pentecostal theologies and practices of salvation, sanctification or holiness, Spirit baptism, divine healing, and eschatology.[27]

The habit of minimal ecclesiological reflection, however, begins at the origins of the tradition. At the beginning, modern Pentecostalism started with an ethos that might be considered not only anti-ecumenical but even anti-ecclesial. The Pentecostal restorationist narrative implied that something had died, or had at least gone cold, in the history of Christianity that required revival. The oft cited opening to the second issue of *The Apostolic Faith* (Los Angeles), the official newspaper of the Azusa Street Revival, from October 1906, propagated and well summarizes this narrative of the partial fall and subsequent restoration of the Church before an end times revival:

> All along the ages men have been preaching a partial Gospel. A part of the Gospel remained when the world went into the dark ages. God has from time to time raised up men to bring back the truth to the church. He raised up Luther to bring back to the world the doctrine of justification by faith. He raised up another reformer in John Wesley to establish Bible holiness in the church. Then he raised up Dr. Cullis who brought back to the world the wonderful doctrine of divine healing. Now he is bringing back the Pentecostal Baptism to the church.[28]

---

25. Kärkkäinen, *An Introduction to Ecclesiology*. Also, Thomas, *Toward a Pentecostal Ecclesiology*.

26. Oliverio, *Theological Hermeneutics*, 78–82.

27. Thomas, *Toward a Pentecostal Ecclesiology*.

28. Azusa Street Mission, "The Pentecostal Baptism Restored," 1.

Early Pentecostals considered themselves part of a restorationist movement, and gravitated toward terms like 'fellowship' and 'mission' and 'assembly' in naming their gatherings and emerging congregations.[29] Their self-understanding was that they were the people of God's 'latter rain' outpouring as God pouring his Spirit out 'in the last days.'[30] The eschatological orientation of early Pentecostalism, influenced by twentieth-century premillennial movements, connected the Wesleyan-Holiness emphases on holiness and revivalism with an understanding that a subsequent baptism in the Spirit provides empowerment for Christian witness.[31]

Since early Pentecostals were interested in restoring the Church, they were critical of 'dead' and 'cold' denominations and what they considered their divisive creeds. Such evaluations of the status of other Christians and their confessions came at the level of their practical spirituality. And Pentecostals were especially associated with believers 'coming out' of these churches into new assemblies and missions, often after their experience of Spirit baptism and charismatic gifts, and often because of rejection by the established churches on account of these experiences.

Such rejection from 'cold' or 'dead' established churches, as well as hostility from Fundamentalists, led to a dual reaction. On the one hand, Pentecostals responded with certitude and absolutism, since God's faithful people had always experienced rejection and even persecution.[32] On the other hand, they just as often displayed a deep impulse for Christian unity with anyone who genuinely believed, although early Pentecostals had a hard time holding that any genuine believer could be associated with some of the 'apostate' liberal Protestant churches let alone the Roman Catholic Church. This is why, with all its subsequent iterations in the global Pentecostal tradition, Nimi Wariboko has characterized the 'pentecostal spirit' as, positively, a dynamic and kairotic spirit, yet negatively—with the caveat that there are appropriate times for such a spirit—as the "division of divisions" or "Apelles' cut," "the tendency toward endless fragmentation . . . a tendency to perpetuate ecclesial disunity."[33]

Yet from its beginnings, Pentecostalism simultaneously exhibited underlying ecumenical impulses, in contrast to surface antipathies toward other churches. In fact, Pentecostalism might be well understood as attempting

29. Blumhofer, *Restoring the Faith*.

30. Archer, *A Pentecostal Hermeneutic*.

31. See Anderson, *Introduction to Pentecostalism*, 19–38; Dayton, *Theological Roots of Pentecostalism*; Oliverio, *Theological Hermeneutics*, 19–30.

32. Wacker, *Heaven Below*, 18–34.

33. Wariboko, *The Pentecostal Principle*, 144–49.

to generate an ecumenical ecclesial renewal as it has deconstructed existing ecclesial structures and practices as 'dead' or inadequate religiosity in order to reconstruct a renewed Church. The charismatic movements and various movements of renewal associated with global Pentecostalism might be considered as a movement to deconstruct in order to reconstruct. The deconstruction comes in the proud brought low, as children, in a renewed Church, as exhibited in the lead story of the inaugural issue of *The Apostolic Faith*:

> Proud, well-dressed preachers come in to "investigate." Soon their high looks are replaced with wonder, then conviction comes, and very often you find them in a short time wallowing on the dirty floor, asking God to forgive them and make them as little children. It would be impossible to state how many have been converted, sanctified and filled with the Holy Ghost. They have been and are daily going out to all points of the compass to spread the wonderful gospel.[34]

But if the proud were brought low and humbled, it was to be raised up in a vision, like the outcome of genuine *koinonia* fellowship found in Acts (2:42–47; 4:32–37), and in the Pauline calls for the unity and dignity of each in Christ (Gal 3:28; Col 3:11).

The original Pentecostal revival at Azusa Street in Los Angeles (1906–9), and much of Pentecostalism, has offered a practical and spiritual breakthrough beyond dominant and oppressive racial, socio-economic, and gender structures. There is no doubting that the Azusa Street Revival, led by a black preacher with little education in the first decade of the twentieth century, was a remarkable occurrence in its deconstruction of powerful social norms on race and other social structures towards a reconstructed *koinonia*.[35] As Frank Bartleman, a white Pentecostal pastor and participant at Azusa Street, famously declared, "The 'color line' was washed away in the blood."[36] There is an underlying ecumenical vision that William Seymour, the black preacher who led the revival, and many Pentecostals since have embraced and embodied. As Walter Hollenweger, the Swiss pioneer of Pentecostal studies,[37] has put it, "Two worldwide Christian movements were

34. Azusa Street Mission, "The Pentecostal Baptism Restored."

35. Robeck, *The Azusa Street Mission and Revival*. It is not a coincidence that Robeck is both the leading historian of the Revival and Pentecostalism's leading contemporary ecumenist.

36. Bartleman, *Another Wave Rolls In!*, 55, cited in Daniels, "God Makes No Difference in Nationality."

37. In Europe, Hollenweger is considered to have founded the field of Pentecostal studies, particularly through his role in founding the Centre for Pentecostal and Charismatic Studies at the University of Birmingham, UK.

founded by non-Europeans. One is the global Pentecostal Movement, the other is Christianity. The former's founder was a black ecumenist from the United States, the latter's a story-telling Rabbi who belonged to the oral culture of the Middle East."[38] Pentecostal ecclesiology has started not from existing power structures but through a reconstruction of social and ecclesial orders with prophetic urgency. Hollenweger, Vondey, and other ecumenical theologians have seen Pentecostalism as a spiritual and theological renewal of Christianity where the Spirit expands and empowers the vision and mission of the Church beyond previous normalities.[39]

When the mainline theologian and missiologist Dale T. Irvin identified a moment in the 1990s when attitudes from and towards Pentecostals concerning ecumenism were changing, he contended that Seymour and the Mission had already "prefigured important themes and commitments that would come to characterize the ecumenical movement."[40] Irvin highlighted *The Apostolic Faith*'s statement that "(God) recognizes no flesh, no color, no names Azusa Mission stands for the unity of God's people everywhere. God is uniting His people, baptizing them by one Spirit in one body."[41] Spirit baptism could be seen as having ecumenical implications from the very beginning, even as it had deconstructive-reconstructive ecclesial implications.

While the early Pentecostal missions did not yet envision Pentecostalism in an ecumenism that sought to bless other Christian churches without necessarily having to join the Pentecostal movement, they did envision a simple and diverse Christian unity. As the nexus of theological convictions from the North American context was exported, very early on, through Pentecostal missions, they were enculturated and reconstructed in ways that allowed for a wider range of ecclesiological structures to develop in relation to indigenous values and traditions.[42] Yet a key characteristic of Pentecostal ecclesial self-understanding across cultures has been that of the Church as *koinonia*, as a charismatic fellowship of love in communion. Kärkkäinen has recognized this as a key to Pentecostal ecclesiology. Pentecostals "have almost from the start appreciated fellowship language over 'institutionalized church.'"[43] This was also recognized by the Third Quinquennium of the Roman Catholic-Pentecostal Dialogue, which had as its topic "Perspectives on *Koinonia*."

38. Hollenweger, *Pentecostalism*, 18.

39. Hollenweger, *Pentecostalism*; Vondey, *Beyond Pentecostalism*.

40. Irvin, "Drawing All Together," 26.

41. Irvin, "Drawing All Together," 27.

42. As the work of Allan Anderson and others has shown, this has been far from a simple process of exporting a form of North American Christianity to the global community.

43. Kärkkäinen, *An Introduction to Ecclesiology*, 75.

Yet none of this means that Pentecostal theologians are at all satisfied with the state of Pentecostal ecclesiology or ecclesial practices. Chan sees both the problem and the promise in Pentecostal ecclesiology:

> Pentecostals are [in addition to evangelicals] also becoming aware that some of the major problems confronting the movement today are at bottom ecclesiological in nature. . . . Whereas there is little within their own traditions that evangelicals could draw from to deal with their deficit, there is a rich implicit theology (*theologia prima*) within Pentecostal faith and experience which could contribute to the development of a coherent Pentecostal ecclesiology.[44]

Chan sees a particular problem in Pentecostal ecclesiology's excessive individualism and pragmatism. Yet he contends that Pentecostalism has the implicit resources to develop a strong and appropriate corrective to its contemporary ecclesiology, especially if Pentecostal churches recognize the greater Christian tradition and the process of 'traditioning' as resources for growth in ecclesial understanding.[45] Chan is blunt here. Pentecostal ecclesiologies "conceived in largely sociological and pragmatic terms" are now acknowledged to be "manifestly inadequate."[46]

This realization has resulted in subtle but potentially significant developments in Pentecostal ecclesiology. Perhaps the most important current statement on the Church in Pentecostal churches, the World Assemblies of God Fellowship's Statement of Faith Article 6, reads:

> The Church and its Mission: We believe that the church is the body of Christ and the habitation of God through the Spirit, witnesses to the presence of the kingdom of God in the present world, and universally includes all who are born again (Ephesians 1:22–23; 2:22; Romans 14:17–18; 1 Corinthians 4:20). We believe that the mission of the church is to (1) proclaim the good news of salvation to all humankind, (2) build up and train believers for spiritual ministry, (3) praise the Lord through worship, (4) demonstrate Christian compassion to all who suffer, and (5) exhibit unity as the body of Christ. (Matthew 28:19–20; 10:42; Ephesians 4:11–13).[47]

---

44. Chan, *Pentecostal Ecclesiology*, ix.

45. Chan, *Pentecostal Ecclesiology*; Chan, *Pentecostal Theology*.

46. Chan, *Pentecostal Ecclesiology*, 10.

47. World Assemblies of God Fellowship, "Statement of Faith."

The Church is understood as the body of Christ, the habitation of God through the Spirit, witness to God's kingdom, and constituted by all who have experienced spiritual rebirth in Christ. The second paragraph states the mission of the Church: proclaiming the gospel, discipleship, and worship—three areas of mission emphasized for most of the past century. Compassion and Church unity are, however, more recent additions. There is clear development here in ecclesial understanding from the earlier versions of the US Assemblies of God's Statement of Fundamental Truths. The original 1916 version read as follows:

> 8. THE CHURCH A LIVING ORGANISM. The Church is a living organ ism; a living body; yea the body of Christ; a habitation of God through the Spirit, with divine appointments for the fulfillment of her great commission. Every local assembly is an integral part of the General Assembly and Church of the Firstborn, written in heaven. Eph. 1:22, 23; 2:22; Heb. 12:23.[48]

As the various forms of Pentecostalism continue to emerge, develop, and form traditions, the question arises about their relation to the greater Christian tradition itself and the kind of ecclesial understanding found in *The Church: Towards a Common Vision*. Before addressing ecumenical and ecclesial issues, it is important to take into account the relationship between Pentecostal ecclesiologies and culture.

Pentecostal Ecclesiologies and Culture

Pentecostal churches have taken on many of the characteristics of late modern culture. They are usually indigenous to the many local cultures but also the global culture of the late modern world. Vondey has argued that Pentecostal culture is properly accounted for neither by a globalization thesis, a typically modern spreading of a homogenizing movement, nor a localization thesis, a typically post modern emphasis on the heterogeneity and incommensurability of the local, but as a 'glocalization.' Despite the awkward amalgamation in 'glocal' it is helpful as "the globalization of Pentecostalism consists of the production and reproduction of the local in the global and the global in the local, the mediation, or more precisely, the encoding and decoding of local distinctiveness and global generality."[49]

---

48. General Council of the Assemblies of God, "Minutes," 11. The minutes of all General Councils are accessible online through the Flower Pentecostal Heritage Center, the official archive of the Assemblies of God (www.ifphc.org).

49. Vondey, *Pentecostalism*, 25.

Pentecostal churches are filled with people who are on a quest to know God and themselves, and who desire to express their longings for life and love. They are situated in manifold socio-economic and political situations where they are often industrious and entrepreneurial, and in many contexts Pentecostals confront oppressing forces.[50] In these situations, from small Pentecostal gatherings in the Islamic world to congregations of all sizes sprawled throughout the countless conurbations on every continent to rural congregations throughout the world, Pentecostal congregations have a strong local and indigenous impulse. Part of this is attributable to the Pentecostal emphasis on experience. But it is even more so because of the underlying Pentecostal conviction that the Spirit is at work everywhere in their lives, and because of the significance of the Pentecost event pointing to the pouring of the Spirit upon all flesh. Pentecostals emphasize God's presence in all situations.[51]

Many Pentecostals have been concerned with syncretism between new global Pentecostal Christian communities and the traditional indigenous spiritual and religious tendencies of those peoples. Western Pentecostal missionaries often focused on biblical teaching and Pentecostal doctrines to ensure that the spiritual impulses which these new Pentecostals drew upon would be channeled into Pentecostal beliefs. Through much of this period, a contrasting concern arose that social and cultural concerns among Pentecostals have been at times reduced to the apolitical or 'other-worldly,' and that this would effectively translate into reactionary conservative politics, in North America and globally.[52]

However, Pentecostal spiritual and cultural resources have proven themselves stronger than any of those tendencies. By the early twenty-first century, concerns about Pentecostalism being an 'opiate of the people' or on the other hand 'so earthly minded that they are of no earthly good' are being labeled largely 'myths,' even if those charges contained some truth. These stereotypes held to some extent for earlier generations, but this has largely changed. Pentecostals are increasingly educated, socially mobile, and integrate spiritual with social concerns.[53] The political stances of Pentecostals are also much more complex than stereotypical.[54]

---

50. Johns, *Pentecostal Formation*; Yong, *In the Days of Caesar*; Miller and Yamamori, *Global Pentecostalism*.

51. Pentecostals also tend to account for divine absence as in the presence of evil. For example, Yong, *Beyond the Impasse*, 164–67.

52. Anderson, *Introduction to Pentecostalism*, 261–67.

53. Miller and Yamamori, *Global Pentecostalism*, 20–22.

54. See Pew Forum, "Spirit and Power."

The underdevelopment of Pentecostal ecclesiology has made Pentecostalism quite adaptable to existing cultural forms and yet by the same token has led Pentecostalism to be susceptible to uncritical acceptance of cultural assumptions and trends. Today, late modern consumerism has emerged as the greatest form of religio-cultural syncretism to challenge authentic Pentecostal faith. Underdeveloped ecclesiology has allowed various cultural understandings of religious communities and their purposes to step in to fill the gap.

In the past several decades, consumerism and capitalistic corporate culture have stepped into this gap in many cases, and not just in North America. This wider culture has taken advantage of the free church model adhered to by most Pentecostal churches. Phrases like 'church shopping,' rather than discerning what local congregation a believer is called to participate in, are normalized. Churches borrow sales models and persuasive rhetoric to gain adherents, even offering giveaways for attending. Abusive practices by some Pentecostal televangelists are well documented. Sociologists like Donald E. Miller and Tetsunao Yamamori speak of Pentecostals "compet(ing) for clients."[55] The wider music industry has co-opted some forms of Christian music to develop a Christian music industry that profits from 'worship music' and has profit as the primary end rather than worship. The ends here tend to be pragmatic and financial rather than spiritual-theological. Theodor Adorno's critique of the 'culture industry,' where a homogenizing industry takes over human creative powers harnessing it for profit, seems like a prophetic voice in this context.[56] Pentecostals are in a mostly unwitting relationship with the 'culture industry,' where pragmatic ends have snuck in and, at times, have replaced the deeper spiritual ends. Pentecostal ontological depths are subtly replaced with shallower purposes.

Yet at the same time, and against these late modern consumerist interpretations of humanity, exemplified by the quest for continual entertainment, Pentecostalism has continued to address the deeper plights of people facing various trials in life. This tension between assimilating late modern consumerism and pushing back against its thin view of human life and purposes can often be seen within the same Pentecostal congregation, or even the same worship service. Pentecostal churches often live in this tension.

Additionally, Pentecostalism has faced marginalization from powerful interests that want to tell humanity other stories about life and reality, usually secular stories whose agendas thinly veil interests of power and profit. Even so, self-disciplined and diligent Pentecostals of various types

---

55. Miller and Yamamori, *Global Pentecostalism*, 15.
56. Horkheimer and Adorno, *The Dialectic of Enlightenment*.

have continued to affirm the goodness of work. Still, the attempt by some to be relevant or to correlate Pentecostal understanding with contemporary culture has led to popularized forms of Pentecostalism correlated with the logic, ethic, and passions of late modern consumerism. This can be seen, in a prime set of instances, in the hermeneutics found in the proponents of the 'health and wealth' gospel that explains the success of this movement, especially promoted by American televangelists and Nigerian preachers.[57] Pentecostal churches have often preached to their people on their dignity, yet these interpretations of power and blessing have also blended in a theology that has drawn more deeply from consumerist and individualist late modern beliefs than from biblical or Christian traditions. These churches run the risk, through witting or unwitting sleight of hand, of moving Pentecostal spirituality away from its deep sources in the biblical narratives to cultural and idiosyncratic sources which too often betray those biblical imperatives and the depths of love for God and love and concern for others found within Pentecostal spirituality.

The 'health and wealth' churches are just one type of ecclesial 'orientation' found within Pentecostalism. These orientations, identified by Miller and Yamamori, transcend Pentecostal denominations, though certain orientations can be found more in one denomination or tradition than in others. For example, the 'health and wealth' orientation is prominent among newer indigenous Pentecostal churches in poorer nations and communities, but is rarer in established Pentecostal contexts. Outsiders to Pentecostalism tend to be more familiar with the orientation of this 'Prosperity Gospel,' and the older but still lingering legalistic and 'other-worldly' orientation. But Miller and Yamamori identify two important and newer ones. There is a routinized orientation that is a less passionate continuation of twentieth-century Pentecostal spirituality mixed with an interest in practical church programming. These churches continue but have softened the sectarian heritage and have embraced some elements of secular culture while rejecting others.[58]

The fourth orientation—beyond the 'prosperity gospel,' legalistic and routinized Pentecostalisms—is where Miller and Yamamori, and I, see the most potential for the future of Pentecostalism in a less recognized but nonetheless driving orientation among contemporary Pentecostals to be 'Progressive Pentecostals.' While they identified this orientation as emerging in

---

57. Miller and Yamamori, *Global Pentecostalism*, 29. Wariboko has offered an economic theory, and financial equation, explaining the assumptions and logic of the 'prosperity gospel' in "Faith Has a Rate of Return," ch. 4 of his *Economics in Spirit and Truth*, 87–104.

58. Miller and Yamamori, *Global Pentecostalism*, 25–31.

the 1990s, it also has been present since Pentecostal beginnings.[59] 'Progressive Pentecostals' are characterized by 'holistic ministry' where "they seek to model their behavior after the lifestyle of Jesus, who constantly blurred the line between the sacred and profane worlds, mixing with sinners and those in need."[60] Though they are almost always theologically orthodox, their practical theology "reflects a deeper theological truth that God's love is to be expressed unconditionally."[61] Evangelism and meeting practical human needs are both part of the mission of the Church. The bottom line for 'Progressive Pentecostals' is that "it is impossible to divorce moral and spiritual needs from physical and economic needs. The two are inextricably linked."[62]

Pentecostal ministries might be seen as in the vanguard of Christian mission here, and, like the growth and development of the early Church in the ante-Nicene era, growing substantially by meeting a nexus of spiritual, relational, and practical needs. And while some Pentecostals have sought attention for their work, many others have gone unrecognized on this front, and sociologists like Miller and Yamamori are left to address the lack of recognition of their work.[63] Pentecostals have often been criticized for not working on the structural levels of injustices. Yet Pentecostals have only occasionally been in a position to do so in the contexts of secular political and social power. Pentecostals instead have found a way through Spirit empowerment to seek and work toward those intimations of God's kingdom and shalom that can be had in the here and now.[64]

Pentecostal ecclesiologies most often have been implicit rather than reflective, pragmatic rather than theoretical. The ecclesiologies in most Pentecostal fellowships result from an understanding, usually generated by local church leaders, that blends what are considered biblical and spiritual principles with indigenous cultural ways of life. These come together in spiritual-cultural dialectics in which Pentecostals have formed an ecclesiology that moves between a vision of Spirit-baptized community and a pragmatic ethos formed in the context of late modernity. On a spiritual-theological level, however, the Pentecostal primal spiritual impulse has represented God's presence among the marginalized, under-resourced, and impoverished. It has meant that the Spirit is there, being 'poured out on all

59. Miller and Yamamori, *Global Pentecostalism*, 30.

60. Miller and Yamamori, *Global Pentecostalism*, 59.

61. Miller and Yamamori, *Global Pentecostalism*.

62. Miller and Yamamori, *Global Pentecostalism*, 62.

63. Anderson, *To the Ends of the Earth*, provides historical work on this.

64. Yong, *In the Days of Caesar*, 310.

flesh,' in spite of the lack of means.[65] Thus, Pentecostal ecclesiology more often than not has been an ecclesiology 'from below,' and it has both benefited
and suffered from this situation. It has benefited from its consonance with
and flexibility towards culture, even as it seems to go against so much that is
prevalent among the powerful cultural forces that it confronts.

A Theology and Ontology of Spirit
Baptism for Pentecostal Ecclesiology

Central to the agenda of this chapter is the conviction that a Pentecostal
ecclesiology, especially an ecumenical-Pentecostal ecclesiology, will not
be fruitful if it simply articulates a justification for the Pentecostal status
quo. Pentecostal ecclesiology is better advised to begin with appreciation
for its own spiritual tradition, intuitions, and implicit ecclesiology in order
to merge that reality with further biblical, theological, and philosophical
resources for ecclesiological development. A lot of the resources will come
through other Christian traditions. At the same time there is a sense among
many Pentecostals that Pentecostal Christianity has indeed brought about a
renewal of certain aspects of the nature and mission of the Church. Perhaps
this hermeneutically organized merging can result in faithful constructive
work toward providing a renewed Pentecostal ecclesiology alongside a renewed ecumenical ecclesiology.

The precedent for this approach has already been laid down. I have argued that a major theological hermeneutic already present among Pentecostal
theologians is what I have called the 'ecumenical-Pentecostal hermeneutic.'
This is a hermeneutic of dialogue and growth through which Pentecostal
theologians seek to draw on other Christian theologians and their traditions
to move towards a more mature and ecumenical-Pentecostalism.[66] Authentic
early Pentecostalism, exemplified by Seymour, had this deeply ecumenical
impulse which sought to transcend the tragedy of Christian divisions in one
baptism of divine love. Throughout Pentecostal history, a number of key figures have represented this impulse in their person and theologies. However,
no one, in my view, has provided more important constructive work toward
an ecumenical-Pentecostal ecclesiology than Frank Macchia. A systematic
theologian and professor at Vanguard University, the regional university of
the Assemblies of God in southern California, he has been a significant participant in ecumenical work and dialogues, including with the WCC/NCC.

---

65. See Johns, *Pentecostal Formation.*

66. See chapter 6, "The Ecumenical-Pentecostal Hermeneutic," in Oliverio, *Theological Hermeneutics,* 253–314.

Macchia's work on the central distinctive doctrine of Classical Pentecostal theology—the baptism in the Holy Spirit—offers a way forward for not only Pentecostal theology of Spirit baptism but for a pneumatological ecumenical ecclesiology. His approach to Spirit baptism in *Baptized in the Spirit* provides a way forward for those concerned with producing an ecumenical-Pentecostal ecclesiology.[67] The Pentecostal practice and doctrine of baptism in the Spirit, and its relation to speaking in tongues, *glossolalia*, has often functioned as a shibboleth defining who is a Classical Pentecostal in good standing and who is not. Macchia, however, has sought to broaden and deepen theological understanding of the biblical 'metaphor' of Spirit baptism, turning a shibboleth into a resource for ecumenism.

Baptism in the Spirit speaks of an experience, yet also a doctrine. As a metaphor, it images immersion into the life and purpose of the Spirit of God, and theological articulation of this part of Christian life. The experience of Spirit baptism is what Pentecostals often cite as their experience of transformation beyond conversion. As Studebaker summarizes, "Pentecostals have routinely turned to the biblical metaphor of Spirit baptism to describe their experience of the Spirit despite the fact that they may disagree over the doctrinal formulation, purpose, and the signs of Spirit baptism."[68] The Classical Pentecostal formulation of Spirit baptism, especially as instituted by the Assemblies of God and other Classical Pentecostal fellowships, is that it is an empowerment for mission and service, and that it has glossolalia as its 'initial, physical evidence,' or, in older Pentecostal parlance, 'its Bible sign.'

Macchia considers that Pentecostals and other Christians do not entirely realize all we have in Spirit baptism. For "Spirit baptism gave rise to the global church and remains the very substance of the church's life in the Spirit, including its charismatic life and mission."[69] As with Irenaeus, "where the Spirit of God is, there is the church and all grace."[70] While Macchia partially affirms Chan's affirmation that the Spirit is the "church-located, church-shaped Spirit,"[71] he broadens this affirmation to see the Spirit as working dialectically between the kingdom of God and the Church. Spirit baptism is a baptism into *koinonia* fellowship and the mission of the Church. As the Trinitarian persons pour into one another in *perichoresis*, then also in creation and redemption, so also is the Spirit present in the Church in its

---

67. Macchia, *Baptized in the Spirit*.

68. Studebaker, *From Pentecost to the Triune God*, 49.

69. Macchia, *Baptized in the Spirit*, 155.

70. Macchia, *Baptized in the Spirit*, 155–56, citing *Adversus Haereses* 3.24.1.

71. Macchia, *Baptized in the Spirit*, citing Chan, "Mother Church," 198. Chan's development of a Pentecostal 'ecclesia-centered pneurnatology' can be found in his *Pentecostal Ecclesiology*.

koinonia and its mission to the world. Thus, for Macchia, "this ecumenical focus on *koinonia* is significant, since there can be no radical disjunction between the kingdom and the church in the light of the Trinitarian structure of Spirit baptism" where "Jesus mediates the Spirit who proceeds from the Father."[72] Therefore, "the love and *koinonia* at the heart of the kingdom both constitute the church and are embodied and proclaimed through the church to the world by the baptism in the Spirit" so that "Spirit baptism means that the *koinonia* of God is not closed but open to the world."[73]

Macchia's approach to Spirit baptism has provided an ecumenical way forward for Pentecostals by, first, affirming it as the "crown jewel" of Pentecostal theology.[74] Yet instead of carefully guarding this jewel through an apologetic of the doctrine as biblically justified, subsequent to salvation, and with tongues as its sign, or rather than diminishing the doctrine as a theological artifact of early Pentecostalism, Macchia has operated with a method that has sought to simultaneously deepen and broaden the doctrine. He deepens Pentecostal understanding of Spirit baptism by looking at the fuller biblical witness, and not just Luke-Acts. A deeper understanding of Spirit baptism then emerges that sees the metaphor imaging Pentecostal charismatic experience of empowerment and life in the Spirit, but also broadens it to incorporate soteriological and sacramental interpretation of the metaphor from the New Testament. Macchia's perspective allows for incorporating aspects of Reformed and Catholic along with other Christian visions of Spirit baptism into an ecumenical theology of Spirit baptism.[75] Macchia's approach is commendable for its spiritual vision since it takes account of what several other Christian traditions have found in their theological understandings of the experience of the Spirit. It simultaneously gives an ecclesiological account that can better support the kind of holistic Pentecostal practices articulated by Miller and Yamamori.

Here, though, I want to suggest that it is the ontology to which his theology of Spirit baptism points that provides a particular contribution to ecumenical theology. It is an ontology of divine love. For Macchia, the central Pentecostal doctrine of Spirit baptism needs to declare not only an empowerment for service *but also* holiness through understanding Spirit baptism as a baptism into divine love. It is a gracious act of God to invite us into participation in divine love.[76] Integrating his ecumenical theology

---

72. Macchia, *Baptized in the Spirit*, 160.

73. Macchia, *Baptized in the Spirit*, 161.

74. Macchia, *Baptized in the Spirit*, 20.

75. Macchia, *Baptized in the Spirit*, 19–88.

76. Land described this need for integration of empowerment and holiness for

with his constructive understanding, Macchia claims that the Catholic and Reformed identifications of Spirit baptism with salvation itself at least implicitly identify baptism, that is, the baptism of Christian initiation, with the discovery of divine love. He reflects that there is an ecumenical mandate "that Christians must rediscover their first love, but in even greater fervency than ever before," which explains the Pentecostal rendition of Spirit baptism as an event subsequent to salvation that represents a deepening or revival of faith by the rediscovery of divine love.[77] Perhaps Pentecostalism might be understood to bring this charism of the renewal of divine love to the Church.

Macchia holds that as Spirit baptism is central to Pentecostal theology, divine love is central to Pentecostal ontology since Spirit baptism is precisely baptism into divine love. This, however, is a chastened ontology, not one that mistakes the theologian's or philosopher's insights or names for that which is itself. Yet it uses the name 'love' strongly, in this case, to identify the nature of God. "Love is God's supreme gift, for it transcends all emotion, conceptuality, and action only to inspire all three. It gives us life and that more abundantly. Love is not only God's supreme gift, it is at the very essence of God's nature as God. There is nothing greater than divine love (I Cor. 13:13). . . . Love is absolute to the nature of God. It is the essence of God and the substance of our participation in God."[78] Thus Macchia concludes that "Theological reflection on Spirit baptism as the organizing principle of a Pentecostal theology must ultimately conclude that the substance of the Christian life is God's love."[79] That is, the Christian participates in godly love as a gracious gift that is from God, and the substance of life in the Spirit.

More precisely, this ontology of love is Trinitarian and eschatological. It is Trinitarian in that the love of the Father and the Son, the Spirit, is poured out as a "redemptive force" imparting God's love to the world.[80] It is eschatological because it is the victory of divine love, a victory not reducible to a charting of the end times. It is the victory of justice and mercy over oppression and indignity that finds its end in God whose identity is 'love' (1 John 4:8, 16). Thus, an ontology of the God who is love could not begin

---

Pentecostal theology in his *Pentecostal Spirituality*. Macchia develops this as participation, in *Justified in the Spirit*, 186–218, 237–41.

77. Macchia, *Baptized in the Spirit*, 258.

78. Macchia, *Baptized in the Spirit*, 259. Macchia quotes Karl Barth in support: "The Christian life begins with love. It also ends with love . . . there is also nothing beyond love. There is no higher or better being or doing in which we can leave it behind us" (*Church Dogmatics*, 371, in *Baptized in the Spirit*, 259).

79. Macchia, *Baptized in the Spirit*, 259.

80. Macchia, *Baptized in the Spirit*, 260. Macchia draws from both Barth and Emil Brunner, *The Christian Doctrine of God*.

with an abstract concept of 'love' which is then applied to God, but must begin with God's self-revelation and self-impartation.[81] Love is not a mere attribute but "God's very nature."[82] Macchia follows Jürgen Moltmann's affirmation that "the divine freedom to love cannot involve a freedom not to love, since love is essential to God's nature" so that "God's freedom is to be understood within the context of divine self-giving and not apart from it." And this includes a genuine love for the "other" so closely connected with God's self-giving love in creating; this is "God for us."[83]

Macchia's theology of Spirit baptism, and its attendant ontology, are exemplified in his summarizing flourish:

> The point is that the God of Spirit baptism is the God who overflows with abundant life and who seeks to embrace the others with life-renewing love. The embrace does not oppress, force, smother, or annihilate the others but rather creates space for them in their unique otherness and fills them with life abundant so that they can be everything they were meant to be in all of their uniqueness. The tongues of humanity were not dissolved at Pentecost by the flaming tongues of God's holy presence (Acts 2:4). The diversity of human cultural self-expression was preserved in all of its uniqueness and differences but caught up in a shared praise, devotion, and witness. God's freedom in this outpouring of divine love is a freedom to overcome all resistance and barriers to reconcile a people into a shared communion.[84]

This ontic affirmation of love has significant ecclesial implications, for "The self-giving God of Spirit baptism produces a self-giving people in mission. The God who seeks to save the lost produces a people who do the same. To love God is to be shaped by that love so as to share its affections and passions."[85] Pentecostalism is called to operate in the 'analogy of love.'[86]

---

81. Macchia, *Baptized in the Spirit*, 261.

82. Macchia, *Baptized in the Spirit*, 262.

83. Macchia, *Baptized in the Spirit*, 263, developing Moltmann, *The Trinity and the Kingdom*, 52–56.

84. Macchia, *Baptized in the Spirit*, 264.

85. Macchia, *Baptized in the Spirit*, 264.

86. David Nichols has suggested that Pentecostals operate not on the 'analogy of being' or 'of faith' but on the 'analogy of love,' which is "the correct existential basis for theology," in "The Search for a Pentecostal Structure," 72.

Pentecostal Ecclesial Vision and *The Church: Towards a Common Vision*

In the Preface of *The Church: Towards a Common Vision*, Canon John Gibaut and Metropolitan Vasilios state that the purpose of the document is twofold: to bring about renewal and to bring about theological agreement on the Church. The call for renewal and theological agreement on the nature and mission of the Church are calls that resonate with purposes deeply felt by many Pentecostal bodies even as Pentecostals typically range from skepticism to cautious optimism concerning ecumenism. Further, and quite importantly, there is a great deal in *The Church* that Pentecostals could and should affirm. In this fifth section, after developing a basis for response in the preceding sections, I will directly respond to the first three of the five questions posed by the Faith and Order Commission in the document:

1. To what extent does this text reflect the ecclesiological understanding of your church?

2. To what extent does this text offer a basis for growth in unity among the churches?

3. What adaptations or renewal in the life of your church does this statement challenge your church to work for?[87]

There are a number of ways in which *The Church* does reflect Pentecostal ecclesiology and offer a basis for Pentecostal unity with other churches. The opening section on "The Church in the Design of God" (I.A.1–4) resonates with core Pentecostal affirmations, such as the centrality of Christ, the work of the Spirit, and the Church as the *koinonia* fellowship central to God's redemptive purposes. As I have been proposing above, *koinonia*, together with Spirit baptism, are locations of potentially fruitful ecumenical dialogue for and with Pentecostals. Further, in the document, beloved Pentecostal scriptural texts—from the Pentecostal canon within the canon—in Acts 1:8, the Johannine Pentecost (John 20:19–23), and the Great Commission (Matt 28:18–20 and parallels)—are treated as constitutive of the Church's mission (I.A.2).The Day of Pentecost itself is regarded as where the Spirit began to equip disciples for mission in the world (I.A.3). In *The Church*, evangelism is affirmed throughout, though contextualized by concerns of other Christian traditions, with emphases, language, and meaning different from those usually found among Pentecostal churches.

It is at this very point that Vondey, as an ecumenical-Pentecostal theologian, offered a criticism of *The Church's* predecessor text, *The Nature and*

---

87. Questions 4 and 5 are addressed below in the concluding section.

Mission of the Church (Faith and Order Paper 198). As a historical theologian, Vondey argues that Pentecostalism holds within it the other major Christian confessions. Pentecostal churches and theologies came out of and have drawn on Catholic, Lutheran, Calvinist, Methodist, Evangelical, and Orthodox churches. Pentecostal ecclesiological understanding is indebted to these confessions but has experienced a transformation away from them as well. Vondey contends that Pentecostalism is a renewal movement within the Church, and, as such, is concerned with transformation, confrontation and urgency *within* the Church as it moves in mission toward the world and thus towards the inbreaking of God's kingdom.[88] He states that, "For Pentecostals, Church is a reflective, discerning reality that finds consensus about its nature and mission not only in formal statements but in an often painful process of repentance, forgiveness, conversion and renewal in and among the churches while the Church proclaims the gospel to the world."[89] Pentecostals might well question whether *The Church* reflects their "passion for the kingdom," a passion that predominantly includes concern for regular, explicit evangelization.[90] On this point, the wider ecumenical movement might seek to understand better this Pentecostal passion and its relation to the growth of the global Church.

While the language and narrative of *The Church* on evangelization are not typically Pentecostal, the document's ecclesiological understanding might resonate with Pentecostals, at least those Pentecostals who have moved beyond sectarianism. For example, the language and narrative of "The Church of the Triune God as *Koinonia*" (II.B.13–24) hold ecumenical potential for Pentecostals. As contended above, the ecumenical rendition of baptism in the Spirit, from Seymour to Macchia, is a significant contribution which Pentecostals present to the greater body of Christ. Spirit baptism is a returning, again and again, to our 'first love,' as we are drawn to the Father with Jesus the Spirit baptizer, so that we are empowered to live lives of holiness and empowerment in *koinonia* fellowship with one another. Jesus' disciples are known by their love for one another (John 13:35). And the ecumenical-Pentecostal rendition of Spirit baptism is a place for openness between Pentecostals and other Christians on a renewed understanding of the Church as *koinonia*, that is, of one another as *in* the Spirit.

The marks of the Church as one, holy, catholic, and apostolic, from the Nicene-Constantinopolitan Creed of 381 CE and as articulated in "The One, Holy, Catholic, Apostolic Church" (II.B.22–24), requires clarification

---

88. Vondey, "Pentecostal Perspectives," 62–66.

89. Vondey, "Pentecostal Perspectives," 65–66.

90. This is Steven Land's emphasis in *Pentecostal Spirituality*.

regarding Pentecostal affirmation of these marks, and are a location where Pentecostal churches and other churches might challenge one another productively.

Whereas *The Church* understands current divisions in the Church as "stand(ing) in contrast to the oneness" (II.B.22), Pentecostals have often seen these divisions as necessary for faithfulness to the gospel, and hold that divisions are the result of the failures of other Christian churches. Pentecostals have tended to affirm the essential oneness of the Church. But in contrast to *The Church* (11.B.23), they understand this unity as that of individuals connected to Christ through faith and in the Spirit, and in this way connected to one another. On this point, many ecumenical-Pentecostal theologians see this as an issue where it is primarily Pentecostal ecclesiology that is in need of growth and change. Chan, for one, contends that "there is a deep interplay between the corporate and personal aspects . . . the corporate, however, is the primal reality."[91] Ecumenical-Pentecostal theologians are challenging an overemphasis on individualism in Pentecostal ecclesiology. As stated earlier, Pentecostals also see institutional or organizational oneness or unity as secondary to spiritual unity. Here, ecumenical-Pentecostal theologians are challenging their Pentecostal brothers and sisters to recognize the corporate nature of the Church's existence, and the necessary interplay between the 'visible Church' and the 'invisible Church.'

Whereas *The Church* speaks the language of holiness (II.B.22), Pentecostals often question the depth of that commitment to holiness among some who belong to and even lead other Christian churches. Pentecostals not uncommonly believe that other Christians are too worldly, and that they are too easily willing to compromise biblical faith and morality for culturally prevalent trends. Further, Pentecostals often resent the criticisms they sometimes hear about their moral stances from other Christians who seem to be allied with worldly interests against theirs. On the other hand, Pentecostals are sometimes just as unaware or cultural sources of their own beliefs. Holiness is a key area of ecumenical hindrance for Pentecostals.

Whereas *The Church* affirms that because of catholicity "the Church's mission transcends all barriers and proclaims the Gospel to all peoples" (II.B.22), Pentecostals have sought to embrace the mission of the Church "to the ends of the earth" (Acts 1:8). The Pentecostal emphasis on the indigenous and on enculturation has seen manifold success, yet Pentecostal churches are in need of maturation in their mission. Here, Chan has called for just that in Pentecostal 'traditioning.' "The strength of Pentecostal traditioning lies in its powerful narratives . . . its weakness lies in its inability to

91. Chan, *Pentecostal Ecclesiology*, 77.

explain itself."[92] In the sense that Pentecostals have brought powerful Christian narratives to the ends of the earth, Pentecostal catholicity has been a success. Pentecostals have brought a passion for the mission of the Church in the world 'to the ends of the earth.' Yet Pentecostal catholicity is also in need of significant growth in the breadth of its ecclesial self-understanding and its understanding of other churches. The good news here is that the resources are often at hand, if Pentecostals are willing to look to the greater *oikumene* of Christian faith.

Whereas *The Church* recognizes that apostolicity calls Christians "to be ever faithful to these apostolic origins" and affirms "apostolic succession in ministry, under the guidance of the Holy Spirit" (II.B.22), Pentecostals have understood the 'apostolic faith' as that which proclaims the true and 'full gospel.' Pentecostals have sensed a directness between themselves and the faith of Jesus' original apostles to the degree that some Pentecostals have had a sense that the greater Christian tradition can be skipped over. As Yong summarizes, "the episcopal notion of apostolic succession in the historical Christian tradition is redefined functionally according to the Spirit-empowered vocation of mission and church planting."[93] Apostolicity in Pentecostal churches can range from a humble desire to be faithful to the apostolic faith, to self-appointed 'apostles' who stand over local hierarchies, to networks of missional communities working on the frontiers of Christian evangelization and re-evangelization. Here as well, ecumenical-Pentecostal theologians tend to call their own churches to recognize the greater and historic apostolicity of the Church. The common Pentecostal understanding of the Church's place in God's design for the world has tended to eschew sacramentality and focuses primarily on the 'invisible Church.' Thus, discussions of the Church as sacrament (II.C.27), on sacraments, and on church offices and authority (III.B.37, 40–57) tend to be non-starters in ecumenical discussions with Pentecostal churches. In my view, as far as ecumenical dialogue towards unity goes, this is a bridge that might be better crossed at a later time, when Pentecostals have developed a more mature ecclesiology, and the relations between Pentecostal and other Christian churches have become more firmly established. Nevertheless, on these matters, some Pentecostal theologians have been at work, and dialogue with those theologians is perhaps the best place for those of other Christian communions to engage in dialogue.[94]

---

92. Chan, *Pentecostal Theology*, 20.

93. Yong, *Renewing Christian Theology*, 174.

94. For example, Chan, *Pentecostal Ecclesiology*; Green, *Towards a Pentecostal Theology of the Lord's Supper*.

However, the document's paragraphs on "Communion in Unity and Diversity" (II.D.28–30) and "Communion of Local Churches" (II.E.3–32) are already themes of greater common understanding. They invoke understanding in line with the 'many tongues' principle when it speaks of the legitimate diversity that enriches the Church. The indigenous emphasis in Pentecostalism also resonates with *The Church*. It holds that legitimate Christian diversity "is compromised whenever Christians consider their own cultural expressions of the Gospel as the only authentic ones, to be imposed upon Christians of other cultures" (II.D.28). This principle also means, then, that condescension towards the sometimes folksy ways of Pentecostals might be reconsidered in light of this good ecumenical principle.

The final section of the document, "The Church: In and for the World" (IV), begins with John 3:16 (IV.A.58), a verse that is precious to many Pentecostals, orienting the Pentecostal imagination concerning God's salvific purposes for humanity and the world. While this final section addresses very important practical issues—religious pluralism, Christian morality in the contemporary world, and the Church-society relationship—*The Church* seems to adopt the strategy of a lower common denominator document for what can be confessed together. It is well noted that while such minimalism is sometimes the best that can be done, this approach also runs the risk of equivocation of meaning among constituencies which have real disagreements.[95]

Toward a Pentecostal Pastoral Theology of *The Church: Towards a Common Vision*

The fourth and fifth questions posed by the Faith and Order Commission are:

4. How far is your church able to form closer relationships in life and mission with those churches which can acknowledge in a positive way the account of the Church described in this statement?

5. What aspects of the life of the Church could call for further discussion and what advice could your church offer for the ongoing work by Faith and Order in the area of ecclesiology?

In this final section, I will primarily address issues underlying Pentecostal response to the fourth question. As far as any advice from the Pentecostal churches to the Commission concerning its further work, the Commission has at its disposal a generation of Pentecostal theologians, such as Macchia, Yong and Vondey, who have already made significant contributions

95. IV.B.63 expresses this problem well.

to ecumenical theology. I have identified the connection between Spirit baptism and *koinonia* as a fruitful Pentecostal contribution to ecumenical theology. In addition, Pentecostal "passion for God's kingdom," especially through explicit proclamation of the gospel, ought to be considered in any document that would like to include Pentecostal ecclesiology in its ecumenical breadth.

The need for Church unity is a matter that Pentecostals have both had great implicit, operational insight on, as in the Seymourian vision, and have also neglected to the point of harm. The common failure of Pentecostals to understand and appreciate other Christians at the local levels frequently has resulted in a sectarianism that has hindered Christian mission. This failure is understandable, and even justifiable in some contexts where regnant or traditional churches have had serious failures to live out the nature and mission of the Church. Yet a better way forward may allow for a vision of Pentecostalism as renewal for all Christians, as Vondey suggests, and the Seymourian-Macchian vision of Spirit baptism as baptism into divine love, a vision which might incorporate perhaps the whole *oikumene* of Christ's people. Too often, however, and contrary to Pentecost, Pentecostals have seen their own tongue as the only faithful one that witnesses to the living God. This has meant practical harm to other churches and to the mission of God's people in *koinonia* fellowship together. Of course, what has been just stated here can be applied to other churches as well.

There are several reasons for the lack of a drive for Christian unity among Pentecostals today. As just mentioned, Pentecostals can question the theological or spiritual faithfulness of other churches. Another reason is a simple lack of understanding of other Christians. Sectioning themselves off, Pentecostals sometimes do not know their Christian brothers and sisters, and quickly write them off because of differences associated with secular, popular, or compromised culture. Concerning this, Pentecostals are often in need of more developed judgment.

Yet, in my judgment, consumerism is perhaps the greatest obstacle to Christian unity among Pentecostals at the current moment, even if its influence often goes unnoticed. The Pentecostal indigenous instinct has sometimes unwittingly taken on secular and consumerist ways, even as Pentecostal spirituality's communal and spiritually edifying tendencies stand in deep tension with them. On this matter, Pentecostalism is at odds with itself. Among the majority of Pentecostal theologians, there is little doubt as to where priorities ought to lie. Pentecostal churches too often end up in a spirit of competition with one another, let alone other Christian traditions. While this 'spirit of competition' can generate creativity and motivation for ministry, it often reinforces wrong motives and is, essentially, another spirit since the Holy Spirit cannot be bought (Acts 8:18–24). The spirit of competition ends in lack of ministry to those to whom God has called his people to go. In some contexts, Pentecostal churches are too busy competing for tithers, influence, notoriety, and numbers—with motivations only thinly veiled—to develop a more mature sense of Christian mission, and to continue going to the more difficult places, a characteristic of the tradition of Pentecostal mission. The deep brokenness of our world ought to call God's people to unity in mission, especially to "the least of these."

Another reason for the lack of drive for Christian unity among Pentecostals is the lack of ecclesial leadership on the issue. Pentecostal theologians have, by and large, been the ones leading the way towards Christian unity. Perhaps a Pentecostal denominational leader will place this matter higher on the agenda for Pentecostals in the not so distant future. While Pentecostal ecclesial leaders have, in general, shifted their stance from a negative evaluation of ecumenism to a cautiously positive one, the next step is needed. Pentecostals have moved from Pius IX to Leo XIII but are still awaiting John XXIII.

Pentecostals must, and I believe will, find their drive for Christian unity because of their baptism into the Spirit, into the love of God and *koinonia* fellowship that has unity in such fellowship as a necessary end. As Seymour was driven toward Christian unity by his experience of the Spirit, so also will Pentecostals who operate on the 'analogy of love.' Because God has loved us Pentecostals (1 John 4:19), we might be empowered to obey the Great Commandment, and love our Christian neighbor as ourselves (Mark 12:29–31 and parallels), even as we urge them on in living out the Great Commission (Matt 28:19–20).

6

Scripture, Experience, and Community

Western theology, as it has come out of the period of the Enlightenment and the age of modern rationalism, has been pressed to deal with the historicity and truth of the Christian faith as a prolegomena to its theological agenda. Wolfhart Pannenberg's short introduction to his larger three-volume systematic theology exemplifies this. The great modern theologian begins not only with the affirmation that Christian faith is always personal, a matter of genuine confession, but by arguing that it necessarily makes historical truth claims. For "the story of Jesus Christ has to be history."[1] Theology must be about truth claims, and even so first, because if this is surrendered, or even equivocated upon, the clergy will "become doubtful about the truth of the gospel, they will replace it by other 'causes,' and the believers will be disturbed, because they no longer get to hear in church what they rightfully expect to be taught there."[2] Claims concerning personal relationship with God must be grounded in historical theological truth claims about God and God's self-revelation to humanity.

Modern theology has also often begun with questions of truth about God through the pressing questions of human existence. Karl Rahner addressed the truth of God's existence, not through historical claims so much as through those great questions. In Rahner's modern Christian existentialism,

---

1. Pannenberg, *An Introduction to Systematic Theology*, 5.
2. Pannenberg, *An Introduction to Systematic Theology*, 6.

theology is necessary because 'man' would not be 'man' without God.[3] The question of God makes us human because it places before us the totality of all that exists, and to be human is to consider that totality. For if ever the word 'God' is forgotten by humanity, "Man would have forgotten the totality and its ground. . . . What would it be like? We can only say: he would have ceased being a man. He would have regressed to the level of a clever animal."[4] Theology begins because we find ourselves before the questions of transcendence, totality, and the meaning of our own existence.

Pentecostal theology has tended to begin differently. Pentecostal theology does deal with the question of the historical truth of Christian faith—it usually assumes it. And Pentecostal theology does address existential questions—it often implicitly and at times explicitly does so. Rather, Pentecostal theology, especially in its less borrowed forms, begins with the Christian's experience of God, with a special emphasis on the presence of God's Spirit. This has also meant that Pentecostal theology has been concerned with the integration of God's story in Scripture in relation to the manifold stories of human experience with the Spirit Pentecostal theological hermeneutics have been identified as constituted by a trialectic that has developed within this young Christian tradition—the interplay of the Scriptures, experience of the Spirit, and life in Spirit-filled communities. This trialectic is central to contemporary Pentecostal theological hermeneutics, and thus central *to* the theological understanding with which many Pentecostal theologians and communities are operating.[5]

Pentecostal Theological Style

The family of Pentecostal theologies tends to approach theology with a pneumatologically-oriented version of the Anselmian-Augustinian *credo ut intelligam*, with an approach that generally moves away from rationalized versions of faith seeking understanding towards a rendition that emphasizes the affective and pneumatic in theological understanding. Pentecostal theology has tended towards an integrative hermeneutic of experiential faith working out its understanding in relation to its readings of Scripture, the world, and human life. As James K. A. Smith has argued, Pentecostalism does not offer a set of propositional truths, rather "a latent but distinctive *understanding* of the world, an affective 'take' on the world that constitutes

3. Rahner, of course, was referring to men and women with a masculine term.

4. Rahner, *Foundations of Christian Faith*, 48.

5. This trialectic has especially been put forth by Archer, *A Pentecostal Hermeneutic*; Archer, "Pentecostal Story."

more of a social imaginary than a cognitive framework."[6] Or, as Steven Land has contended, Pentecostal theology is embedded in its spirituality. Pentecostal theology is about not just orthodoxy and orthopraxis but also orthopathy.[7]

For much of the century-plus history of Pentecostalism, Pentecostal theology has been primarily embedded in the songs, preaching, oral traditions, testimonies, devotional practices, and lived experiences of Pentecostals, even as the past several decades have seen the growth of formal Pentecostal theological work. The family of Pentecostal theologies has sometimes been judged as deficient by scholarly standards, and while there is some justification for this general criticism, much of the condescension is the result of a failure of understanding among those condescending. This is, in part, because Pentecostal theology has operated with a dissenting formula concerning the mix of the spiritual and the rational in theology, one which attributes a greater role to the spiritual in its constitution. As Douglas Jacobsen puts it, although Pentecostal theology does not exist in a class by itself, it has a "different center of gravity" than other theological traditions.[8]

While some have emphasized the seeming focus on experience among Pentecostals at the expense of theological reflection, Pentecostals have, in fact, understood the need for theology as a second order reflection on the Christian life, working out and developing that which is embedded in interpretive experiences of spiritual life. It is simply a human need to reflect and understand. So the first and then subsequent generations of Pentecostals redeveloped a formula for theology which emphasized experiential spiritual understanding. They developed a hermeneutic that read the Bible, God's actions among them, and their life experiences as ways of knowing God. Yet against the misreading of Pentecostalism that it merely represents generalized spiritual experience, Steven Studebaker has argued that this cannot be the essence of Pentecostal ism because Pentecostal experience involves a latent theology embedded in such experience of the Spirit-that is, it *is* experience of the Triune God.[9]

To dichotomize experience and thought decisively is to misunderstand the ways humans understand and interpret life and reality. Hermeneutics always involves embedded understanding formed by language, tradition, proclivities and habits that, while often taken for granted and left unreflected or minimally reflected upon, nevertheless provide the interpretive

6. Smith, *Thinking in Tongues*, 31.

7. Land, *Pentecostal Spirituality*.

8. Jacobsen, *Thinking in the Spirit*, 7.

9. Studebaker, *From Pentecost to the Triune God*, 11–35, 189–92.

structures not only for second order conscious, reflective understanding but also first order intuitive experiences, including spiritual experiences, which embed much prior understanding into human experiences.[10] First order interpreted experiences of life give rise to second order reflections and evaluations. This second order thinking interprets and disciplines first order habits, pressing its interpretations back down on them. Yesterday's interpretations become today's preunderstanding; today's interpretations become tomorrow's preunderstanding.

Pentecostal theologies have tended to place greater weight on the first order experiences, as both source of theological understanding as well as one of its ends. To the critics of Pentecostalism who have claimed that there is little in Pentecostal theology to be explicated, Studebaker offers the analog of the Christian understanding of God as Trinity prior to Nicaea in 325. There is much implicit in Pentecostal understanding that, with time and some patience, will providea more mature theological tradition that is now in the making.[11] Pentecostal theologians, perhaps especially ecumenical-Pentecostal theologians, are already doing so.

A surge in that maturation process might be understood as having begun in the 1990s when Pentecostals began to develop a theological approach that sought to drink from the wells of the tradition's own resources while nondefensively drawing upon ecumenical sources for furthering Pentecostal theology. The early 1990s saw a number of calls for Pentecostals *to* resist the reduction of their spiritual-theological vision to a sub-division of Evangelical theology; rather, they called Pentecostals to drink from their own wells, and to work *out* their own intuitions and spiritual understanding into a more mature and authentic theology.[12] D. Lyle Dabney's call to develop a 'theology of the Third Article' of the Creed, beginning with the Spirit—to throw off 'Saul's armor' and take up 'David's sling' was his metaphor—epitomized the paradigm shift that began in the 1990s and which has become

10. The work of the Nobel Prize winning psychologist Daniel Kahneman, and his late research partner Amos Tversky, has developed psychological theory based on human understanding consisting of two systems that continually interact with one another: System 1 and System 2. Kahneman has argued that while System 2, our "conscious reasoning self that has beliefs, makes choices, and decides what to think about and what to do" is often seen as being in charge of human knowledge, it is System 1 that guides most of human understanding as it "continually constructs a coherent interpretation of what is going on in our world at any instant . . . the complexity and richness of the automatic and often unconscious processes that underlie intuitive thinking . . . these automatic processes explain the heuristics of judgment." See Kahneman, *Thinking*, 13, 21.

11. Studebaker, *From Pentecost to the Triune God*, 191–92.

12. Dempster, "Paradigm Shifts and Hermeneutics"; Faupel, "Whither Pentecostalism?"; Johns, "The Adolescence of Pentecostalism."

predominant in the contemporary Pentecostal theological community by the second decade of the twenty-first century.[13] Subsequently, Kenneth J. Archer's constructive vision of Pentecostal hermeneutics as narratival and advocating this trialectical interaction between the Spirit, Scripture, and the interpretive community came to the fore.[14] Amos Yong published a paradigmatic work on theological hermeneutics early in his writing career in which he articulated a dynamic interrelation of Spirit-Word-Community.[15]

Further, the pneumatic element in Pentecostal hermeneutics has come to be understood as a point of distinctive emphasis for theology in the Pentecostal tradition. In recent years, this has come to even greater stress in formal Pentecostal theologies. These more recent explicit developments have sought to work out this element as having been deeply embedded in Pentecostal hermeneutical practices in ways that were not yet adequately articulated. Against forms of scholasticism and rationalism, Pentecostal theological hermeneutics have tended towards an affirmation that at the core of one's interpretive disposition of the things of God are the affections or desires, even as some Pentecostal theologies mimicked scholastic and rationalist forms.[16] While modern rationalisms have sought to distance themselves from such affections as improper prejudices in the quest for knowledge, Pentecostal theologies have embraced them as proper expressions of the deepest human inclinations.

For Pentecostalism, theology and theological interpretation are living and spiritual exercises of the self in Christian community. The early Pentecostal educational and doctrinal pioneer D. W. Kerr expressed this, albeit in his early twentieth century American conceptual frame, as "facts on fire."[17] So also Land considered orthopathy an essential aspect of Pentecostal theology as Pentecostal hermeneutics has, by and large, tacitly affirmed an anthropology in which the spiritual aspect of human understanding makes rationalist approaches to theological matters unfitting and thus unreliable. Pentecostal theology turns the table on the Enlightenment critique that affections distort and need to be overcome. Yong's philosophically sophisticated *Spirit-Word-Community* emphasized that theological hermeneutics ought to be a hermeneutics of life.[18] Nevertheless, Pentecostal theologians

---

13. Dabney, "Saul's Armor."

14. Archer, *A Pentecostal Hermeneutic*; Archer, "Pentecostal Story."

15. Yong, *Spirit-Word-Community*. I have argued that this work was central to his early theological agenda in "An Interpretive Review Essay on *Spirit-Word-Community*."

16. See Jacobsen, "Knowing the Doctrines of Pentecostalism."

17. Kerr, "Facts on Fire," 5.

18. Yong, *Spirit-Word-Community*, 1–7.

spent much of the twentieth century attempting to fit Pentecostal intuitions into the theological forms of their Evangelical siblings.

Early Pentecostal and Evangelical-Pentecostal Theological Hermeneutics: Originating and Evangelicalizing Pentecostal Theology

Early and mid-twentieth century Pentecostals seem to have turned to Evangelicalism for several reasons.[19] First, as Jacobsen stresses in his history of early Pentecostal theologians, many Pentecostal theologians came from Evangelical traditions, and their subsequent theologies as Pentecostal converts included continuities with those previous Evangelical and revivalist theologies and their attendant hermeneutical tendencies.[20] Second, it seems that second and third generation Pentecostal theologians sought to do theology through emulation, and they turned to the approaches used by what they considered their most trusted fellow Christians. It did not seem to have occurred to some of them to the degree that it has to contemporary Pentecostal theologians, that Pentecostal understanding and experience is much more than a theological addendum to Evangelical theology. More importantly, it did not occur to many theologians of those generations that Evangelical forms and hermeneutical approaches might be inadequate to the task of developing Pentecostal spiritual intuitions into a more thoroughgoing Pentecostal theology. Third, Pentecostals turned to Evangelicalism simply because their conclusions concerning doctrine most closely coincided with Evangelical doctrine. There seemed to be a shared affirmation of the status of the Bible and other commonalities on important matters like soteriology and the primacy of evangelism.

In the first decades of the twentieth century, early Pentecostal theology made a series of awkward attempts to identify with the fundamentalism that had arisen out of nineteenth century Evangelicalism[21] There were continuities between the two constituencies, especially in their anti-modernism, which itself included a deep if subtle modern influence on Pentecostals and fundamentalists. Early twentieth century Christian anti-modernism, perhaps more unwittingly than conscientiously, assumed much of the rationalism that it sought to oppose.[22] While fundamentalists embraced some

19. For further evaluation of the relationship between Evangelicalism and Pentecostal hermeneutics, see my *Theological Hermeneutics*, 83–184.

20. This is a recurring theme in Jacobsen, *Thinking in the Spirit*.

21. Blumhofer, *Restoring the Faith*, 5–6; Blumhofer, *The Assemblies of God*, 15–16.

22. Archer, *A Pentecostal Hermeneutic*, 47–88.

of this rational ism because they held to its tenets, Pentecostals seemed to have done so much more unwittingly and awkwardly. The distrust between Pentecostals and fundamentalists was based on real differences in ontologies. The Pentecostal affirmations of contemporary activities of the Spirit and openness to revising Christian doctrine not only characterized the first generation of Pentecostal theology but also represented constitutive differences from fundamentalism.[23] The immediacy of the Spirit to Pentecostals meant that Pentecostals interpreted Scripture as norming contemporary Christian life.

Archer has named what emerged among early Pentecostal biblical hermeneutics as their 'Bible Reading Method,' a narratival hermeneutic that focused its effort on the spiritual life of Pentecostal communities. On the one hand, this method took on the scholastic Protestant tendency to proof-text and harmonize biblical texts into doctrinal statements, operating with a pre-critical understanding of the Bible.[24] On the other, the Pentecostal 'Bible Reading Method' brought an alternative narrative and pathos to biblical interpretation. Pentecostals typically brought a different historical and eschatological story through which they read Scripture, and they found contemporary Christianity at a different point in that story than their Evangelical and fundamentalist siblings.[25] Though a case can be made that at least a somewhat broader narrative was at hand, Archer well identifies the 'Latter Rain' motif among early Pentecostals as governing that historical narrative. Pentecostals considered themselves a community poor and humble enough to allow for God's 'Latter Rain' outpouring to manifest itself, and that understanding filtered right through the paradigm of early Pentecostal hermeneutics.[26] This early hermeneutic was also primarily characterized by a continual dynamic between readings of the Bible and life experiences, and it usually involved a naïve version of common sense realism, while it had Pentecostal renditions of the "Full Gospel" funding its content. This original Pentecostal hermeneutic was a hermeneutic of origination, a hermeneutic of openness to doctrinal reformulation and innovation, and a radicalization of the Protestant conviction concerning the perspicuity of Scripture, with

23. Jacobsen, *Thinking in the Spirit*, 355–58.

24. Archer, *A Pentecostal Hermeneutic*, 99–102.

25. Sheppard, "Pentecostals and the Hermeneutics of Dispensationalism," 5–34.

26. Early Pentecostals used the Old Testament motif concerning the two rainy seasons in Palestine as indicative that God a 'Latter Rain' outpouring of the Spirit available beyond the original outpouring on the apostles and the early Church. Archer, *Pentecostal Hermeneutic*, 136–50.

the perspicuity only coming to those who were spiritually and morally right with God and open to the work of the Spirit.[27]

The second and third generations of Pentecostals regulated the openness to revise traditional Christian doctrine found among the first generation. This openness had too easily led to continual theological innovations. And while openness was sought, too much openness created alt kinds of problems as the hermeneutic could lead to constant revisions to doctrine. These generations of Pentecostals mainly regulated this openness by returning to Evangelical hermeneutical tendencies that sought to justify Pentecostal doctrines as properly biblical ones.[28] Pentecostals who felt God very deeply in their worship even turned towards a 'Pentecostal scholasticism' exhibited in the works of several Pentecostal theologians in the 1930–50s whose work was widely used in ministerial training, especially Myer Pearlman's *Knowing the Doctrines of the Bible* (1937) and Ernest Swing Williams's three-volume *Systematic Theology* (1953).[29]

Christopher A. Stephenson has shown how these works stand in continuity with the late-nineteenth century Princetonian method of Charles Hodge. They assume that the proper way of doing systematic theology is through an inductive approach that investigates the Bible in order to harmonize and arrange the doctrines that emerge from the texts. This approach thus begins with a theological epistemology that understands God's revelation to have been faithfully and inerrantly delivered through the inspired biblical authors. Biblical readers need to seek illumination to understand the Bible faithfully, thus enabling the arrangement and harmonization of biblical doctrines. The method remained Hodgean while the content found in the reading of Scripture was Pentecostal.[30] The alliance between white Pentecostals in North America and the National Association of Evangelicals in the early-1940s led EvangelicalPentecostal hermeneuts to see what Pentecostals brought to the theological table as addenda to Evangelical theology rather than as more integrally affecting the whole, like many late-twentieth and early-twenty-first century Pentecostal theologians will insist.[31]

The more explicit turn to evangelical theology in the mid- and late-twentieth century among Pentecostals led them towards a theological hermeneutics that stood in a line of continuity with the hermeneutics of

---

27. Oliverio, *Theological Hermeneutics*, 31–82.

28. Oliverio, *Theological Hermeneutics*, 83–132.

29. See Jacobsen, "Knowing the Doctrines of Pentecostals"; Stephenson, *Types of Pentecostal Theology*, 11–27; Oliverio, *Theological Hermeneutics*, 116–29, 264–71.

30. Stephenson, *Types of Pentecostal Theology*, 22–24.

31. See Cross, "The Rich Feast of Theology."

not only Hodge but also the author-centered hermeneutic theory of the Yale philosopher E. D. Hirsch Jr.[32] This method integrated certain Evangelical-Pentecostal theological affirmations with Hirsch's author-centered theory, and it allowed this Evangelical-Pentecostal approach to find a philosophical ally that provided them with supportive arguments for its hermeneutics. Key to this approach was the issue of the meaning of 'meaning,' which Hirsch reserved for what could be discerned of authorial intention. This integrated well with a theological and epistemological foundationalism that affirmed the inerrant Scriptures as providing biblical principles which, then in turn, are topically organized in systematic theology. Experience was not to be primary for interpretation; rather, experience was to result from obedience to Scripture. Though it was usually recognized that there was a back-and-forth between experience and biblical interpretation, the proper method was for Scripture to guide experience, and not vice versa. Scripture is to norm experience.[33] They were also comfortable with employing historical-critical methods in biblical studies, as long as they employed an affirmation of God's faithfulness in self-revelation in the Scriptures by employing a 'believing criticism.'

Still, many of these Evangelical-Pentecostals emphasized the pneumatic aspect of Pentecostal hermeneutics.[34] The Spirit is involved in illumination in reading the biblical texts, and guides believers in application. The Spirit illuminates the Scriptural word for the Christian community of interpreters, and the pneumatic emphasis among Pentecostals allows them to understand better the inspired Scriptures. Following Hirsch, though, the Scripture still has a singular ideal meaning, even if certainty about that meaning is never humanly attainable. Nevertheless, doctrines are discovered in the intention of the biblical authors, and their significance is applied to the particular situations of believers in Pentecostal communities. Several Pentecostal theologians, especially Roger Stronstad and Robert Menzies, emphasized that the search for authorial intent included the use of redaction and narrative criticism that could find the intent in the editing and narration of the biblical authors, especially as this pertained to Pentecostal doctrines as developed from Luke-Acts.[35] Still, even with the addition of this pneumatic emphasis, Evangelical-Pentecostal hermeneutics remained

32. Hirsch's *Validity in Interpretation* is the paradigmatic work.

33. Exemplars of this method among Pentecostals include Gordon Anderson, Gordon Fee, Stanley Horton, and Robert Menzies. For analysis of this method, see Stephenson, *Types of Pentecostal Theology*, 16–21; Oliverio, *Theological Hermeneutics*, 133–81.

34. For example, Ervin, "Hermeneutics."

35. Stronstad, *The Charismatic Theology of St. Luke*; Menzies, *Empowered for Witness*.

focused on textual interpretation and the movement from biblical to systematic theology; and then to practical theology and application.

Contextual-Pentecostal Hermeneutics: Situating Pentecostal Theology

Beginning in the 1990s, the Evangelical-Pentecostal hermeneutical approach came under criticism from Pentecostal scholars who, in general, rejected several underlying assumptions of that hermeneutical type. A first objection was to the methodological primacy of biblical hermeneutics. Sometimes taken as an objection to the authority of Scripture, most of those Pentecostal theologians who voiced dissent to the Evangelical-Pentecostal approach did so while still holding to a high view of Scripture's authority. They often argued that failing to account for hermeneutics on a broader level, including that of human preunderstanding, undermined rather than preserved biblical authority. Yong, for example, contended that while biblical hermeneutics is necessary for good theological hermeneutics, a failure to develop a hermeneutics of the extra Scriptural world will, in the end, "sabotage the theological task."[36] Biblical interpreters inevitably interpret more than Scripture, on the basis of much more than Scripture, and thus increased self-awareness of what theological and other assumptions Pentecostal interpreters bring to bear upon biblical and theological interpretation is needed for good theology.

A second objection has to do with the nature of hermeneutics more generally. Contextual-Pentecostal theological hermeneutics were often influenced by Continental philosophical hermeneutics, and especially the work of Hans Georg Gadamer.[37] In this philosophical tradition, hermeneutics is foremost about human understanding and preunderstanding. Thus hermeneutical prejudices, rather than standing as those things which need to be overcome in order to get to an objective understanding of anything, including an author's intention, are the very conditions through and in which human understanding takes place. Situatedness is how humans understand, not something that can or should necessarily be overcome. Preunderstanding is inevitable and always a part of the meaning interpreters find in texts like the Bible; the question is rather which preunderstandings best account for what is there in texts and bring their truth to bear upon the present, as forms of illumination. Further, it is language, through and in which we understand. And language comes through inherited traditions. Smith, in

36. Yong, *Spirit-Word-Community*, 2.
37. Gadamer, *Truth and Method*.

his earlier and more Pentecostal work, furthered the claim that all human understanding is always mediated by our finitude and situatedness. For Smith, Pentecostal and other Christian hermeneutics were more faithful to the biblical narrative when they recognized that a Christian theological anthropology meant that our knowledge is always limited, partial, and mediated, and that this situation was also the case in humanity's prelapsarian state, not just after.[38] Interpretation is not a result of the Fall but constitutes a description of how finite and situated humanity knows. The Fall added sinfulness to that originally good situation.

Third, contextual-Pentecostal theologians argued that contextual hermeneutics were more authentically Pentecostal, that is, more faithful to the ethos of the tradition and especially its early years. In this way, the critique of Evangelical-Pentecostal hermeneutics turned into constructive contextual-Pentecostal hermeneutics. Archer's *A Pentecostal Hermeneutic for the Twenty-First Century* picked up on a development that had been manifesting since the early-1990s, namely, that Pentecostals, in order to continue the original witness of their forebears, needed to drink from their own hermeneutical wells. These wells were primarily narratival, and they eschewed modern rationalisms, including the ways in which modern methodologies had influenced Evangelical-Pentecostal hermeneutics. The ethos of these contextual Pentecostal hermeneutics resonated more with postmodern hermeneutics than modern. While some, including Archer, affirmed contextual-Pentecostal hermeneutics as postmodern, a number of Pentecostal theologians affirmed aspects of postmodern hermeneutics while pushing back against other aspects.[39] Cheryl Bridges Johns, for instance, analyzed the turn among Pentecostals towards broader cultural influences and the turn to Evangelicalism as the twentieth century progressed as part of the adolescence of Pentecostalism. It was, she contended, an attempt to substitute another's identity because of one's own sense of shame in one's own identity. In order to move beyond this adolescent substitution, she called for Pentecostal theology to speak its own language and urged Pentecostal scholars that they should "not feel obligated to relate to the tyranny of Evangelical rationalism nor . . . acritically jump on a postmodern bandwagon."[40] Pentecostalism could have and develop a legitimate sectarian identity while learning from others, especially from the larger Christian tradition.

---

38. Smith, *The Fall of Interpretation*. This is developed for Pentecostal hermeneutics in Green, *Sanctifying Interpretation*; Oliverio, *Theological Hermeneutics*, 315–61.

39. Also see Noel, *Pentecostal and Postmodern Hermeneutics*.

40. Johns, "The Adolescence of Pentecostalism," 17.

Ecumenical-Pentecostal Hermeneutics: Deepening and Broadening Pentecostal Theology

In her 1994 address to Pentecostal scholars, Johns pointed Pentecostals to such a way forward. Rather than substituting another's identity for their own, as an adolescent in an immature state, she called Pentecostals to the constructive work of integrating the future identity of Pentecostalism with its past and with the good that can be found from other traditions in its manifold surrounding contexts. To be able to do so, Pentecostals need to "know their ontological vocation."[41] A legitimate identity will result from a vocational calling that both stands against those powers which remain in hostility to the holiness of God and develops the community's own legitimate sectarian voice. Pentecostal identity ought to be hopeful and future-oriented as it finds existential strength in an ontological Christian understanding of vocation rather than a never ending modern quest to find identity. It is not that identity does not continually become; it is that the identities of persons and communities must become in relation to their vocation.[42] To Johns, it has been since the Second World War, that Pentecostals have been tempted to substitute identities found in the broader consumer and political culture, beyond subsuming their own identity under Evangelical rubrics. Rather, maturation as a spiritual and theological tradition requires growth by integration rather than substitution.[43] While she took later twentieth century Pentecostalism to task for its adolescence, Johns identified signs of a potentially mature approach to identity within the tradition's infancy.

In the first issue of the Azusa Street Mission's newspaper, *The Apostolic Faith*, the mission proclaimed that "Azusa Mission stands for the unity of God's people everywhere."[44] This was based upon a vision of spiritual unity and equality. Yet early Pentecostals immediately struggled with the negative judgments and disparagements from other Christians. An article in the second issue of *The Apostolic Faith* saw Pentecostals as welcoming the prodigals returning to the Father at Azusa St, and implied that their Christian critics were the elder brothers in Jesus' Parable of the Prodigal Son.[45]

Early Pentecostals read the Scriptures as calling all true Christians to deep spiritual unity. Yet they also interpreted Scripture in light of their marginalization, mocking, and rejection not only by non-Christians but even

---

41. Johns, "The Adolescence of Pentecostalism," 10–11.

42. Green echoes this theme in his *Sanctifying Interpretation*.

43. Johns, "The Adolescence of Pentecostalism," 10–11.

44. Azusa Street Mission, "Beginning of the World Wide Revival," 1.

45. Azusa Street Mission, "The Elder Brother," 2.

other Christians. Nevertheless, early Pentecostals generally reported a sense that the Spirit was leading them to humility and unity with other believers. Yet this sense contrasted with another set of impulses that held sway among them. This hermeneutical logic considered that since the Spirit and Word were immediate to them as they testified to the closeness of God's presence, their interpretations of biblical truth were the very truth of God for all. Among many Pentecostals, this sense of immediacy was taken to require certitude and absolutism in their theological interpretations, which in turn led to some very anti-ecumenical tendencies.[46]

While it is possible to generalize concerning types or families of hermeneutics, as here with Pentecostal hermeneutics, differences and conflicting approaches nonetheless exist even within the development of these types. Within the broader family of Pentecostal hermeneutics, internal differences concerning ecumenical impulses have been significant. Early ecumenical-Pentecostal desires were met by early divisive and absolutist theological approaches, and many other approaches and temperaments in between. This tension has had a prolonged history in the tradition.[47]

With what might be characterized as an ontological resilience, an ecumenical-Pentecostal hermeneutical stream found its way from Azusa Street, through a century of pioneering work, to the current it represents in Pentecostal theology today. Such a hermeneutic ecumenically broadens the sources for developing Pentecostal theology by consciously drawing on the wider Christian tradition. It has taken Pentecostal ecumenical pioneers like David du Plessis and Cecil M. Robeck Jr., with many others, to further practical relations with other Christian traditions.[48] Yet Pentecostal theologians, from Ernest Swing Williams in the mid-twentieth century to Veli-Matti Kärkkäinen and Frank Macchia today, have developed and employed an ecumenicalPentecostal hermeneutic. They have deepened Pentecostal understanding as they have found resources in other Christian traditions that have enriched Pentecostal theology.

A certain stereotype of ecumenism sees it as reducing beliefs to lower common denominators, watering down theology in order to find common ground. There is, of course, some warrant for this stereotype, though it would grossly mischaracterize the ecumenical movement as a general description. By and large, however, ecumenical-Pentecostal hermeneutics

46. Grant Wacker has accounted for these latter impulses in *Heaven Below*, 18–34.

47. For example, consider the tension and conflict concerning ecumenism between David du Plessis and Thomas Zimmerman, two prominent twentieth century Pentecostal leaders. See Ziefle, *David du Plessis.*

48. Perhaps the crown jewel of this is the International Roman Catholic-Pentecostal Dialogues (1972–present).

have avoided a simplistic lower common denominator strategy. They have sought to deepen Pentecostal theological understanding by broadening it. The particularities of the ecumenical-Pentecostal strategy have been productive for a nexus of reasons. They include a move away from a static modern rationalism towards a more dynamic ontology. Contemporary ecumenical-Pentecostal hermeneutics typically understand theology as testifying to the Triune God whose self-revelation in the economy of creation, salvation, and the coming kingdom is best understood through multiple theological testimonies. Yong's development of the 'many tongues' principle, in which the tongues of Pentecost represent the proper testimony to the one True God in multiple languages and articulations, affirms that multiple theological articulations and disciplines provide for more fruitful and more adequate theological understanding than singular doctrinal principles could. On this model, theological truth is seen, in concert with the divine economy, as better understood in terms of aggregation and difference as well as unity of understanding. The Triune God is not a static entity best spoken about in monolithic statements, even if there is unity and commonality in Christian confession and experience. The multiplicity of the biblical witness is affirmed as modeling the multiple witnesses of Christian traditions.[49] On this ecumenical-Pentecostal model, the way forward is through deepening as much as broadening, and turning to the wider Christian *oikumene* as an authentic theological resource has provided the most significant sources for such deepening.

Yong models the approach where space is opened up for an ecumenical-Pentecostal theology through a revision of received philosophical categories. While I have previously typified Yong as a contextual-Pentecostal theologian, there is a good case to be made that he can be well understood, perhaps primarily so, as an ecumenical-Pentecostal theologian.[50] Yong has opened up philosophical space for ecumenical broadening and deepening, using concepts like the 'pnuematological imagination,' 'the many tongues' principle, and the trialectic of Spirit-Word-community. These concepts have created space for a wider agenda for Pentecostal theologies.[51]

While ecumenical-Pentecostal hermeneuts have tended to agree with the approaches advocated by contextual-Pentecostal hermeneutics, the distinction between the two is in their agendas, which draw upon different

49. See Yong, *Renewing Christian Theology*, 12–23; Oliverio, "The One and the Many"; Stephenson, "Reality, Knowledge, and Life in Community."

50. Oliverio, *Theological Hermeneutics*, 232–47; Stephenson, *Types of Pentecostal Theology*, 82–110.

51. Yong, *Spirit-Word-Community*; Yong, *Renewing Christian Theology*, 1–27. For interpretation and evaluation, see Oliverio, "An Interpretive Review Essay."

disciplines and sources for Pentecostal theology. While contextual-Pentecostal hermeneutics tend to focus on the conditions of theological understanding, ecumenical-Pentecostal hermeneutics have tended towards the systematic and constructive theological matters themselves.[52] Chris E. W. Green, for example, states that contemporary theology needs to move away from talk about talk about God to "genuine talk about God."[53] Or, to put it in terms of the disciplines involved, thus far the contextual-Pentecostal hermeneutic has primarily employed philosophical theology and the ecumenical-Pentecostal theology constructive or systematic theology, though both have and can employ a variety of disciplines, theological and otherwise.

The ecumenical-Pentecostal hermeneutic has focused on first order theological truths, even as it has sought to develop theological understanding from other traditions and integrate it into its theological identity. The hyphenation here implies genuine and primary identity as Pentecostal, with the kind of integration spoken of by Johns. Others' voices are heard, and Pentecostal identity grows and is deepened through this interaction. This entails a mature relationality in which Pentecostals interact in genuine friendship, fellowship, and theological conversation, giving and expecting respect—even Christian love—in those relationships. It also entails the ability to make distinctions and disagree. The ethos of the ecumenical-Pentecostal hermeneutic is to move away from the shame-based approach that seeks attention and affirmation, and to believe that Pentecostal theology, as it matures, provides a contributing voice to contemporary Christian theology in general. This broadening and deepening among Pentecostal theologians is exemplified in the theological work of Pentecostal theologians like Johns, Yong, Simon Chan, Frank Macchia, and Studebaker, among others. Each of them considerably utilizes the broader Christian tradition as a resource for developing Pentecostal theology.

While Chan's diagnosis of the need for Pentecostal maturation has much in common with that of Johns, he has added his contention that the lack of attention to the nature and role of tradition in Pentecostal theology has created a problematic situation for it in general and its ecclesiology and practices in particular. He represents the side of ecumenical-Pentecostal theological hermeneutics that tends to see the wider Christian tradition as providing needed correctives to Pentecostal identity. With Chan, the wider tradition is like an older sibling that is helping a younger sibling mature

52. These early trajectories in the history of these hermeneutical approaches do not, of course, imply that other trajectories could not develop. For instance, it is not hard to imagine a stream of ecumenically-oriented Pentecostal biblical hermeneutics emerging in the near future, or contextually-oriented Pentecostal constructive theologies either.

53. Green, *Sanctifying Interpretation*, 3.

in her gifts, even as the younger sibling might avoid taking on her older sibling's faults.

The charismatic nature of the Church has been taken by many Pentecostals as a rejection of the Church's historicity since God's presence can be immediate, and thus historicity bypassed. Chan, however, rejects this logic and the sense that the Church's experience of and freedom in the Spirit can or should sever the present Body of Christ from its historical roots.[54] The visible and invisible Churches are joined. It is the subtle influence of modernism that has led Pentecostalism to individualistic rather than communal, and ahistorical rather than historical, interpretive tendencies.[55] Chan contends that pitting tradition against the newness of the work of the Spirit has been an important theological mistake made by many Pentecostals.[56]

Instead, tradition and 'traditioning' are central to Chan's proposal for the way forward for Pentecostal theology. So also is reviving the Church's historical sense that theology is a unitary discipline concerned with spiritual knowledge.[57] As Stephenson explains concerning Chan, "the use of the verbal derivative from *tradition* underscores the active nature of the formation process in which the church must intentionally engage to perpetuate Christian faith to successive generations"; this includes two main aspects-integrating systematic theology and spiritual theology, and situating one's own tradition within the larger Christian tradition. Both are ways in which Pentecostal theology and its methodology require growth.[58]

On Chan's register, experience has been overemphasized in the Pentecostal tradition because Pentecostal theological explanations, in the form of doctrines, have been poorly developed. This is in part attributable to the mini mal attention paid by Pentecostals to the resources available in the broader and historical Christian spiritual tradition. Case in point: "the central doctrine called 'baptism in the Spirit' is far richer in Pentecostal *experience* than in Pentecostal explanation."[59] It is the greater Christian spiritual tradition that provides the resources for developing theological explanation.

54. Chan, *Pentecostal Ecclesiology*, 67–70.

55. Chan, *Pentecostal Ecclesiology*, 77–80.

56. Chan, *Pentecostal Theology*, 22–23.

57. Chan, *Pentecostal Theology*, 28.

58. Stephenson, *Types of Pentecostal Theology*, 48–49.

59. Stephenson, *Types of Pentecostal Theology*, 10. Chan does acknowledge what he considers helpful theological work on Spirit baptism, citing Hocken, "The Meaning and Purpose"; Macchia, "Sighs Too Deep for Words." Chan develops Spirit baptism within George Lindbeck's cultural-linguistic framework in *Pentecostal Theology*, 40–72. For summarization and evaluation of Chan's ecclesiology in relation to his theological method, see Stephenson, *Types of Pentecostal Theology*, 48–58.

An important reason for this methodological conviction is Chan's ontological conviction concerning the Church. Chan rejects as inadequate the notion that the Church is the collection of individuals who have placed their faith in Christ. Rather, "The church *is* the unity and communion of the Holy Spirit"; the Church is caught up in the life of the Triune God. The Church is constituted by the presence of the 'ecclesia-shaped Spirit' so that the Church is linked to theological truth *historically* and *charismatically*, The Church has its linear history, yet may transcend those historical limitations because of the presence of the Spirit.[60] For Chan, then, Pentecostal theology needs to pay attention to the way tradition works so that Pentecostal theology might better take up the task of 'traditioning' in Pentecostal churches because that history is much the history of the work of the 'ecclesia-shaped Spirit,' not a history to be bypassed or overcome. In the historicity of the Church and in its ontology as the Body of Christ, it is, together with Christ, the *totus Christus*. Therefore, the greater *oikumene* is not only a resource for Pentecostal theology, but the Church in its very historicity, *is* what theology is explicating.[61]

Frank Macchia represents another leading voice in ecumenical-Pentecostal theological hermeneutics. His development of the doctrine of Spirit baptism is perhaps the most developed exemplar of ecumenical-Pentecostal theological hermeneutics to date. Macchia regards Spirit baptism as the 'crown jewel' of Pentecostal theology. Thus, rather than reducing the doctrine so that it might be made more palatable to other Christian traditions, Macchia deepens and broadens a theology of Spirit baptism in order to integrate other Christian theologies of Spirit baptism into a fuller Pentecostal theology, one that incorporates their theological insights into his Pentecostal vision. Finding where to broaden in order to deepen is key to the ecumenical-Pentecostal strategy. The choice of which other Christian voices are best for developing Pentecostal theology has been crucial. Macchia develops Spirit baptism by contending that a sense of *koinonia* is at the essence of the doctrine, and the philosophical-theological category of participation in God and the Christian community as another key concept. Both of these add ecumenical emphasis to his theological method. When these elements are brought together with the breadth of theological resources he draws upon in constructing Pentecostal theology, Macchia provides

---

60. Chan, *Pentecostal Theology*, 64–65.

61. "If the church as the body of Christ is the extension of Christ the Truth and the embodiment of the true Tradition (which is Christ himself, the first Tradition sent from the Father), the church as the temple of the Spirit explains how this tradition is alive and moving inexorably toward its appointed End" (Chan, *Liturgical Theology*, 32).

an ecumenical-Pentecostal theological hermeneutic that is an exemplary model for Pentecostal ecumenical theology.[62]

More specifically, in *Baptized in the Spirit*, Macchia engages Catholic and Reformed theologies of Spirit baptism while he broadens the canonical sources for further development of a Pentecostal theology of Spirit baptism. As he integrates wider Christian and canonical sources into a constructive proposal, he draws on the core insight of the Pentecostal father William Seymour that Spirit baptism is a baptism into divine love, where we return again to God as our 'first love', a Pentecostal rendition of the doctrine that incorporates Catholic and Reformed theologies.[63]

Studebaker represents a final constructive exemplar whose work advances key aspects of the ecumenical-Pentecostal approach. His *From Pentecost to the Triune God: A Pentecostal Trinitarian Theology* is one of the most important contributions to Trinitarian theology by a Pentecostal theologian to date. This text exemplifies the development and fruition of the ecumenical-Pentecostal theological hermeneutic, and its approach has much hermeneutical continuity with Macchia's broadening-deepening and use of the canon, and with Yong's use of revised philosophical concepts to open up conceptual space for ecumenical-Pentecostal theology. This latter task has often meant broadening conceptions and sometimes meant sliding Pentecostal thought away from unhelpful philosophical ideas that inhibit articulation of Pentecostal truths.

This can be seen when Studebaker questions received notions of hierarchies and distinctions among experience, practices, tradition, and Scripture, as often assumed by Pentecostals. Rather, he reconceptualizes these theological sources as in a nexus in which these sources exist in a number of dynamic relations. He makes a similar hermeneutical affirmation of a continual dynamic between theological understanding and experience altogether. While he affirms Scripture's authority and normativity for Christian life, he maintains that "experience can sometimes point to a better understanding and embodiment of biblical truth than can the received interpretation of Scripture."[64]

Studebaker takes up the task of revising philosophical categories in order to develop Pentecostal pneumatology. He makes connections between

---

62. Another example of Macchia's ecumenical-Pentecostal approach is his *Justified in the Spirit*. There, Macchia develops a theology of justification that results in participation in the Triune God as he engages, at length, Catholic and Protestant traditions on justification, drawing upon and rejecting elements from each, and integrating them with a Pentecostal rendition of the doctrine that, again, draws upon a wide canonical witness.

63. Macchia, *Baptized in the Spirit*.

64. Macchia, *Baptized in the Spirit*, 23.

the biblical witness and Christian experience with these revised categories. For "the Spirit's identity and work is manifested most expressly as the
Spirit of Pentecost. The Spirit of Pentecost has three characteristics: liminal,
constitutional, and consummative (or eschatological)."[65] He uses liminal-
ity as a bridge across spirit-matter and other dualisms; constitutionality to
overcome the reduction of the Spirit to an instrument; and the Spirit as
consummative to move to wards an understanding of the Spirit as the agent
that brings God's purposes for creation into their transition to another existential plane that will come to fulfillment in the eschaton. Such an approach
provides an integrative hermeneutic that works with biblical hermeneutics
and philosophical hermeneutics and weaves them into, in the end, a theological hermeneutic. This can also be seen in how he moves between theological understanding in the Christian tradition and the functions of *ruach*
and *pneuma* in Scripture, interpreting the biblical terms and their use in
the Christian tradition each on their own terms before reintegrating them.
While using the biblical text as a source for developing Trinitarian theology,
he nevertheless affirms that "The Spirit of God in Genesis 1:2, with respect
to the theology of ancient Israel, is not the Holy Spirit of later Christian theology. 'Spirit of God' is probably the presence of God in creative action."[66]

Studebaker also works *to* open up conceptual space in a manner similar to Macchia, by moving between biblical and theological hermeneutics,
and drawing on theological understanding developed by those from wider
Christian traditions, in developing a Pentecostal Trinitarian theology. Like
Macchia, he draws on the resources provided by the constructive theologies
of leading theologians from other Christian traditions, dialoguing with them
and then integrating helpful elements into his Pentecostal theology. Like
Macchia, Studebaker exhibits breadth in doing so. He identifies key traditions that are necessary to draw upon for developing Pentecostal Trinitarian
theology, in the form of historic Eastern and Western Trinitarian theologies,
but also turns to other particular sources he sees as providing insight. Here,
it is the Reformed evangelical tradition and the wider charismatic tradition,
drawing on sources from Jonathan Edwards to Clark Pinnock.[67] In the end,
Studebaker's voice provides us with an example of Pentecostal theological
maturity, unashamed of Pentecostal theology, constructively giving and taking in conversation with the wider tradition.

Hermeneutics are approaches and habits that allow humans to abstract from the utter complexities of what is. Of all types of hermeneutics,

---

65. Macchia, *Baptized in the Spirit*, 53.

66. Macchia, *Baptized in the Spirit*, 66.

67. Macchia, *Baptized in the Spirit*, 101–207.

theological hermeneutics abstract from the totality of all that is, and seek to create habits of interpreting what is beyond, in the transcendent God. Since Pentecostal theological hermeneutics are Christian theological hermeneutics, they are finding their place not only in interpreting the Scriptures but an entire vision of Christian understanding, and developing their own voice among Christian traditions. This voice is particularly attuned to speaking of the Spirit, the affective, and the particularities of Christian spiritual experiences, especially as they have been manifested in Pentecostal communities. The ecumenical-Pentecostal theological hermeneutic takes Pentecostal readings of Scripture, the guidance of the Spirit, and the acknowledgement of the role of Pentecostal communities in their theological interpretations, and then purposefully draws on wider resources from the Christian tradition. In the end, this hermeneutic becomes a catalyst for a richer Christian unity and helps to correct the pneumatological deficit in the Christian world and within the ecumenical movement.

7

Religion and Holy Affections

In the midst of the formative years of his young adulthood, while pastoring in New York City, summering in East Windsor, then pastoring in Bolton, Connecticut, and into his years tutoring at Yale, Jonathan Edwards kept a book of resolutions.[1] The full list of seventy resolutions is a revealing instance of what Michael McClyrnond and Gerald McDermott have described as Edwards' understanding of creaturely participation in God as these meet the dispositions, loves, and habits that govern a person—both key components of the great 'symphony" found in Edwards' life and corpus.[2] Among these stands Resolution 28: "Resolved, to study the Scriptures so steadily, constantly and frequently, as that I may find, and plainly perceive myself to

---

1. Edwards, "Resolutions," 756.

2. McClymond and McDermott, *Theology of Jonathan Edwards*, 3–9. In the opening of *Theology of Jonathan Edwards*, McClymond and McDermott compare the work of Jonathan Edwards (1703–58) to a symphony played by five instrument sections. The first constituent of the symphony, the violins in their image, is the self-communication of the beauty of the trinitarian God. The second, the other strings, is creaturely participation in God, as divine beauty confers spiritual beauty upon others. The horns, the third constituent, represent Edwards' necessitarian dispositionalism where all beings, including God, have at their essence dispositions or habits, those human loves and affections that most truly reveal personal identities. Fourth, as the woodwinds, Edwards' Calvinism sounds forth in its theocentric voluntarism, as God continually sustains all reality. As the percussion section, the fifth section of the symphony is Edwards' harmonious constitutionalism in which he found harmony in the entire course of redemptive history. McClymond and McDermott suggest that the totality of Edwards' works produces this symphony, even as some interpretations of Edwards "capture one or another part of the symphony, yet fail to construe the sound and flow of the whole" (8).

grow in the knowledge of the same."[3] To judge from the vast proliferation of the use of the Bible in his written works, the conclusion is compelling that Edwards missed little opportunity to steadily, constantly, and frequently study the Bible.

For Edwards, biblical interpretation was no dispassionate or technical exercise. He came to the important doctrinal conclusion that "true religion, in great part, consists in holy affections," the central thesis of his *Religious Affections* (1746).[4] Yet Edwards was also a remarkable philosophical theologian who utilized innovative and complex philosophical convictions as he theologically interpreted Scripture. Standing among those who turned away from the idea that human reason could serve as the arbiter of all things during the period of the Enlightenment, Edwards came to understand the affections and the intellect as fused together because he considered that "the affections are no other, than the more vigorous and sensible exercises of the inclination and will of the soul."[5] His biblical hermeneutics can thus not be properly described in merely technical terms, but they must account for the primacy of the spiritual in his interpretation of Scripture.[6]

Pentecostals have likewise operated with a strong affirmation of the role of the affections in an authentic Christian life. Like Edwards, pentecostal hermeneutics have stood against rationalisms and merely academic or technical hermeneutics of the Bible. They, too, though not as often recognized, have come to the biblical texts with important philosophical, ontological, and theological assumptions as they have interpreted Scripture for its spiritual content.[7] Nevertheless, the affections or feelings have been central to all major pentecostal hermeneutical types. Steven J. Land's thesis that pentecostal theology is found in its spirituality, and that pentecostal theology is not just about right belief or right practices but centered on right feelings, concluded that pentecostal spirituality and theology are about affections shaped by a longing for the kingdom of God.[8] Pentecostal biblical hermeneutics have likewise placed significant emphasis on the affective and the role of the Spirit.[9]

3. Edwards, "Resolutions," 755.

4. Edwards, *Religious Affections*, 95.

5. Edwards, *Religious Affections*, 96.

6. Cherry, "Symbols of Spiritual Truth"; Stein, "The Quest for the Spiritual Sense."

7. Identifying these was a key task of mine throughout *Theological Hermeneutics*.

8. Land, *Pentecostal Spirituality*, especially 125–64.

9. Archer, *A Pentecostal Hermeneutic*; Martin, *Pentecostal Hermeneutics*; Martin, "Longing for God." Keener has significantly developed contemporary pentecostal hermeneutics in *Spirit Hermeneutics*.

Pentecostal hermeneutics is a broad and general category to compare to the hermeneutics found in the work of a particular person, even that of a theological and philosophical giant like Edwards. Pentecostalism is itself a category that is complicated and contested, as Pentecostalism includes the Classical Pentecostals who find their roots in the early movement, of which the Azusa Street Revival was its exemplary original manifestation, through to the vast varieties of the five hundred million plus Pentecostals worldwide today, and their relation to broader charismatic and renewal movements.[10] Pentecostalism is itself best understood when accounted for as simultaneously local and global, particular and general.[11] Further, both pentecostal hermeneutics and Edwards diverged from the hermeneutical canons of Enlightenment modernism, and so certain assumptions common in modern thought have been brought into question. The hermeneutics at Azusa Street, 1906–9, and the hermeneutics of Edwards, who pastored in Northampton from 1726 to 1750, continued and further initiated alternatives to standard forms of Enlightenment modernism and their approaches to Scripture.

This chapter, while focusing on biblical hermeneutics, operates with an approach to hermeneutics that also stands, with Edwards in particular and Pentecostals in general, in contrast to the Enlightenment's attempts to elevate its naturalistic and foundationalist epistemic canons as the proper ones for human knowing. Along with some forms of Christian thought, much of late modern or so-called postmodern thought has concurred so that the result has been that hermeneutical understanding has superseded the foundationalist epistemologies established during the Enlightenment, for what are, at least in my estimation, some compelling reasons.[12] Most importantly, the hermeneutical approach has trumped Enlightenment epistemic conceptions because the ontological, metaphysical, anthropological, theological, epistemic, and other assumptions built into foundationalist approaches are themselves contested. Those conclusions are built into the epistemologies which serve as arbiters of further ontic affirmations. Reductive materialism, for example, cannot simply beg the question of its truth. Declaring a particular epistemology the indubitable foundation for human knowledge is either to assume the triumph of or to beg the question of all these assumptions.

---

10. Anderson, *An Introduction to Pentecostalism*; Jacobsen, *Thinking in the Spirit*, 1–15; Jacobsen, *Global Gospel*, 34–39; Yong, *The Spirit Poured Out on All Flesh*, 17–30.

11. Vondey, *Pentecostalism*, 25–26.

12. For some narrations of the supersession of epistemology by hermeneutics, see Taylor, "Overcoming Epistemology"; Westphal, *Overcoming Onto-theology*, 47–74.

As Merold Westphal has efficiently formulated it, the late modern or postmodern turn contends that, instead, "hermeneutics is epistemology."[13] What this hermeneutical approach means for comparing the biblical hermeneutics of Edwards and Pentecostals is that the biblical hermeneutics of both, while a critical center and source for their theologies, are interdependent in relation to their entire paradigms of understanding life and reality, and thus the funding of conceptions is multidirectional.[14] In a paradigm as bountiful and as ingenious as that of Edwards, a rich biblical hermeneutic both funded and emerged from his theology and philosophy. This chapter, as with this entire volume, might only begin to put Edwards into dialogue with Pentecostalism.

Elements of Edwards' Biblical Hermeneutics

McClymond and McDermott estimate that the combined exegetical elements found in Edwards' written works, from his sermons to the primarily exegetical material found in his other works, run around 5,000 printed pages. Edwards' dedication to scriptural knowledge and interpretation came from his theological conviction that any true knowledge of God comes from divine revelation as well as his resolution to study such.[15] The mid-twentieth-century resurgence of interest in Edwards focused on his metaphysical genius and often underestimated the place of Scripture in his thought.[16] Recent decades have seen a surge in interest in the biblical interpretation that played a crucial role in Edwards' thought.[17]

Edwards' biblical interpretation might be well understood, though, from today's vantage point, as primarily theological interpretation of Scripture.[18] For theological reasons, he rejected the emerging modern canons of

13. Westphal, *Overcoming Onto-theology*, 50.

14. I describe this paradigmatic approach to hermeneutics in more detail in my *Theological Hermeneutics*, 319–54.

15. McClymond and McDermott, *Theology of Jonathan Edwards*, 167–69.

16. Stein, "Quest for the Spiritual Sense," 99–101. The appreciation of his metaphysical genius and depreciation of his love of Scripture follows the lead of Miller, *Jonathan Edwards*.

17. Among these are Brown, *Jonathan Edwards and the Bible*; Cherry, "Symbols of Spiritual Truth," 263–71; McClymond and McDermott, *Theology of Jonathan Edwards*, 167–80; Sweeney, *Edwards the Exegete*; Stein, "Editor's Introduction (*Notes on Scripture*)"; and Stein, "Editor's Introduction (*Blank Bible*)." Further, Marsden's *Jonathan Edwards* provides regular attention to Edwards' hermeneutics.

18. See, for example, The *Journal of Theological Interpretation*, for contemporary discussions regarding theological interpretation of Scripture.

historical-critical scholarship, themselves still young in development and far away from Edwards' own context on the American frontier. Edwards' biblical interpretation was deeply informed by his core theological affirmations. These core theological affirmations were deeply informed by his reading of Scripture, though it seems that the whole tended to have more noetic authority than the part in Edwards' hermeneutical circle. Edwards' sermons typically exposited a verse of Scripture in the Puritan style of proclaiming a doctrine abstracted from the text to be followed by application or improvement for the hearers.

Commonly seen as one of his most revealing sermons, "Divine and Supernatural Light," originally delivered in Northampton in August 1733, is an exposition of Jesus' affirmation of Peter's confession that he is the Christ, the Son of the living God in Matthew's gospel. In the Authorized (King James) Version used by Edwards, it reads, "And Jesus answered and said unto him, Blessed art thou, Simon Barjona: for flesh and blood hath not revealed it unto thee, but my Father which is in heaven" (Matt 16:17).[19] In the sermon, Edwards exposits the doctrine that "there is such a thing, as a spiritual and divine light, immediately imparted to the soul by God, of a different nature from any that is obtained by natural means;"[20] All knowledge, for Edwards, is, of course, imparted by God. Material things operate as mediate or secondary causes of knowledge. But the special divine and supernatural knowledge that he speaks of here is immediately imparted by God.[21] That is what appears in this passage in the Gospel of Matthew, according to Edwards, as this light of a different nature has been imparted to Peter. He uses the theological distinction between common grace and special grace to explain what has happened to Peter's understanding. If it was merely a sense of his own sinfulness and misery or the anger of God that Peter had sensed, men in their natural condition may experience that, for "common grace only assists the faculties of the soul to do that more fully, which they do by nature."[22] But here Edwards sees the Spirit of God acting upon Peter in special and regenerative grace where the Spirit "acts in the mind of a saint as an indwelling vital principle."[23]

Edwards' sermon and interpretation of Matt 16:17 is a theological and philosophical exposition that seems to burst forth spiritual meaning from the statement found in the text. He explains how the divine light does

19. Edwards, "A Divine and Supernatural Light."

20. Edwards, "A Divine and Supernatural Light," 410.

21. Edwards, "A Divine and Supernatural Light," 409.

22. Edwards, "A Divine and Supernatural Light," 410.

23. Edwards, "A Divine and Supernatural Light," 411.

not spring from the human imagination but affects it, that it suggests no truths not revealed in the Word of God, and that not every lofty affection is a movement of the divine light. He teaches that the light is an apprehension of the divine excellency of what the Word of God reveals. The light removes the hindrances placed by man's reasoning, and moves attention to a clearer view of the truth of the objects of reason and their mutual relations. Toe divine excellency is perceived, and it removes all doubt that it is from God, not man. He defends the rationality of his doctrine of the divine light as well. He argues that if transcendent things do exist, they should be exceedingly different from other things, that it is not irrational to then see such things, and that it is logical that God should give them immediately and not by natural means.[24] But he also justified the doctrine as scriptural on the basis of other texts. He cites other texts as describing this supernatural knowledge as a seeing or knowing. Still other biblical texts portray this light and knowledge as always only immediately given from God. This kind of knowledge distinguishes the saved from the unregenerate, according to the witness of Scripture.[25] Edwards' use of other biblical texts in reference, here, as in his other works, could be characterized as encyclopedic.

There is little doubt that the whole works strongly on the part in Edwards' hermeneutics, but also that, as in this exposition of this biblical text, we find a part that contributes to and integrates itself with that intricate whole. Edwards' whole was robust in content and influence. Against the fragmentation of modern approaches to the Bible, Edwards prioritized the whole, which, in his case, led to a prioritization of the spiritual sense. McClymond and McDermott aptly explain how this operates, and its implications for interpreting the larger story of Scripture:

In Edwards' biblical hermeneutics the whole has epistemological priority over the parts. This is one reason the spiritual sense is so crucial. The spiritual interpretation of Scripture allows the interpreter to put the pieces together into a coherent whole. Without the spiritual sense, the events of the Old Testament might seem like a set of random and disconnected events, having little relationship to one another and even less connection with the New Testament.[26]

The theologically formed historical narrative Edwards operated with oriented his reading of Scripture and his understanding of what Scripture meant for himself and his audience.

24. Edwards, "A Divine and Supernatural Light," 411–15, 420–23.

25. Edwards, "A Divine and Supernatural Light," 416–19.

26. McClymond and McDermott, *Theology of Jonathan Edwards*, 174.

Yet cultural elements were also factors. George Marsden, as one of his leading biographers, found Edwards continually interpreting the Bible in relationship to contemporary events "through the lenses of his millennialist categories and Constantinian assumptions."[27] Edwards interpreted the parts of Scripture, along with current events, through his larger affirmations of postmillennialism and what he saw as God's hand at work in furthering the gospel through Protestant political governments. Much of what governed his narrative, by which he interpreted Scripture and the world, was his theological narrative of history. It was his plan to complete two works articulating that narrative when he arrived at Princeton in early 1758, and which were left uncompleted at his death. One was supposed to be his master work, to be entitled *A History of the Work of Redemption*, to be a theology in the form of a history.[28] In it, "history; prophecy, types, and doctrine would center in Christ's redemptive work," providing a cosmic history that was playing out in Edwards' periodization of history.[29] The other plan was to write a text harmonizing the Old and New Testaments with a focus on the relationship between Christology and typology.[30]

Edwards' Puritanism, of course, also loomed large. His reading of the Bible drew on favored commentators and theologians, while his arguments regularly contested with Arminians (though occasionally siding with them in issues of Christian apologetics), deists, and skeptics.[31] He predominantly read the Bible as an orthodox Calvinist who, in Marsden's words, was "an apologist for 'Calvinistic' theology versus 'the modern writers.'"[32] Still, he drew on Enlightenment ideas, and especially Locke, though primarily with the motivation of using the new learning in defense of Christian theology; even as he adopted aspects of Locke's system of ideas and empiricism. Edwards had investigated Enlightenment philosophy since his teenage years, and had found a continual theological and philosophical enemy in what he considered the pernicious philosophies that sought to elevate the human in judgment over God and to reject and ridicule Christian doctrines like that

27. Marsden, *Jonathan Edwards*, 424–25.

28. Edwards, *"History of Redemption" Notebooks*.

29. Marsden, *Jonathan Edwards*, 481–89, esp. 482.

30. Edwards, *"History of Redemption" Notebooks*.

31. Marsden, *Jonathan Edwards*, 474, regards Matthew Poole, Matthew Henry, Moses Lowman, and Philip Doddridge as among his favored sources; Holifield, *Theology in America*, 103–4, notes the theological influence of Petrus van Mastricht, along with Poole and Henry; Stein, "Editor's Introduction (*Notes on Scripture*)," 6–9, considers Poole and Henry foremost as his trusted sources, while Edwards sought out interesting exegetical ideas from a variety of sources.

32. Marsden, *Jonathan Edwards*, 437.

of original sin and its epistemic and moral ramifications. While Edwards appreciated the emphasis on observation and the scientific interest of the day, as the book of nature is the self-communication of God, and having written a scientific paper on spiders as a young man (1714), he found the optimistic anthropologies and epistemologies produced by Enlightenment thinkers to be enemies of true religion.[33]

The doubt of the proper spiritual condition of the human mind led such a brilliant mind as Edwards' to consider proper spiritual understanding of the Scriptures as necessitating a regenerated heart and mind. This was, of course, standard Calvinist doctrine, but Edwards' idealism, as can be seen in "A Divine and Supernatural Light," took this to new heights. And Edwards' sophisticated defense of Calvinistic determinism and criticism of the supposed freedom of the will also provided an important theological tenet that informed his interpretation of Scripture.[34] As Marsden explains, "Edwards' philosophy started with his theology. While his opponents were starting with principles of human morality and psychology and from those inferring what God's moral government of the universe must be like, Edwards was starting with what God must be like and then examining the human condition in that light."[35] Robert Brown concluded similarly that "the great task of Edwards' theological career was to reconstruct and reinterpret the rationality or cogency of Christian belief with reference to the intellectual assumptions of the age."[36] Brown characterizes the approach of Edwards to the Enlightenment and to deist attacks on Scripture as a 'modernizing traditionalism' that held to the basic historical outlines of the Bible by arguing for their truth.[37]

Edwards' biblical interpretation operated with this 'modernizing traditionalist' approach. This can be seen in the longest of the notes found in his notebook, "Notes on Scripture," No. 416, essentially an apologetic treatise defending the Mosaic authorship of the Pentateuch.[38] In it, Edwards argued by producing lengthy scriptural demonstrations. He pieced together the evidence of Mosaic authorship by, first, cataloguing and often quoting in full the places in the Pentateuch and elsewhere in the Old Testament where it was stated or remembered or referred to that it was Moses who had been

---

33. Edwards, "Of Insects," 154–63; Edwards, *Original Sin*.

34. Edwards, *Freedom of the Will*.

35. Marsden, *Jonathan Edwards*, 442, made this comment in relation to Edwards' *Freedom of the Will*.

36. Brown, *Jonathan Edwards and the Bible*, xv.

37. Brown, *Jonathan Edwards and the Bible*, xvii.

38. Edwards, "Notes on Scripture," 423–69.

tasked with writing the covenantal history. In the Yale *Works* edition, this goes on for twenty pages, as Edwards moves into connecting the covenantal law and history so that Moses, entrusted with the law, is likewise entrusted with the history, as "history and law are everywhere so grafted one into another, so mutually inwrought."[39] He argues that it is more reasonable to consider the primeval history in Genesis as Mosaic than not on the grounds that it is attested by the reliable history that follows Gen 11:26, and referred to as genuine and Mosaic just as Moses is throughout the Old Testament.[40] He catalogs 163 instances, events or themes in the Pentateuch that appear elsewhere in the Old Testament, corroborating their reliability through multiple attestations.[41] He puts forth a further historical argument on the basis of the assertion that 'it is certain' that the book of the law that was taken into the Babylonian captivity was the same that came out.[42]

Edwards fervently defended his notions of theological history as he ardently studied the progress of the contemporary Protestant cause of his day, all of this standing in historical continuity with the narrative he constructed concerning biblical, past, and contemporary history as it led to the forthcoming postmillennial triumph of the church.[43] His argument would be unconvincing to anyone who did not assume the authentic spiritual nature of Scripture, but that result coheres with his Calvinistic assumptions about knowledge of God.

While Edwards had as a lifelong project, his development of a grand narrative of history that informed his reading of the Bible and which was a central part of his overall theological hermeneutic, his biblical hermeneutics might also be considered spiritual hermeneutics. For Edwards, spiritual truths came from the believer's perception of Scripture, which is properly spiritual and affective.[44] Right reason did not conflict with revelation, though neither revelation nor the illumination of Scripture could be had without a supernatural light in the first place. Edwards, in fact, held to the tradition that what other religions and deists have that is truth comes from remnants of divine revelation that had been unwittingly absorbed in cultural traditions—that is, the *prisca theologia*.[45] Additionally, the excellencies

---

39. Edwards, "Notes on Scripture," 441.

40. Edwards, "Notes on Scripture," 438.

41. Edwards, "Notes on Scripture," 443–53.

42. Edwards, "Notes on Scripture," 457.

43. Marsden, *Jonathan Edwards*, 481–89.

44. Brown, *Jonathan Edwards and the Bible*, 76–86.

45. Holifield, *Theology in America*, 106. Also see McDermott, *Jonathan Edwards Confronts the Gods*.

of the divine were to be found in images and shadows of divine things found in nature as well as Scripture. In his notebook on "Images (or Shadows) of Divine Things," he explains:

> The book of Scripture is the interpreter of the book of nature two ways, viz., by declaring to us those spiritual mysteries that are indeed signified and typified in the constitution of the natural world; and secondly, in actually making application of the signs and types in the book of nature as representations of those spiritual mysteries in many instances.[46]

The two books, Scripture and nature, are divine self-communication. Material realities existed at the will of the divine, and so reality is essentially about personal relationships. Passing things are the signs or expressions of divine love. Though Edwards drew from Locke and Newton, he also held that "created reality was not independent of the minds that engage it . . . the universe most essentially consisted of personal relationships. All of creation was a system of powers to communicate."[47]

Edwards held that God especially communicates through types, which are not the product of human imagination but a discovery of God's self-communication. The presence of the Spirit in the exegete could perceive spiritual truths so that there was a harmony between heart and text. To put it in Gadamerian hermeneutical terms, Edwards held to something along the lines of a spiritual 'fusion of horizons.'[48] The spiritual sense was not limited by the literal, even as the literal held a certain prominence: "The plethora—and indeed, the inexhaustibility—of the Bible's meaning was basic to Edwards' hermeneutics. Without abandoning the foundational role of the literal sense, he showed a tilt toward the spiritual sense. The fecundity of the Bible, its wealth of hidden meaning, overflowed the literal sense."[49] Edwards used typology, in line with Puritan precedent, as a way to avoid fanciful allegories as well as wooden literalism and to honor the spiritual nature of Scripture.[50]

But it was the affections, "the more vigorous and sensible exercises of the inclination and will of the soul," which were Edwards' key to rightly interpreting the Bible, and a key resonance with pentecostal hermeneutics.[51] Edwards is well known for his involvement in the religious awakenings in

46. Edwards, "Images of Divine Things," 106.

47. Marsden, *Jonathan Edwards*, 504.

48. Gadamer, *Truth and Method*.

49. McClymond and' McDermott, *Theology of Jonathan Edwards*, 173.

50. Cherry, "Symbols of Spiritual Truth."

51. Edwards, *Religious Affections*, 96.

which he was a key figure. Against the anti-revivalist, conservative Puritan Old Lights, on the one hand, and the more liberal but orderly Anglicans on the other, Edwards and the New Lights sought to be both faithful to the Puritan heritage and fervent in faith so as to eagerly desire awakenings and revivals. Edwards' leadership of the revival in Northampton in 1734–35 and his *Faithful Narrative* of the revival placed him at the forefront of this movement.[52] His subsequent involvement with the awakenings in the early 1740s and his ongoing leadership in the revival movements made him an important advocate of experiential religion. Edwards' work on the proper role of human affections in religion is also telling of his biblical hermeneutics.

Edwards' *Religious Affections*, published in 1746 in the midst of difficult times for him in Northampton, begins, in sermonic fashion, with an exposition of 1 Pet 1:8, "Whom having not seen, ye love; in whom, though now ye see him not, yet believing, ye rejoice with joy unspeakable, and full of glory" (KJV). Edwards interprets the scriptural text by tending to the spiritual content of the words of the Apostle Peter, taking what later hermeneutic theory would refer to as the text's own literary context at the face value it appeared to have to him, and by swinging the very meaning of the words he is interpreting (i.e., love, joy, and others) as proper Christian affections back onto the text in his hermeneutical method.[53] True religion and true knowledge of Scripture is affected and fervent: "'That religion which God requires, and will accept, does not consist in weak, dull and lifeless wouldings, raising us but a little above a state of indifference: God, in his Word, greatly insists upon it, that we be in good earnest, fervent in spirit, and our hearts vigorously engaged in religion," upon which he cites, in full, quotations Rom 12:11, Deut 10:12, then 6:4–5, and 30:6 as scriptural demonstration of this truth.[54] The bulk of *Religious Affections* is, first, an exposition of a dozen things that are not but may pretend to be genuine signs of gracious, that is, divinely given, affections, followed by twelve genuine ones. The gracious signs are God-centered and produce good spiritual fruit while the signs that offer no proof focus on appearances.[55] In these, we have the integration of spiritual, biblical, theological, and philosophical hermeneutics in Edwards' signs and false signs, together in a comprehensive paradigm in which his

---

52. Edwards, *The Great Awakening*, 96–210.

53. Edwards, *Religious Affections*, 93–99.

54. Edwards, *Religious Affections*, 99.

55. Edwards, *Religious Affections*, 127–461. McClymond and McDermott, *Theology of Jonathan Edwards*, 676, consider *Religious Affections* (1746) as tending toward caution concerning charismatic manifestations as compared to more openness in his earlier *Distinguishing Marks* (1741) with a middle ground between the two found in *Some Thoughts Concerning the Revival* (1743).

biblical hermeneutics continually funded and was continually funded. For Edwards, those who have the power of godliness are baptized in the Spirit:

> The Spirit of God in those that have sound and solid religion, is a spirit of powerful holy affection; and therefore, God is said to have given them the spirit of power, and of love, and of a sound mind (2 Tim. 1:7). And such, when they received the Spirit of God, in his sanctifying and saving influences, are said to be baptized with the Holy Ghost, and with fire; by reason of the power and fervor of those exercises the Spirit of God excites in their hearts, whereby their hearts, when grace is in exercise, may be said to burn within them; as is said of the disciples.[56]

Edwards, then Pentecostals, both read the scriptural texts which spoke of Spirit baptism and saw their importance. Both made connections between Spirit baptism and the affections, recognizing that a living and affected experiential faith is what is needed to rightly interpret Scripture.

Edwards and Pentecostal Hermeneutics

In the humble conditions of the revival that took place among the holiness Christians led by William Seymour at Azusa Street (1906–9) in Los Angeles, scriptural passages that spoke of a baptism in the Spirit had been reinterpreted as teaching an empowerment from God that followed God's gracious works of salvation and sanctification. This hermeneutical and doctrinal move, combined with other social, theological, and practical factors, originated a new movement within Christianity that blossomed into the manifold movements that comprise contemporary Pentecostalism, though modern pentecostal origins also came from beyond Azusa Street.[57] I have contended that this original pentecostal hermeneutic ought to be understood as the original pentecostal paradigm, and as one that has since organically developed into other hermeneutical types: evangelical-pentecostal, contextual-pentecostal, and ecumenical-pentecostal hermeneutics.[58]

As with Edwards, the place of the affections in pentecostal hermeneutics cuts across Enlightenment rationalisms. This can be seen in Land's thesis that orthopathy has been as essential to pentecostal identity as

56. Edwards, *Religious Affections*, 100.

57. Robeck, *The Azusa Street Mission and Revival*, considers the Revival the 'Grand Central Station' of early Pentecostalism. The broader origins are accounted for, among other sources, by Anderson, *An Introduction to Pentecostalism*; Anderson, *To the Ends of the Earth*; Hollenweger, *Pentecostalism*.

58. Oliverio, *Theological Hermeneutics*.

orthodoxy and orthopraxis. Or in James K. A. Smith's claim that, against the "de facto naturalism of market-driven, technological construals of the world . . . pentecostal spirituality fosters a more expansive, affective understanding of what counts as knowledge and a richer understanding of what we know."[59] Or in Wolfgang Vondey's characterization that "the affections inform, shape, and direct the pentecostal worldview as not merely an objective understanding of the world but as active involvement in the world's transformation."[60] Pentecostalism represents a broad tradition of Christianity that has emerged since the turn of the twentieth century. It is difficult to account for the hermeneutical approach of a tradition of roughly a half billion people that has no central structure and allows for a variety of tendencies, even if there are identifiable continuities. This is why Vondey's *Guide for the Perplexed* explains Pentecostalism through a series of contrasts and syntheses: local and global, holistic and extreme, ecumenical and denominational, orthodox and sectarian, socially engaged and triumphalist, egalitarian and institutional, scholarly and anti-intellectual.[61] The variety of pentecostal hermeneutics, moreover, has identifiable resonances with Edwards' hermeneutics.

Among Classical Pentecostals, with roots in the traditional pentecostal denominations coming out of Azusa Street and representing slightly under half of global Pentecostals, I have identified four types. The original classical pentecostal hermeneutic, as aforementioned was a hermeneutic of origination. It moved dialectically between Scripture and experience to construct new doctrines and experiences that came to constitute early Pentecostalism. This openness called for regulation, so an early version of an evangelical-pentecostal hermeneutic did so by arguing for the biblical justification of classical pentecostal doctrines. By the mid-twentieth century, that hermeneutic developed more sophisticated and academic uses for biblical scholarship and more thoroughgoing methods of integrating interpretations of the intent of biblical authors into doctrinal and systematic theologies in a contemporary evangelical-pentecostal hermeneutic. By the 1990s, a contextual pentecostal hermeneutic had arisen that emphasized, primarily from a philosophical rather than cultural standpoint, the contextuality of all interpretation, in line with hermeneutic philosophy.[62] The constructive goal of these contextual hermeneutics was to get to the subject matter of the

59. Smith, *Thinking in Tongues*, 59.

60. Vondey, *Pentecostalism*, 33.

61. Vondey, *Pentecostalism*.

62. Here I refer to the tradition following Gadamer, Ricouer, Westphal, and others as drawn upon by Christian theologians. See the essays in Archer and Oliverio, *Constructive Pneumatological Hermeneutics*.

text by legitimizing the contextuality of the interpreter as well as the text, often in line with Gadamer's 'fusion of horizons.' Picking up on the trickle that remained from the early ecumenical impulses at Azusa Street and other early pentecostal movements, an ecumenical-pentecostal hermeneutic explored pentecostal readings of Scripture alongside those of other Christian traditions in order to broaden, deepen, and mature pentecostal theology.[63] Consonances can be found between Edwards' hermeneutics and each pentecostal hermeneutical type.

The quest for the spiritual sense of Scripture is often found in popular pentecostal hermeneutics as a quest for experience of Jesus and the Spirit through the revelation of the scriptural text and is readily seen in the more original type of pentecostal hermeneutics. An exemplary instance of this can be seen in the founder of the African American Church of God in Christ (COGIC), Charles Harrison Mason (1866–1961). When he visited Azusa Street in early 1907, Masson struggled to accept the new pentecostal doctrine of baptism in the Spirit. Mason wrestled with the spiritual meaning of the Scriptures that were used in the proclamation that this third blessing of the Spirit was available, and that it had *glossolalia* as its 'Bible sign.' After great endeavor, Mason testified to receiving Spirit baptism after having a deeply affective experience in which his insight resulted in humility before God that brought great joy, so that "from that day until now." He later also testified that "there has been an overflowing joy of the glory of the Lord in my heart."[64] For both Edwards and Mason, biblical interpretation was inextricably linked to the spiritual meaning of the text so that the end sought was a living experience of the spiritual truth that was the result of the gracious work of the Spirit. Such living experience of the text has been paradigmatic for the core of what constitutes 'pentecostal' in pentecostal hermeneutics. Lived experiences of the Spirit, moreover, have been essential to the subsequent development of other types of pentecostal hermeneutics. Nevertheless, for reasons developed in *Religious Affections*, Edwards would likely have been a critic of the wider spiritual hermeneutics utilized by early Pentecostals like Mason—for example, the latter's interpretation of unique vegetable roots as spiritual signs from God. But it would also be hard to find deeper testimonies of the living and affected knowledge of Scripture promoted by Edwards than what has been found among early Pentecostals from Seymour and Mason through to the present.[65]

63. Oliverio, *Theological Hermeneutics*, esp. 15–18, 315–18.

64. Mason, *The History and Life Work of Elder C. H. Mason*, 27–30; Clemmons, *Bishop C. H. Mason*, 6–23.

65. For instance, McClymond and McDermott, *Theology of Jonathan Edwards*, 172n26, find that "though Edwards might have approved some aspects of the

Yet another early founder, Daniel Warren Kerr (1856–1927), who showed more conservative hermeneutical tendencies that helped (re)turn pentecostal hermeneutics toward an evangelical-pentecostal hermeneutical type, is perhaps the Pentecostal whose biblical and spiritual hermeneutics most closely stands in line with those of Edwards. Quietly an influential figure for early Pentecostalism as the primary author of the Assemblies of God's original Statement of Fundamental Truths (1915/16), as well as the founder of several institutions of higher education, Kerr sought the spiritual realities that Scripture revealed for his Bible doctrines while persisting in foregrounding the spiritual realities. That is, for Kerr, the spiritual experiences were primary and the proper ends, while the theology was secondary yet still of importance.

In interpreting the Bible, Kerr did not just want biblical facts, he wanted 'facts on fire.'[66] While not using the same terms as Edwards' spiritual and speculative theologies, Kerr offered similar categories as he advocated the preeminence of 'spontaneous theology' over 'systematic theology.'[67] It is 'spontaneous theology' that should take 'first place' as the "Bible is a supernatural revelation from God to men . . . the discourse of God concerning Himself."[68] 'Systematic theology' is like the dry, factual structures which, while true, do not contain life. For Kerr, "the secret of 'spontaneous theology' lies in the word of Jesus, "He that willeth to do His will shall know of the doctrine whether it be of God or whether I speak for myself; John 7:17."[69] Kerr also drew on images in a manner similar to Edwards' 'images' or 'shadows,' finding the organic nature of 'spontaneous theology' to contain spiritual life in images like 'fire,' 'water,' and 'rain.'[70] The quest for a spiritual sense of Scripture, the preeminence of this spiritual knowledge over the systematic or speculative, the development and justification of such as scriptural doctrine, and Kerr's own 'modernizing traditionalism' in his theological narrative of history, sound tones quite similar to those of Edwards.[71]

This 'modernizing traditionalism' is also another key point of confluence with Edwards and evangelical-pentecostal hermeneutics. McClymond

---

twentieth-century Pentecostal Charismatic movement, the practice he condemned in *Religious Affections* has a parallel in the contemporary Charismatic notion of the 'rhema word' or specific text of Scripture that comes vividly to mind—purportedly through the power of the Holy Spirit."

66. Kerr, "Facts on Fire," 5.

67. See Ramsey, "Editor's Introduction," 47.

68. Kerr, "Spontaneous Theology," 3.

69. Kerr, "Spontaneous Theology," 3.

70. Kerr, "Spontaneous Theology," 3; Kerr, *Waters in the Desert*, 17–20.

71. Oliverio, *Theological Hermeneutics*, 88–104.

and McDermott consider 'hybrid traditionalism,' their preferred category for the class of exegetes in which Edwards is properly placed in his approach to the historicity of Scripture, as being defined by holding to traditional views while not merely assuming them but arguing for them.[72] In doing so, Edwards could defend things, like the Mosaic authorship of the Pentateuch, in ways that would strain historical judgments of many believing scholars today. This 'modernizing traditionalism" or 'hybrid traditionalism' has also been used in various renditions of 'believing criticism' among contemporary evangelical-pentecostal hermeneuts since the development of a more scholarly tradition within Pentecostalism in the mid-to-late twentieth century. This development can be seen, for instance, in the way history and biblical interpretation are integrated in the earlier evangelical-pentecostal theologian Myer Pearlman's (1898–1943) works published in the 1930s. Pearlman's oft-used *Knowing the Doctrines of the Bible* (1937) drew on ancient historical and cultural contexts as they merged with the present so that the text presents a theological, even eschatological, narrative of human history. A more sophisticated use of historical-critical methods, and especially redaction criticism, has since developed in late-twentieth and early-twentieth-century evangelical-pentecostal biblical scholars like Roger Stronstad and Robert Menzies.[73] Edwards and early forms of the evangelical-pentecostal hermeneutic, however, produced readings of history that have often ended in awkward historical judgments, especially regarding their eschatologies. For Edwards, this can be seen not only in his hoped-for Protestant world triumph which came amid his postmillennial schema of history but also among many Pentecostals, often in more cataclysmic readings of history rooted in their forms of premillennialism.[74]

A more fruitful resourcing of Edwards and his legacy for Pentecostals continues to be found in how the substance of Christian theology and the human affections meet, like they did for early hermeneuts like Seymour, Mason, and Kerr. Contemporary pentecostal theologians, including many who can be categorized as doing theology and interpreting the Bible in light of the sense of the utter contextuality of all human understanding, a sense which has become acute in late modernity, have also placed a strong emphasis on the centrality of the affections for pentecostal biblical interpretation.

72. McClymond and McDermott, *Theology of Jonathan Edwards*, 168–72.

73. My account of Pearlman's hermeneutics is available in *Theological Hermeneutics*, 121–30. For Stronstad, see *The Charismatic Theology of St. Luke*; Stronstad, "Pentecostal Experience and Hermeneutics"; Menzies, *Empowered for Witness*.

74. My thanks to Oliver Crisp for pointing to this similarity in history and eschatology during our panel discussion on Edwards and Pentecostalism at the 2016 Annual Meeting of the Society for Pentecostal Studies.

Many of these contextual-pentecostal theologians, like Amos Yong, have understood the affections as not only central to pentecostal theology, but have also emphasized the centrality of love for Christian theology altogether, and for the pentecostal cardinal doctrine of Spirit baptism more particularly. Following Land's lead, Yong and other pentecostal theologians have affirmed that the affections, the "abiding dispositions which dispose the person toward God and the neighbor in ways appropriate to their source and goal in God,"[75] are to be shaped by an orthopathy, that is, right affections, and are to be combined with right practices and right beliefs for fruitful Christian living, theology, and biblical interpretation.[76] Some Pentecostals have turned to an 'analogy of love' (*analogia agape*) not at the exclusion of the *analogia entis* or the *analogia fidei*, but seeing each as bringing the others to completion in a perichoretical relationship.[77]

The ecumenical-pentecostal impulse in contemporary pentecostal hermeneutics has also, by an almost second nature impulse, turned to the affections in its readings of the Bible. Ecumenical-pentecostal approaches have sought to draw on the historical Christian traditions and contemporary *oikumenē* in order to nurture pentecostal and other churches with rich theology. The overall agenda is exemplified by Simon Chan's call for pentecostal 'traditioning.'[78] But the Old Testament scholar Lee Roy Martin's post-critical, ecumenically oriented, and nurturing approach to the 'hearing' of texts provides a key contemporary exemplar of pentecostal affective hermeneutics that resounds with Edwards' in an approach to Scripture where the affections come to the fore in garnering spiritual fruit from the interpretation of Scripture.

For Martin, "the affective approach calls for the hearer to attend to the affective tones that are present in the text and to allow the affections of the hearer to be shaped by the text."[79] Martin turns to 'hearing' over 'reading' on account of its more biblical basis, so that the constitution of the text presupposes God's speech and calls for obedience and transformation, while this orality also reflects pentecostal self-understanding.[80] Such an affective hearing can combine with a variety of approaches and take place in different contexts, among diverse traditions. Further, it need not ignore critical

---

75. Land, *Pentecostal Spirituality*, 136.

76. See Yong, *Spirit of Love*, esp. 75–91.

77. For development of the 'analogy of love,' see Yong, *Spirit of Love*, esp. 85–91; Macchia, *Baptized in the Spirit*, 257–82; Nichols, "The Search for a Pentecostal Structure in Systematic Theology"; Oliverio, "Spirit Baptism in the Late Modern World," esp. 57–60.

78. Chan, *Pentecostal Theology*, esp. 17–39.

79. Martin, "Longing for God," 55.

80. Martin, "Longing for God," 55n2; see also Martin, *The Unheard Voice of God*.

scholarship, as Martin advocates a post-critical rather than pre- or a-critical approach. This approach distinguishes itself from other modern ones that tend to focus on the dissection of the structure of a text and other historical-critical issues with little to no attention placed on the emotional dimensions, though such are prominent in texts like the Psalms which Martin focuses on. Rather, a hearing of the text "aims to develop emotional and moral sensitivities" and informs not only belief and action but "the imagination."[81]

Pentecostal hermeneutics that have tended to the affections have understood such as a way of knowing, a positive response in attitude and reception that is compatible with late modern hermeneutics and anthropology, as well as a pentecostal sense of the manifold witness to truth and understanding in order to construct spiritual understanding, discern, and build Christian communities of empowered and loving witness. Edwards' hermeneutics were much more conservative than many late modern, that is, contemporary pentecostal hermeneutics, though the depth of his theological vision and the affirmation of the affections, rightly understood, are points where pentecostal hermeneutics might learn from the great American theologian.

Further, Edwards was insufficiently aware of the influence of British-colonial and Puritan cultural norms upon his spiritual and theological interpretations of the Bible. The black pentecostal theologian Estrelda Alexander has noted how, though Edwards preached and sought the salvation of blacks, he theologically interpreted the Bible as implying that the hierarchical social order on earth in fact reflected God's intent, and that even in heaven there would be differing 'degrees of glory' for whites and blacks.[82] Contemporary pentecostal hermeneutics would, almost unanimously, be critical of smuggling in these types of cultural assumptions into theological hermeneutics. Nevertheless, popular pentecostal hermeneutics also commonly reflect cultural assumptions quite deeply, loosely interpreting biblical texts in light of contemporary ideas as they take initial spiritual and theological readings of the Bible at face value, oftentimes without suspicion concerning interpretive motives or sufficiently developed theological, biblical, or philosophical resources for discernment.

Dialogue between the dual impulses to relate to culture and affirm the affections can create the desire for an approach, like Martin's, that is unafraid of scholarship and critical readings but is nevertheless productive of sanctified and empowered affections for hearing the biblical text.[83] What

81. Martin, "Longing for God," 59.

82. Alexander, *Black Fire*, 64–65.

83. See also Green, *Sanctifying Interpretation*.

Edwards and many Pentecostals have understood is that the affections are a way of knowing. The affections are not reduced to irrational reactions to be overcome by colder and supposedly more rational ways of understanding. The affective is an inevitable aspect of human being-in-the-world. Humans are lovers. Such loves orient us toward the ends that we most greatly desire.[84] They form the agendas of what we read in the Bible, and they open our ears to hear. They tend our intentions to that which we attend.

Conclusion

Edwards' approach to the affections seeks the spiritual sense of Scripture with a discipline that is rigorous and that casts suspicion on mere outward appearances. Pentecostals have tended to openness in interpreting experienced affections as righteous or gracious. The confluence of the attention to the affections here is also met by contrasting theological anthropologies and narratives for the path of salvation and the Christian life. For Pentecostals, Edwards' theology of the affections in *Religious Affections* may be utilized in helpful critique of overly optimistic and accepting readings of the human affections that mistake too wide a variety of feelings for gracious ones, or any spirit for the Spirit. Edwards' Calvinistic approach is untenable for most Pentecostals, yet his theological criteria for identifying affections might lead Pentecostals to develop further theological criteria of their own. Pentecostals do not need to put on the 'Saul's Armor' of Edwards' theology for developing a more robust account of the affections, for biblical interpretation or otherwise.[85] Like the best of ecumenical-pentecostal hermeneutics, though, Pentecostals may see an example in the Christian tradition and not merely imitate it but seek to learn from it, to draw salient understanding, and then to reconstruct and integrate a deeper and more theologically sound approach to the affections in tune with pentecostal identity. Martin's work, in particular, exemplifies this as he has integrated such into his scholarly work in interpreting the Old Testament.

84. Smith, *Desiring the Kingdom.*
85. Dabney, "Saul's Armor."

8

Breaking Out of the Immanent Frame

In the title essay of his collection of popular writings entitled *The Devil Reads Derrida* (2009), Jamie Smith articulates a trickle-down theory of cultural formation. That essay compared the influence of the French deconstructionist to a theory of cultural influence exemplified in a tense scene in the 2006 film *The Devil Wears Prada.*[1]

In that scene, Miranda (played by Meryl Streep), the tyrannical editor of a fashion magazine (based off of *Vogue*'s Anna Wintour), deconstructs her naïve young assistant, Andy (Anne Hathaway), for referring to fashion as "this stuff." Miranda takes the moment to educate Andy on the formative role of the fashion industry. She informs Andy that despite her naiveté the "people in this room" have made the very fashion that Andy is herself wearing. Andy's "lumpy blue sweater," Miranda chides, is cerulean, "not just blue or turquoise or lapis." Cerulean was the fashion a few years back, she lectures, because of the proclivities and tastes of people in the fashion industry, even if it was later found in the cheap imitation Andy had picked out of some clearance bin at some "tragic Casual Corner." Smugly, Miranda dresses Andy down for being "blithely unaware"—so that "it's sort of comical how you think that you've made a choice that exempts you from the fashion industry when in fact you're wearing a sweater that was selected for you by the people in this room, from a pile of 'stuff.'"[2]

This episode epitomizes a guiding principle for Smith's work as a Christian philosopher and theologian. His work is predicated on the conviction

1. Smith, "The Devil Reads Derrida."
2. Frankel, *The Devil Wears Prada.*

that "philosophical currents . . . have an impact on the shape of cultural practices."[3] Thus his writings have bridged the depths of the existential and linguistic queries of Continental philosophy in order to span them across to educated and not just academic audiences in a series of texts that have included *Who's Afraid of Postmodernism? Taking Derrida, Lyotard, and Foucault to Church* and the first two installments of his planned Cultural Liturgies trilogy—*Desiring the Kingdom: Worship, Worldview, and Cultural Formation* (2009) and *Imagining the Kingdom: How Worship Works* (2013). In these texts, part of Smith's method is to leave with the gold of Egypt (secular philosophy) to enrich Christian communities (Exod 12:35–36).

Such a trickle-down theory of cultural formation and understanding presents an answer to the perlocutionary agenda of this short and dense book on a monumental work, Charles Taylor's *A Secular Age* (2007). This time, though, Smith draws from an influential Christian philosopher. However, one may consider *A Secular Age* the most important book written on religion in the West so far this century. In it, Taylor recounts that our contemporary secular age is here because of a trickle-down of ideas, practices and sensibilities, and Smith provides here a summation and retelling that is itself a trickle-down of Taylor's deconstruction of the standard "subtraction stories" for an alternative genealogy of the secular.

For the Pentecostal educator, Smith's work ought to receive special note since he came from us. Converted as a teenager at a Pentecostal Assemblies of Canada congregation in Ontario, Smith has gone on to make his mark in the Christian academy and in wider scholarly circles—and he has done so as an unashamedly Christian philosopher. Smith has made a turn towards the Reformed tradition, teaching philosophy at Calvin College in Grand Rapids, Michigan. Yet deep Pentecostal impulses remain in his work.[4] His 2010 *Thinking in Tongues: Pentecostal Contributions to Christian Philosophy* was a foray into the implications of Pentecostal spirituality for Christian philosophy. He was the key figure in founding the Philosophy Interest Group of the Society for Pentecostal Studies (c. 2000) and was its first Interest Group Leader. Most importantly, Smith's continued articulation of the role of the whole person for Christian theological and philosophical understanding displays his charismatic-Pentecostal roots which continue to produce regular intellectual fruit. Smith has been about legitimizing an account of the human that serves as a corrective to modern rationalism.

---

3. Smith, "The Devil Reads Derrida," 136.

4. Do we have higher educational institutions in the Pentecostal tradition capable of allowing a Christian philosopher of this caliber to flourish?

But why would a leading Christian philosopher write an entire book on a book? Because the trickle down to Christian communities in this case is that important as one could well argue that *A Secular Age* is that important. *A Secular Age* could be the most significant book written so far this century on religion in Western culture.[5]

Throughout his career, Taylor has functioned as a subtle and non-defensive apologist for religion in general, and for even what may be called deep Christian philosophical intuitions about reality.[6] He has provided a sustained defense of the plausibility structures and importance of religious understanding, frequently in an indirect manner. Taylor's philosophical writings have most often come in the form of winding stories about the emergence of sets of ideas. These philosophical narratives, rarely easy reads, are still winsome and illuminating. Truth claims, for Taylor, find adequacy as our best accounts of human experience in the worlds which we inhabit.[7]

Frankly, in my view, every contemporary Western Christian theologian, especially every philosophical theologian or Christian philosopher, should read both Taylor's *Sources of the Self* and *A Secular Age* as essential texts to understanding the contemporary setting for theological work. Pressures on scholars and educators, however, are often quite limiting. Therefore, Smith's *How (Not) to Be Secular* provides a guide and summation of Taylor's important work for those who, may not have the opportunity to attend to the primary text. It could also serve as a supplement or dialogue partner for those who wrestle with Taylor's account of the secular condition of the contemporary West.

Smith does not approach Taylor and *A Secular Age* as some neutral arbiter. As a creative and capable writer, he is strategic in his summarization. It is clear that Smith has been influenced by Taylor's work and is in general sympathy with his agenda. In Smith's reading of Taylor, one can sense care for the latter's ideas and their attending contexts. In fact, Smith's careful attention to detail and subtext in Taylor's agenda may lead the reader to feel

5. Taylor received the Templeton Prize in 2007, largely for his work on *A Secular Age*. The 776-page (before endnotes and indexes) tome from the Canadian Catholic philosopher was published by Belknap Press of Harvard University Press, an imprint known for publishing modern scholarly classics, as the culmination of one of the most important philosophical careers in recent decades. See, also, the collection of essays from prominent scholars addressing *A Secular Age* in Warner et al., *Varieties of Secularism in a Secular Age*.

6. That Taylor is a philosophical realist, and what kind of realist, is further articulated in Dreyfus and Taylor, *Retrieving Realism*.

7. The full title of his other monumental work, *Sources of the Self: The Making of the Modern Identity*, is particularly telling of his overall philosophical agenda and its emphasis on philosophical anthropology.

as if she is in a seminar on Taylor's book led by the author, she would be on to something. This due to the fact that the text is, in part, a result of a spring 2011 senior level undergraduate philosophy seminar Smith held on *A Secular Age*.[8] Nevertheless, Smith on Taylor is of course more than exposition. Smith's illustrations from contemporary literature and his lengthy footnotes serve as professorial riffs that are quite revealing of Smith's own take on Taylor.[9]

On another level, Smith's Augustinianism might be understood as the driving force behind his interest in Taylor. *How (Not) to Be Secular* might be understood as a late modern embodiment of Augustine's famous maxim, *credo ut intelligam*, "I believe in order to understand," over and against the canons of modern rationalist epistemologies. Further, Smith's Augustinian emphasis on how our bodies and affections, desires and love, play critical roles in our theological and philosophical understanding finds consonance with Taylor's more romantic (as in Taylor's affinity for eighteenth- and nineteenth-century German Romantics like Herder and Humboldt) and Hegelian (Taylor started out as a Hegel scholar) tendencies.

Smith and Taylor are in general agreement in their stance against Enlightenment rationalism. For instance, in a significant essay from Taylor entitled "Overcoming Epistemology," he takes the canons of modern foundationalist epistemology to task for claiming to hold the proper method of ascertaining true knowledge but not owning up to their deeply held assumptions—spiritual, anthropological, ontological and moral—which betray their supposedly neutral, scientific, mechanistic and mathematical methodology.[10] Augustine, Taylor and Smith are all thus aligned against this sort of epistemic stance to the way the human understands. And this rationalist stance has undergirded the common sense that modern Western people so often have that transcendence is to be ruled out of the domain of genuine knowledge, relegated to the domain of opinion and speculation, and disregarded as an epistemic relic of a bygone age.

---

8. Smith, *How (Not) to Be Secular*, xii.

9. The four figures used to illustrate Taylor's account of the secular, like the first (63) in *How (Not) to Be Secular* which shows how the forces of transcendence-immanence and enchantment-disenchantment played on the 'buffered self' to create the 'nova effect' of the fragmentation of visions of reality in modernity, function as the chalkboard sketches in the seminar he offers readers. The glossary of Taylor's terminology (140–43), with the terms bolded in the body of the text, saves the reader a task that usually exacts patience in reading Taylor—gradually understanding what he seems to be expressing (and not just referring to or designating) in his use of certain terms. The way words work is important to Taylor, and Smith.

10. Taylor, "Overcoming Epistemology."

In the Preface, Smith tells the reader that he is writing this book for a variety of people—religious and non-religious, though with a certain tending toward those in Christian work amidst the kind of secularism he and Taylor will describe—who need an alternative to the stories about religion and secularity told by those on each side who "retreat to homogenous zones of shared plausibility structures."[11] Rather, as he stresses in the Introduction, "Our Cross-Pressured Present: Inhabiting a Secular Age," we live in an age where *both* belief *and* unbelief are 'haunted' by lingering doubts so that "the haunting is mutual."[12] We live in an age where we are 'cross pressured' as we face the "simultaneous pressure of various spiritual options"—transcendent and immanent—producing the 'nova effect' of an explosion of multitudinous options for belief and meaning. So, living in this secular age is living in a pluralistic age, though one with some common underlying assumptions.

Taylor's account of the secular takes care to distinguish types of the secular to avoid the conflation of ideas, and resulting equivocations. He does not merely describe the non-religious alongside religious ways of life ('Secularity 1') or public and political secularism that works alongside decreasing religious belief and practice ('Secularity 2'), but he especially focuses on the underlying plausibility structures of belief where religious belief or belief in God has become contestable and often enough assumed to be untrue ('Secularity 3').[13]

These plausibility structures are deep in those tacit assumptions which Taylor refers to as our 'unthought.' In what has already become a well cited line from *A Secular Age*, Smith quotes Taylor's guiding question for his next seven-hundred-plus pages: "Why was it virtually impossible not to believe in God in, say, 1500 in our Western society, while in 2000 many of us find this not only easy, but even inescapable?"[14] Taylor will have to tell a story to unravel this, explaining *how* this happened, and he will do so against the 'subtraction stories' which held that "religion and belief withered with scientific exorcism of superstition."[15] An alternative story is needed.

This story is important—for Christian educators, theologians, philosophers and pastors, as well as engineers, teachers, students, homemakers, plumbers, retail store clerks, retirees, and others.

---

11. Smith, *How (Not) to Be Secular*, xi.

12. Smith, *How (Not) to Be Secular*, 10.

13. See Smith, *How (Not) to Be Secular*, 20–23, for his explanation of "Taylor's taxonomy of the secular." See Taylor, *A Secular Age*, 1–4.

14. Taylor, *A Secular Age*, 25.

15. Smith, *How (Not) to Be Secular*, 24.

Smith tells Taylor's story of the becoming of our secular age by structuring the five chapters of his book in correlation with the five parts of Taylor's much larger work (139 pages on 776 pages in the bodies of these respective texts). Nevertheless, Smith echoes Taylor's agenda throughout. This is especially the case in their methodological agendas in the sense that both want to reorient the discussion about religion and secularism in the current age, redrawing the contours of the 'existential map of our present' when it comes to religion and secularity.[16]

The idea of philosophy as map making draws on one of Smith's favorite metaphors for what he is doing in his writing—cartography.[17] His appreciation for Taylor's skill in this is clear: "It is Taylor's complexity, nuance, and refusal of simplistic reductionisms that make him a reliable cartographer who provides genuine orientation in our secular age. *A Secular Age* is the map of globalized Gotham, a philosophical ethnography of the present."[18]

Smith begins his narration with a critical concept for Taylor—the 'immanent frame.'[19] This is the social space that is taken as normal in much of Western (or North Atlantic, as Taylor sometimes likes to put it) culture. It frames human life within a purely 'natural' framework of immanent causation and precludes 'supernatural' reasons as legitimate for public discourse. If you want to speculate on your own time and in the privacy of your own home or house of worship, so be it—that is your right. But the normal social imagination (the 'social imaginary'[20] is another important 'Taylorism') frames your life within this immanence. Transcendence is a ghost of the past or an unwarranted set of beliefs still defended by those who just cannot let go. According to these 'subtraction stories,' secularization has been in a long but triumphant journey (at least eventually, with the inevitable ups and downs) of lopping off these past superstitions, 'subtracting' until we are left with only genuine reality.

It is just these 'subtraction stories' that Taylor's *A Secular Age* contests. Yet it is far from a fundamentalist reaction or the kind of apologetics that

16. Smith, *How (Not) to Be Secular*, 3.

17. Smith also thinks of what Taylor is doing as archeology that works in concert with cartography of the present, "giving us both the lay of the land and a peek at the strata beneath our feet," Smith, *How (Not) to Be Secular*, 18. Taylor's work is more archeology than cartography while Smith's is proportionately more cartographical.

18. Smith, *How (Not) to Be Secular*, 3.

19. The importance of Taylor's reframing the terms of the discussion of religion and secularism can be seen in the title of the official blog of the Social Science Research Council of Canada's Program for Religion in the Public Sphere. They began and entitled it "The Immanent Frame" just months after the original publication of *A Secular Age* in 2007.

20. See Taylor's *Modern Social Imaginaries*.

accepts the terms of the debate set by modern rationalism. Taylor (and Smith) contest the 'subtraction stories' by leveling the playing field. Repeatedly they push the point, that the 'subtraction stories' *are* constructive accounts of reality, developed with contingent and historical ideas, which posing as the 'true story' of reality. These stories pretend at incontestability. Using political terminology, Taylor speaks of this approach as 'spin' rather than a contestable account of reality, or a 'take.'[21]

This is how Smith summarizes Taylor on this matter (emphases in italics, here and throughout this essay, are those of the original author):

> Taylor is most interested in considering (and contesting) the "spin of closure which is hegemonic in the Academy" (p. 549 [of *A Secular Age*]). This is the spin that is dominant amongst intellectuals and elites who would actually see the 'open' take on the immanent frame *as* 'spin' and see their own 'closed' take as *just the way things are*. For these secular 'fundamentalists,' we might say, to construe the immanent frame as closed is to just see it as it *really* is, whereas construing it as 'open' is a mode of wishful thinking. In effect they say: we 'closed' framers are just facing up to the facts of the case; its 'open' framers who are *interpreting* the world *as if* it would be open. The immanent frame is *really* closed even if some persist in *construing* it as open (p. 550 [of *A Secular Age*]). For those adherents of the closed reading, *it's not a 'reading.'*[22]

In an important sense *A Secular Age* is about undermining the 'spin' that the immanent frame is all there is and all there ever will be. Rather, Taylor (and Smith) contend, it is a 'take' on what is—itself an ontology.

Ontology, or a philosophical account of what is there, is critical to Taylor's work, even though his philosophical work has sought to avoid strong metaphysical claims about the nature of reality. Smith's approach to this matter is similar. Neither is attempting to construct a great metaphysics nor even a robust ontology, though ontic claims are made and implied throughout the writings of both men. Each often argues, with various degrees of subtlety that Christian intuitions about reality are at least philosophically legitimate, perhaps even compelling.

Both also claim that our 'secular age' is one that has been 'fragilized.' That is, differences in faith commitments in our day—your next door neighbor may hold a very different take on reality than you—tempt not only believers to doubt their faith, but also atheists to doubt their atheistic faith. All

---

21. Smith, *How (Not) to Be Secular*, 93–97.
22. Smith, *How (Not) to Be Secular*, 95.

shades of belief experience similar questioning given common contemporary plausibility structures.

It is not that this is the state of belief for the entirety of Western culture. Taylor and Smith know it is more complicated than this, that there are zones of largely shared plausibility structures (from a certain kind of Christian college campus to the left-leaning or 'progressive' part of town to the Bible Belts), but these multiple and conflicting zones is part of what Taylor, in fact, means by Secular 3. You cannot take belief in God for granted these days because an 'exclusive humanism' (that is, a worldview or imaginary that excludes transcendent realities and goals) is plausible today given reigning contemporary plausibility structures. Yet the Catholic Taylor and the Pentecostal become Reformed Smith are both believers in the midst of this secular age.

Taylor's story about the becoming of this age is also one that reveals his defense of particular things against the Enlightenment quest for universals. As Smith puts it, this "reflects Taylor's Hegelian side—a deep appreciation for the contingencies of history. So we can't tell a neat-and-tidy story of deduction from abstract principles."[23] Things could have turned out differently, but the way they did tells us a lot of truth about reality.

Rather than telling the story of secularization as that of lopping superstitions off of a theistic worldview, Taylor accounts for the artifacts of our ideological and cultural history with an archeology that describes the construction of an exclusive humanism from at least initially medieval Christian roots. Those roots begin with the move for 'Reform.' Part 1 of *A Secular Age* (the first five chapters and two hundred pages itself) is thus entitled "The Work of Reform."

Taylor contends that Reform, the movement within high and late medieval Christendom to move from a Christian society where there were various options as to degrees of religious commitment to one where everyone was meant to be a deeply and totally committed Christian, was a driving force behind the rise of secularism. This first part, and sometimes misunderstood, aspect of Taylor's narrative is a detailed account that deals with more facets of the movement of Reform than can be adequately recalled here. However, his thesis is that reform was the engine that, when met with some shifts in intellectual ideas, allowed for the constructions of what will become 'exclusive humanism.' Reform pushed people and created intolerance for social and individual lapses in the quest for betterment. Smith explains the results succinctly: "If people aren't meeting the bar, you can either focus on helping people reach higher or you can lower the bar.

---

23. Smith, *How (Not) to Be Secular*, 25.

This is why Reform unleashes both Puritanism and the '60s."[24] On the other hand, Reform affirms what Taylor refers to as 'ordinary life,' where grace and fulfillment might be found in the normal person's vocational and domestic life, not just in the life of the heroic or religiously dedicated person.

When this movement for Reform combined with that set of intellectual movements, and especially nominalism,[25] which undermined the 'enchanted' worldview of medieval Christendom, an important shift occurred. In this 'enchanted' ontology, things everywhere functioned semiotically to point to higher truths, exemplified in the Western Platonic-Aristotelian heritage. Beginning with this shift towards disenchantment, meaning was no longer seen as inherent in things but in individuals who are agents that generate knowledge.

This led to profound religious and communal consequences. Smith puts it this way: "Once individuals become the locus of meaning, the social atomism that results means that disbelief no longer has social consequences. 'We' are not a seamless cloth, a tight-knit social body; instead, 'we' are just a collection of individuals—like individual molecules in a social 'gas.'"[26] Religiously, this played out in the disenchantment that was part of the Protestant Reformation—or, as Smith puts this, "the Reformers' rejection of sacramentalism is the beginning of naturalism, or it at least opens the door to its possibility. It is also the beginning of a certain evacuation of the sacred as a *presence* in the world."[27] Sometimes Taylor is misunderstood as being anti-Protestant. Rather, he is against the 'excarnation' that, in part, was facilitated by the Protestant Reformation, though funded by nominalism.

The second part of *A Secular Age* ("The Turning Point," two chapters and 80 pages) is often taken by many narrators of secularism as the starting point. The anthropocentrism of the Age of Enlightenment and the emergence of deism are standard in other accounts of secularity as the beginnings of modern secularism. But Taylor emphasizes the ideological construction in the process of immanentization that took place and thus its prehistory in medieval Christendom.

24. Smith, *How (Not) to Be Secular*, 37.

25. See Taylor's subtle but important use of Dupré's *Passage to Modernity* (94, 144 in *A Secular Age*). For Smith on this, see *How (Not) to Be Secular*, 40–46.

26. *How (Not) to Be Secular*, 31.

27. *How (Not) to Be Secular*, 39. Taylor's account of disenchantment is important for understanding the way his account of secularism differs from the 'subtraction accounts.' For Taylor, disenchantment starts especially with medieval Latin Christendom and Reformation era criticisms of magic. The criticisms lead to a different sense of what is there before a person, and a more flattened and less full ontology. Taylor understands Romanticism as the beginning of a reaction against such a flattening. For a summary of Taylor's account, see McPherson and Taylor, "Re-Enchanting the World."

This early modern immanentization, however, occurs through four 'eclipses.'[28] The first is the most important one—the eclipse of a transcendent purpose in favor of immanent ends. The importance of a *telos* beyond 'human flourishing' is made optional. Instead, a new providential order is introduced, but with immanent ends. These are human flourishing and mutual benefit, especially economic, as Adam Smith, John Locke and Hugo Grotius introduced a providential understanding of God's ordering of the world.[29] The eclipses of grace (in favor of work), mystery (in favor of perspicuity), and transformation (in favor of therapy) largely result from the first eclipse. It is not a large step, then, to lop off the providential order, or at least make it optional.

Taylor articulates the movement towards an ethics based on an impersonal order, the abstraction of the Christian faith, along with the movement away from embodiment and sacramentality of faith in early modern religion as 'excarnation.' Religion finds its place in supporting the basic assumptions of society as 'civil religion' while society has taken the place of ordering the ends of life in, as Smith puts it, "a civilizational or cultural Pelagianism: the confidence that *we* make *this* world meaningful."[30]

That we make this world meaningful rather than discover meaning in it resulted in a revolution in how we understand our own believing. So now we live in "an age in which the plausibility structures have changed, the conditions of belief have shifted, and theistic belief is not only displaced from being the default, it is positively *contested*. We're not in Christendom anymore."[31] But this does not mean Taylor, or Smith's, storytelling is done.

The 'nova effect'—also the title of part 3 for Taylor—and subsequent 'supernova' are metaphorical explanations for what happens when the modern self is pressured by alternately enchanted and disenchanted views of the world, and an immanent framework met by a lingering and haunting sense of transcendence. The 'nova' is the buffet of beliefs that emerged in the modern world, exemplified by the traditional American mantra: "go to the house of worship of your choice." This is followed by the "supernova," a

---

28. Smith, *How (Not) to Be Secular*, 48–50.

29. Taylor speaks of this as the "neo-Durkheimian" dispensation, the hinge between the "paleo-Durkheimian" and "post-Durkheimian" dispensations. Named after the sociologist Emile Durkheim who marked the connections between conceptions of divinity and social orders, in *A Secular Age* and other works Taylor marks the movement from the conception of the divine ordering and justifying societal structures altogether (paleo-) to providentially establishing an impersonal order for the benefit of humanity (neo-) to the secularized disjunction between social order and transcendent purpose (post-Durkheimian). See also, Taylor, *Varieties of Religion Today*.

30. Smith, *How (Not) to Be Secular*, 55.

31. Smith, *How (Not) to Be Secular*, 60.

late-modern explosion of further options for meaning—the blur of multiple visions beyond the varied traditional local options. For example, today in the Upper Midwest of the United States, the options are no longer nominal or devout Lutheran, Catholic, Protestant or pietist; or even later developing options like contemporary Evangelical, modern Pentecostal, late modern educated secularist or the largely areligious working and drinking man; but a secondary explosion from these and other options to new constellations of variants. The new constellations are our neighbors today, resulting from the spiritual 'supernova' we currently inhabit.

Taylor is telling his story, and Smith his exposition of it, in order to undermine the inevitability of the 'closed world structures' of the 'immanent frame.' This story is being told to show how the 'unthought' of the 'immanent frame' is a 'take' and not the very truth it purports to be. Taylor and Smith are working a long argument against the 'subtraction theories' of secularization, arguing through demonstration that those theories are 'begging the question' rather than simply telling us the adult truth about the way reality is. They are politely flipping the table. This is the adult story of secularism told at the adult table, and Dawkins and his ilk (as well as some of the simplistic stories told by religious fundamentalists) are sitting at the kids' table.

Taylor's own work, as I claimed earlier, is subtly apologetic. In *A Secular Age*, and elsewhere, Taylor is challenging his readers to explain the ontology implicit in human agency, our ethics and aesthetic responses. Materialism does not, he strongly implies, account for the 'fullness' of reality as we experience it. The tensions involved in modern religious life occur, then, in an 'expressive individualist' context where the dilemmas of modern meaning are worked out in a variety of settings within this more general context. Taylor understands three fundamental stances in the typical Western context—those who continue to acknowledge transcendence, exclusive humanists who are nevertheless still committed to the good of humanity, and what he generalizes as neo-Nietzschean anti-humanists.

Though he tells a much more complicated story about this (in the nearly five hundred pages of Parts 4 and 5), in the end Taylor sees the religious account of reality as a transcendent and transformative experience essential to the kind of religious life that Christians experience and testify. Smith, for his part, emphasizes this transformationist point to his readers. Smith seems especially concerned that contemporary Evangelicals are tempted to forsake transcendent meaning and the transformationist understanding that is essential to Christian faith, because there is a desire to be relevant to current immanent concerns like the goodness of creation, social justice, and the short attention spans in late modern consumerist culture.[32] Smith is no reactionary, anti-worldly conservative here. He presses this point because he believes in the axis of the incarnation where transcendence embeds itself in immanence, which is at the essence of Christian faith.[33]

Nevertheless, there are things you will be unable to find in Smith's helpful reading of Taylor. Despite the quality of Smith's narration, this text cannot replace Taylor's great book. It will not provide the reader with the same depth of understanding as Taylor's long and winding, yet winsome philosophical storytelling. A key instance would be Taylor's erudite philosophical reading of Western secularism in part 4, chapters 12–14 ("The Age of Mobilization," "The Age of Authenticity," "Religion Today"). Many will find themselves, their parents and grandparents in these chapters, along with explanations of those of other ideological approaches to modern life, and Smith's brief summations cannot do justice to a full reading of *A Secular Age*.

And despite the high quality of his text, Smith has largely missed or underemphasized a few key themes. One is Taylor's dialogue with theorists of secularization. The influence of a small cadre of Christian sociologists on Taylor is skimmed over by Smith, even though the influence of the work of David Martin and his ilk on Taylor's account of secularism looms large. Taylor might even be seen as offering a thicker account of Martin's influential sociological work.[34] Taylor's very thick account resources Martin,[35] though we might turn the table and let Martin help us understand what Taylor and Smith are doing.

In his *A General Theory of Secularization*, Martin included an assessment of the clerical response to the basic stages of the secularization of societies at large (ideas which encompass Taylor's Secular 1–3).[36] While Taylor is no cleric, his explicit Catholicism (some of his favored iterations of faith include that in the 'God of Abraham' and Christian life in the mode of Francis of Assisi) closely resembles two modes of clerical responses which Martin describes as characteristic of the 'professional guardians' of religion.

In a deeper phase of secularization, where religion has not only lost its dominance but even its unity as a robust minority position, Martin speaks

---

32. See Smith, *How (Not) to Be Secular*, 49, 138–39n10.

33. See Smith's *Speech and Theology*.

34. See Martin, *A General Theory of Secularization*; Martin, *On Secularization*. For his work on Pentecostalism, see Martin *Pentecostalism* (2002); and his earlier *Tongues of Fire* (1990).

35. Martin appears ten times in the index of *A Secular Age*, 864, though the weight of Martin's ideas outstrips what can be counted.

36. See "Crisis amongst the Professional Guardians of the Sacred," chapter 7 of Martin, *A General Theory of Secularization*, 278–305.

of "voluntary associations of Christians, segmented and partial in their in-fluence and often concentrating at particular status levels."[37] In this context, Martin's sociological work found several typical responses from the 'profes-sional guardians.' Two of these may be characterized as responses which translate and transpose meaning. The first emphasizes going out from the religious community to the secular world, using evangelism and apologetics to translate and transpose religious meaning into secular terms. The other is translating and transposing secular terms back into the religious vernacu-lar, showing the authenticity of the religious, over and against the secular. Among those who have tended to take this second approach, Martin sees 'the charismatic invocation of the Spirit' as an exemplar. Pentecostals are used to this mode.

Taylor, however, goes both ways with subtlety. Some see his back-and-forth movement as a betrayal of a deeply Christian ontology, so that Taylor, in the guise of opening up space for religious, and more particularly Chris-tian, faith, ends up as much an apologist for deeply secular convictions.[38] While Taylor's Christian critics may have a point that he does not display a fully adequate Christian ontology in his philosophy, this is a misunder-standing of Taylor's agenda. Rather, Taylor's agenda in *A Secular Age* and elsewhere is much better understood in the form of this back-and-forth movement. His philosophical work has gone out to the secular world to speak to it so that we might be understood on our own terms, but then also moves back in from the world with the gold from Egypt to rearticulate Christian faith. We might say the same for Smith, though he is a notch or two more explicit in his agenda than Taylor.

Taylor's Christian critics are also right to sense in Taylor that he is, in fact, also an advocate for a version of Secular 1—one where visions of the transcendent do have a place in the public and the political but are never-theless not allowed to dominate. In this sense, Taylor is also a multicultur-alist.[39] Taylor does see the space created between religious and governing visions as a positive achievement. I think we all might get Taylor's primary point here if we envision what our society might look like if the political visions of some of our fundamentalist friends materialized.[40] Thus, rather

37. Martin, *A General Theory of Secularization*, 29.

38. See Rose, "Tayloring Christianity."

39. Taylor the multiculturalist is the end of Taylor that some Christian scholars tend to either criticize or shy away from. See his central contribution in Taylor et al., *Multiculturalism.* Taylor has his own Christian grounds for multiculturalism, but he is interested in finding common ground with others who have shared convictions on these political and cultural principles.

40. Personally, I shudder. This space keeps even rival Christian visions from dominating

than approaching Taylor with a hermeneutic of suspicion, one that is not warranted on account of his virtuous philosophical and personal attributes, it is best to see the opening of the immanent frame as the central purpose of Taylor's philosophical agenda. That, and his genuine desire to give the best philosophical account he can concerning our secular age.

As a Christian philosopher, Taylor has achieved a great deal. Smith wants a wider audience, like Pentecostal educators, to understand the importance of the alternative narrative which Taylor offers us concerning secularism. Smith is also at pains to urge contemporary evangelicals to not cut off our emphases on transcendent goods for solely immanent ends, with the attendant Christian understanding of the goodness of creation and the embedding of the spiritual in the material. We are an incarnational not ex-carnational people.

Finally, for the Pentecostal educator, neither Taylor nor Smith will provide you with a deeply Pentecostal response to secularism (whether in form 3, or 1 or 2). Their work, however, calls you to such. Smith is full of strong pointers along the away, like his summarization of Taylor's four eclipses of transcendence or his hint at an Augustinian analysis.[41] Rather, Taylor and Smith's work call for deep responses from communities like ours who sense a greater fullness than that of the 'immanent frame'—and this ought to lead us to unpack the ontologies implicit in what we claim to have experienced. They have left this task to our communities.[42] The latent and shadowing influence of secularism over Pentecostalism in the West, and the question of its future relation to global Pentecostalism, should lead Pentecostal educators to pay attention to this issue and avoid the mistakes of which Smith and Taylor warn.

---

one another, and forces us to dialogue and respect one another in a space created by common dialogue and the inability to dominate others—even if the waters of current political realities often wash over the bulwark of these ideals embedded in the structures of our contemporary democracies.

41. See Smith, *How (Not) to Be Secular*, 69n13, for example.

42. Smith, *Thinking in Tongues*, has offered some philosophical starting points for Pentecostals.

PART THREE

Interpretations of Pentecostal
Hermeneutics

9

Spirit-Word-Community

Amos Yong has emerged as a pioneering Pentecostal theologian. Moving beyond the usual theological concerns of the Classical Pentecostal tradition, his inquiries have expanded the palette of Pentecostal theology. While his earliest work focused on philosophical theology and theology of religions, his more recent writings have also engaged the dialogue between science and theology, theology of disability and political theology. Among his earlier writings, *Spirit-Word-Community* is perhaps the best entry point into Yong's thought as it sets out his original vision.[1]

In this review essay, I will be making several key contentions about *Spirit-Word-Community*. First, though it has seemingly attracted the least attention of any of his monographs, it is paradigmatic to his theological project. A dense and wide-ranging work in philosophical theology, it fleshes out Yong's early theological program so that, in a sense, it is autobiographical. Second, I find a particular brilliance in it as he offers a constructive effort at theological hermeneutics, boldly forging a holistic vision which develops an ontology, metaphysics, epistemology and hermeneutics together into an account of what theologically interpreting the world entails. There is much to appreciate here. But such audaciousness also opens him up for criticisms, several of which I will anticipate. Third, I find Yong's hermeneutical paradigm helpful on a quite basic level. His approach to human understanding in general, and theological reflection in particular, fits into the emerging category of 'hermeneutical realism.' This recognition that doing theology is

1. *Spirit-Word-Community* received the 2005 *Pneuma* Book Award from the Society for Pentecostal Studies, the award given by the Society for what is deemed the best new work in Pentecostal studies.

always an interpretive activity is an important matter of self-awareness for the theologian that I consider advantageous. Yet before I further articulate these three claims, I will synopsize his intricate paradigm of theological interpretation.

Synopsis

Yong's thesis is that theological hermeneutics occurs in the hermeneutical trialectic of Spirit, Word and Community. Part 1 (chapters 1–3) deals with metaphysics and ontology from a Trinitarian and especially pneumatological approach. Part 2 (chapters 4–6) conceives of epistemology in terms of a pneumatological imagination. And part 3 draws on the convictions of the previous two in proposing his methodology: "The Acts of Interpretation: Spirit" (chapter 7), "The Objects of Interpretation: Word" (chapter 8), and "The Contexts of Interpretation: Cornmunity" (chapter 9). Through this, he seeks to form a 'hermeneutics of life' which interprets the nexus of 'God-selfworld' where he "strives to describe theological interpretation as it actually occurs, and prescribe a model of doing theology relevant to the Church catholic and directed toward the eschaton" (316).

Yong considers that theological interpretation is a dynamic process in which Spirit, Word and Community are always involved. This understanding of hermeneutics broadens the issue well beyond biblical hermeneutics without simply becoming a general hermeneutics. Instead, a theological hermeneutic "aims at interpreting the totality of human experience—and that includes God and God's relationship with human selves and the world as a whole—from a perspective that is specifically and explicitly formed by faith" (6). But in the process of articulating his theological hermeneutics, he does in fact articulate a general hermeneutics coming from his epistemology, metaphysics and ontology. Yong considers doing theology as entailing a manner of interpreting the world since it "is a strictly second-order affair that proceeds in abstraction from first-hand experience. . . . Theology broadly understood concerns the totality of God and God's relationship to human selves and the world understood from the perspective of faith" (2–3). However, he notes that this is not the only way of cognitively reflecting upon one's world since other disciplines also legitimately approach reality from their own respective starting points.

He also chastens this project with an epistemological fallibilism, stressing the partiality of all knowledge claims and the dynamic nature of reality itself. Still, he is unafraid to engage in categorical thinking because he considers categories themselves "heuristic tools for thinking" (28). He reasons that since human understanding begins within the finitude of human experience *a posteori*, he should decline to consider his own categories *a priori* on account of his own lack of transcendental perspective. But he finds this fallibility to not only characterize human "creaturehood, but also fallen creatureliness" (182). He most often considers sin as an overreaching of one's appointed reason for being, and such has noetic effects.

The key inspiration for his epistemology and metaphysics is the American pragmatist philosopher Charles Sanders Peirce whose metaphysics Yong correlates with his reading of biblical pneumatology (see chapter 1) and Trinitarian ontology (see chapter 2). He adopts and modifies Peirce's metaphysics which consider the character of reality, phenomenologically read, to emerge in three basic categories: the qualities of things abstracted from experiences (Peirce's 'Firstness'), the concreteness of actual things or facts in their differentiation from one another (Peirce's 'Secondness'), and the general laws which relate these together (Peirce's 'Thirdness'). "'Thirdness' is dynamic while 'Firstness' and 'Secondness,' respectively, represent the abstract and concrete. In Peirce's philosophy, all things participate in each of these three aspects of the becoming of reality.[2]

Correlating his Trinitarian ontology with Peirce's categories, he holds that while the Father is the "qualitative source of creative efficacy" and the Son is "the decisive sign or image of the Father through whom the Godhead is embodied and efficaciously interacts with the world," it is the Spirit who is "the interpretant of the divine relationality both ad intra and ad extra" (95). Thus Peircean 'Firstness' with its attendant abstraction is correlated with the Father, the concreteness of 'Secondness' with the Son, and the dynamism of 'Thirdness' with the Spirit.[3]

Not only does Yong correlate Trinity and Peircean metaphysics here, but he is also making a methodological point. He makes another set of correlations as Spirit, Word and Community are, respectively, understood in terms of subjectivity, objectivity and contextuality in interpretation. The created order is grounded in the being and relations of the Trinity. Interpretation begins with subjectivity, but it always includes the objects of interpretation and the contexts in which interpretation occurs. This is also exhibited in the structure of the book. Reversing the usual modern order, method comes last

2. Also see Yong, "The Demise of Foundationalism."

3. Yong's Trinitarian theology utilizes both the 'mutual love' model of Augustine and the 'two hands of God' model from Irenaeus. He seeks to resolve the tension between them, and their attendant disagreement on the *filioque*, through the 'return model' proposed by David Coffey and the similar proposal of Thomas G. Weinandy in which "the Spirit is thereby the mutual love between Father and Son, and the link between God and the world" (71). See Coffey, *Deus Trinitas*; Weinandy, *The Father's Spirit of Sonship*.

(in part 3). Rather, he begins with an ontology and metaphysics (part 1) and then moves toward an epistemology considered in terms of a 'pneumatological imagination' (part 2), demonstrably arguing for the interdependence of each part with the others and rejecting any notion of a 'view from nowhere' or a methodology and epistemology that claims to be devoid of an ontology and metaphysics. The metaphysics from which this hermeneutics operates thus begins with his 'foundational pneumatology.'[4] A foundation is used in a Lonerganian sense in order to sustain the spiritual nature of all reality.[5] He holds that while it is both communal and contextual in its origination, it strives toward universal application. This type of foundationalism is thus 'heuristic' or 'shifting' and is a correlative of his fallibilism.[6]

What should not be lost here is the very basic claim Yong is making in contrast to a reductionistic or naturalistic account of reality.[7] Similar to Karl Rahner's transcendental anthropology, he offers an alternative account of the status of the human and, further, the entire world as essentially spiritual,

---

4. The Jesuit theologian Donald Gelpi has been an important source from which Yong has drawn on here. See Yong, "In Search of Foundations."

5. In Bernard Lonergan's *Method for Theology* he placed 'foundations' as the fifth of eight functional specialties, not the first. In his theory, foundations follow research, interpretation, history and dialectics. But they are the level at which conversions take place. Conversions can be of many different types, but they all involve a shift in fundamental beliefs and attitudes. See Lonergan, *Method in Theology*, 125–45.

6. Yong clarifies that, "It is therefore not an epistemological or Cartesian foundationalism that is erected on incorrigible beliefs. Instead I prefer to image it in terms of a heuristic or shifting foundationalism since it is attentive to the continuously expanding data of experience" (*Spirit-Word-Community*, 100). Like Peirce, he seeks to bring together the best of empiricist and rationalist tuitions while overcoming what he considers their shortcomings. On this view, experience is interpreted by second-order reflection which in turn shapes future experiences.

7. Despite his sympathies with the phenomenological tradition in philosophy, Yong rejects the more radical finitude found in the non-static and a-theological (as in purposefully devoid of the theological) hermeneutics of Martin Heidegger and Hans-Georg Gadamer since he holds to a dynamic ontology that is sustained by the Triune God. He further argues for the inevitability of foundations and frameworks: "I have posited a foundational pneumatology precisely in order to defend a rational, critical, and communal realism. Toward that end, my conviction is that if foundations are equivalent to warrants, then all rationalities and epistemologies are foundational in that sense. The question then is not whether or not any particular rationality is foundational, but what kind of foundations are being appealed to and how they operate" (*Spirit-Word-Community*, 100). Yong's epistemology could be characterized as similar to the postfoundationalist approach yet with the difference that he adds a third, dynamic, non-synthesizing aspect. For examples of the postfoundationalist approach, see Shults, *The Postfoundationalist Task of Theology*; Huyssteen, *Essays in Postfoundationalist Theology*. Postfoundationalism claims that while foundations are inevitable, they are always subject to criticism and revision; they are not self-evident but a result of a complex process.

graced by *the* Spirit in his 'foundational pneumatology.' But it also entails a different parsing of the God-world, divine-human, grace-nature and naturesupernature distinctions than does the usual metaphysics of classical theism or Thomism.[8] Against a Hegelian dialecticism, on the one hand, or a dualism, on the other, his proposal builds upon the metaphysics of Peirce to claim that a dynamic relational pneumatology mediates the poles of the abstract and concrete as an essential third force. Interpretation has its source in this Trinitarian dynamics. So, "only a pneumatological rationality is sufficiently dynamic, historical and eschatological to drive the dialectical movement of thought" (104). Thus a synthesis does not overwhelm the other poles, but there exists a respect for each.[9] So a trialectic, which is differentiated from a triad on account of its dynamism, is superior to a synthesis.[10] The Triune God upholds this reality as both 'the one' and 'the many' simultaneously are and require one another as they are dynamically related.

This pneumatological foundation also upholds Yong's account of the human activity of interpretation. Though he does this less here than in *Discerning the Spirit(s)* and *Beyond the Impasse*, he conceives of 'spirit' as a complex of tendencies which shape the behavior of any thing. This can represent things at various levels of aggregation, be they individuals, communities,

8. While the first two of these distinctions are clearly there, the latter two are a point at which I wonder whether more analytical clarity could have been helpful. Yong comments that while "the Holy Spirit could meet us in the depths of our own hearts (Augustine), in the face of the other (Levinas), and in the future that beckons and welcomes us (Pannenberg). . . . Kierkegaard's qualitative distinction between time and eternity, between creation and the creator, needs to be noted. This means that the transcendence toward which the Spirit inspires us must always be more than what we encounter in ourselves, in others, and in our futures" (*Spirit-Word-Community*, 227).

9. Yong contends that this move alleviates some of the problem created by subject-object dualism or the collapse of such a distinction: "While pneumatology in abstraction gives rise precisely to the theological and philosophical wrong turns of speculative or absolute idealism (Hegel), a robust pneumatological theology brings vagueness and generality together with the distinctiveness, particularity, and individuality of concrete actualities. Here the subject-object distinction or difference is not only preserved but insisted upon, yet not in the Cartesian sense of reasserting a metaphysical dualism between the knower and the known. It is also precisely for those reasons that the logic of pneumatology resists all forms of totalism: absorbing the other into oneself, defining the other according to oneself, or neglecting, ignoring, or abusing the other as not valuable according to standards established by oneself. Both the self-deferential character of the Spirit vis-à-vis the mutuality of the Father and Son in the immanent Trinity and the gracious donation of the Spirit to establish difference and other in the work of God economically considered combat the ideology of totalization. Further, insofar as fallibilism is also negotiated communally, it acts as a means through which the Spirit checks the abuse of intellectual power" (*Spirit-Word-Community*, 104).

10. Yong also considers his hermeneutics triadic as well as trialogical, but it is foremost a trialectic.

institutions or things in the natural order. What seems to qualify something as 'spirit' on his understanding is that it has volition and that it is
in motion—it is living.[11] Thus he considers the subjective moment of interpretation a matter of 'spirit.' And further, "the Holy Spirit is the divine
mind that illuminates the rationality of the world to human minds" (123).
Consequently, theological interpretation works when, through a person's
pneumatological imagination, the Spirit breaks in and gives a 'creative fidel-
ity' in understanding the faith which has been passed down. Knowing that
one is responsibly doing theological interpretation requires a discernment
that is related to one's general spiritual discernment, a graced capacity that
he conceives of more generally than as a specific spiritual gift.[12] Following
von Balthasar, he acknowledges that "the Spirit is the transcendental condition of the human experience of God" (228). Thus we know, theologically,
only by, through and in the Spirit so that "all theologizing is charismatic
in the sense that it is enabled by and through the Spirit" (229). Pneumatic
moments in interpretation thus serve correctively in one's theological work
as the Spirit resists the normal givens of theological knowledge, providing
the possibility of newness in theological interpretation.[13] Yet, though in the
Spirit, the human interpreter is not purely elevated from their given contexts
but encounters the theologically transcendent in a 'mediated immediacy.'[14]
Hence he employs Peirce's semiotics.

11. Drawing some similarities with Hegel's *Geist* seems inevitable here despite his
trialectic's differentiation from a Hegelian synthesis. Yong's use of the concept of 'Spirit/
spirit' is not simple. While 'Spirit' refers to the Holy Spirit, especially in reference to his
Trinitarian ontology, 'spirit' has rhetorical, anthropological, and metaphysical connota-
tions. Rhetorically, it refers to ethos, atmosphere and even tradition. Anthropologically,
it deals with what is common in humanity, in human experience and rationality. Meta-
physically, it also refers to that which sustains commonality, but it is also cosmic, "the
energetic or field dimension that sustains the concrete or phenomenological aspects of
things in the world" (*Spirit-Word*-Community, 15). Yong finds himself following the
pneumatological and eschatological orientation of theologians such as Wolfhart Pannenberg, Jürgen Moltmann and Michael Welker.

12. Yong finds that because "it is important not to exalt the human imagination as
an autonomous faculty or human freedom as an autonomous activity" (*Spirit-Word-
Community*, 229), the human interpreter who truly perceives the theologically transcendent sees 'in the Spirit' who has indwelled the interpreter.

13. A key distinction in Yong's method is between the 'pneumatic,' that is, the experience of the spiritual and the 'pneumatological,' which is second-order reflection upon it.

14. He contends that the given objects of interpretation are nor static but fluctu-
ate in time and space in their biological, natural, cultural, and ecclesial worlds, thus
necessitating the need for dynamic categories of understanding. This requires that the
mediation of the cultural with biblical and theological traditions goes both ways. Social, natural, economic, political, and other forces influence, shape and, at times, even
dictate interpretation.

Yong's three primary objects for theological interpretation are experience, the Word of God, and the ecclesial/theological tradition. Such a claim moves him beyond the conservative Protestant methodology of developing a systematic theology from a biblical foundationalism. He legitimizes the theological exegesis of experience as he finds this, in actuality, to be inevitable in theological hermeneutics. And since he holds that language is inextricable from perception, he accounts for experience as both the medium of interpretation and one of its objects. His conception of the Word of God is also widened. It is found in the life, death and resurrection of Jesus Christ, who can be "interpreted only insofar as he is engaged concretely, interpersonally, and intersubjectively" and in the normative Word of Scripture (257–58); he also recalls Ignatius of Antioch's formulation that the three speeches of God are creation, incarnation, and Scripture.[15] Taken as such, the divine Word is not an object to be manipulated; rather, it interprets us by the power of the Spirit, standing over and against us as an 'other.' While holding to the original author's intent and reader's reception of a text as a center of gravity for its meaning, he also claims that a pluralizing hermeneutic is needed to handle the biblical texts because of both the plurality of biblical sources as well as the need for openness to multiple readings for many texts.[16] In engaging the biblical texts, Yong thus rejects 'arbitrarily' systematizing biblical materials through a single theme or motif in favor of doing so pluralistically as worlds are opened up in their readers by texts. Yet he constrains this pluralizing hermeneutic by arguing that "the original meaning as intended by the author and as received by the audience" (256) limits the interpreter.[17] This corresponds to his notion of the hermeneutics of tradition. A variety of local confessions serve to provide accountability for one another, criticizing the parochial, ideological, or partisan agendas of other local theologies. Further, this also means that "no one event, creed,

15. Following the philosophical approach of J. L. Austin and Speech Act Theory, he understands that the Word of God "confronts us as an other, a locution. It also makes demands of us, as an illocution. Finally, it actually transforms us as a perlocution" (*Spirit-Word-Community*, 256). In Speech Act Theory a 'locution' refers to an actual utterance of words or other sounds, an 'illocution' is what one is doing when saying something, and a 'perlocution' is what one brings about, or hopes to, in such an utterance.

16. Yong holds that texts vary on a continuum between closed readings (those closely connected with the author's intention) and more open readings (chose directed toward the reader's response).

17. Yong offers only a brief explanation of his biblical hermeneutics (see *Spirit-Word-Community*, 253–65), though he summarizes his understanding as follows: "In short, meaning and interpretation is grounded at least in a two-fold manner: in author(s) or text(s) insofar as the biblical language functions communicatively (Word), and in performative or interpretive activity insofar as the biblical language functions transformatively (Spirit)" (*Spirit-Word-Community*, 257).

doctrine, etc., can carry the weight of the entire Christian theological tradition" (271). On the other hand, the historical engagements of Christian theology, within their varied contexts for theological hermeneutics, ideally seek to produce doctrines to be "believed everywhere, always and by all" (294). For Yong, theological interpretation "proceeds upon the conviction that all truth is God's truth, wherever it may be found, and that all persons are created in the image of God and therefore possibly reflect aspects of the truth in and through their lives and thinking" (306).

Evaluation

This last statement, in fact, seems to function as a maxim in all of Yong's work. His interest in theology of religions might well be understood as a result of such a conviction. This correlates with my assertion, at the beginning of this essay, that the hermeneutics found here is paradigmatic to Yong's entire theological project. While offering a more substantiated argument is beyond the space I have here, let me briefly note how I think this is true in relation to his theology of religions. It is his Peircean fallibilism and foundational pneumatology, when combined with his ontological commitment to the Trinitarian God, that drive his openness to the work of the Spirit in non-Christian religions alongside his strong commitment to the truth of Christian faith. While *Discerning the Spirit(s)* did offer an approach for working this out in relation to theology of religions, it is *Spirit-Word-Community* that developed the commitments implicit in it.

My second claim was that this project demonstrates Yong's brilliance as a constructive theologian. He draws from a variety of sources in the biblical tradition, systematic theology, the Christian tradition, hermeneutic theory, and philosophy as he ambitiously attempts to bring it all together in a 'consensual hermeneutic.' There is much that he has rethought here beyond the multiplicity of hermeneutics already found among Christian traditions, including his own. But sometimes this project seems to suffer from vagueness. Some of this may be caused by the difficulty for the reader to keep up with the manifold correlations that he is making. But at other times it appears to be the result of the conflation of concepts under the use of a common term. Does he stretch 'Spirit/spirit' beyond what this sign can handle? And at others he brings aspects of so many visions together that it seems that he should have offered more analytical clarity along the way.[18] Further, it is also

18. For instance, Yong offers an illuminating theory of truth which draws on aspects of pragmatic, correspondence, and coherence theories (see *Spirit-Word-Community*, 164–75), yet such could use a more sustained articulation and justification in order

not altogether clear when Yong is describing how theological hermeneutics in fact occurs and when he is prescribing how it ought to occur. Much of this, though, is the result of his laudable attempt to propose his hermeneutical vision in its fullness. At the time of its publication, there was no fuller hermeneutical proposal from a Pentecostal theologian.

Third, I maintained that Yong's project is, at least very basically, offering a sensible account of human understanding since it is both hermeneutical and realist. His characterization, throughout, is that this project embraces a 'critical realism' which "grounds knowledge in otherness rather than solely in cognitive processes" (83). I find it to embrace Kevin Vanhoozer's call to a 'hermeneutical realism' which, while confirming that everyone always comes to reality with their own descriptive frameworks, also affirms that "we can come to know something other than ourselves when we peer into the mirror of the texts."[19] As such, Yong affirms the contextual, communal, and linguistic nature of theological understanding while still holding that there are better and worse, truthful and false, and helpful and unhelpful interpretations of 'God-self-world.' In doing so, he is to be commended for putting forth a significant creative proposal on theological hermeneutics.

---

to defend it against potential objections. However, it would be helpful if this section of *Spirit-Word-Community* could be a starting point for philosophical reflections on the nature of truth claims and their justification among Pentecostal theologians and philosophers.

19. Vanhoozer, *Is There a Meaning in This Text?*, 31. Though this matter of the status of meaning in relation to texts is a much more complicated matter, Vanhoozer's location of meaning in the communicative action of a speech act rather than an author's mental intention is a helpful distinction which Yong does not affirm without qualification, even though he does draw upon speech act theory. This is because Yong recognizes chat there is no pure access to meaning available. Concerning the truth of a speech act he says: "in Peircean terms, demonstrating truth is a semiotic (and, therefore, interpretive) process that is potentially infinite, except when it satisfies doubt so as to enable resumption of habitual activity. For this reason, even if one were to trade in Peirce's definition of meaning as pragmatically defined for Vanhoozer's definition of meaning as intrinsically related to an author's communicative action, one is still no better off in accessing meaning since doing so requires the ongoing activity of interpretation (involving what Peirce calls interpretants and what Vanhoozer calls signification)" (*Spirit-Word-Community*, 169).

10

The One and the Many

In his celebrated essay on Leo Tolstoy's view of the course of history, Isaiah Berlin offers a binary typology of the modern-day intellectual. He describes the intellectual landscape as a "great chasm between those, on one side who relate everything to a single central vision . . . a single, universal, organizing principle . . . and, on the other side, those who pursue many ends, often unconnected."[1] Citing the Greek poet Archilochus that "the fox knows many things, but the hedgehog knows one big thing," Berlin speaks of foxes and hedgehogs as the opposite poles of the classic problem of 'the one and the many.' While the tendency of a hedgehog is to insist on a universal vision, the tendency of a fox is to entertain the scattered, diffused, and plural elements of life. These classifications are, Berlin insists, helpful even if oversimplified. Berlin found Tolstoy to be a complicated case, since he "was by nature a fox, but believed in being a hedgehog."[2] Amos Yong's provides us with a similar case of complexity.

More than any major Pentecostal theologian before him, Yong has dwelled in the pluralities and the differences, playing around like a fox with various disciplines of inquiry, perspectives, contexts, and traditions. Characteristic of his work is the readiness to dialogue with perspectives from outside his own traditions. Yong moves from theology of religions to hermeneutics, from metaphysics and ontology to pneumatological theology in global contexts, from theology of disability to interreligious practices, from political theology to theology and science. Yong appears to be a fox,

1. Berlin, *The Hedgehog and the Fox.*
2. Berlin, *The Hedgehog and the Fox,* 7–12.

roving around to inquire at the margins. Yet, there are stronger reasons to believe that he is, rather, 'a hedgehog in fox's clothing,' inquiring into the plural, the many, as he investigates the dynamism which comes through the relation of the many to the one.

This essay analyzes and situates the theology of Amos Yong as an ecumenical-Pentecostal theologian who has come to address the late modern version of the classical philosophical problem of 'the one and the many' It is both a classical concern in human thought and an acute problem in a world of many faiths in this era of globalization. We live in an era where theologians face the problem of how their particular claims about the truth of their beliefs can account for the practiced faiths of others, both within and without the particular religious or theological tradition which the theologian represents. This conversation marks the foundational context for Yong's work. He engages this conversation by continually mining, pressing, and working out his understanding of the outpouring of God's Spirit 'upon all flesh.' In Yong's own terms:

> On the day of Pentecost, the crowd asked, "What does this mean?" Peter answered that this was the last days' outpouring of God's Spirit upon all flesh. Today our theological question is, What does it mean that God did so then and continues to pour out the Spirit on men and women, young and old, slave and free (Acts 2:17–18; cf. Joel 2:28–29)? The beginnings of a response to this question will take us toward a Pentecostal theology for the late modern world.[3]

Despite the seeming simplicity with which Yong states the task, his agenda is varied and complex. Underlying its motivation is an alternative account to the prevailing sense of the dissolution of meaning in the late modern world. This chapter, first, provides a brief generalized account of late modernity and the significant burden it places on the late modern theologian. The middle portion of the chapter considers Yong's place in late modern theology as someone who although tending to pluralities, has made a trinitarian ontology the unifying center of his thought. The chapter then traces Yong's response to the dissolution of meaning by accounting for the pluralities of reality and corresponding theological methods or hermeneutics. The chapter concludes with a general characterization of Yong's project amidst the challenges of the one and the many.

---

3. Yong, *The Spirit Poured Out on All Flesh*, 31.

The time is 'now,' so modernity claims.[4] The modern era has been one of imminence as well as immanence.[5] The sense of a closed order to reality, in space-time, has been considered axiomatic by many late modern thinkers, especially those in Western culture.[6] What is considered acceptable for belief is only that which is found comfortably in, as Charles Taylor has coined it, 'the immanent frame,' a closed order where thick and transcendent pictures of reality are relegated to the realm of privatized belief, and only thinned out accounts of matter or nature remain in bounds for general discourse.[7] As a result, late modern culture emanating from the West has found itself in a status where the immediate presence of things has failed to carry with it any necessarily inherent meaning, or only a thinned out sense of it.[8] The logical result of this lack of connection between that which is experienced and its inherent meaning has been both a plurality of constructed meanings and the dissolution of definitive or authoritative accounts of meaning. While in one regard this tension has created space for developing personal convictions and a high regard for the dictates of conscience,[9] both no small accomplishments, there has also been a corresponding emptiness.

In the midst of this confrontation, classical Pentecostalism and (in part) its outgrowth in global Pentecostalism have been considered antimodern,

---

4. Reflecting on the Latin *modo*, 'now' or 'just now,' as the etymological root of 'modernity,' D. Stephen Long helpfully characterizes modernity as "a perpetual preparation for the now, a perpetual change that must always presents itself as new and different, even when it is the same old thing endlessly repeated and simply repackaged with minor changes" (Long, *Theology and Culture*, 85–86). For his assessment of how modernity has influenced theology; see Long, *Speaking of God*, 21–81.

5. Some helpful works on how modernity's immanence has been a major theme in modern Christian theology are Grenz and Olson, *20th Century Theology*; and Charles Taylor's account of the emergence of 'closed world structures' which seem "obvious, unchallengeable, axiomatic" in *A Secular Age*, 539–93.

6. I am referring here to those intellectual frameworks in much of modern thought strongly skeptical towards any form of transcendence, from nineteenth-century figures like those of Durkheim, Feuerbach, Freud, Marx, and Nietzsche and various atheistic and strongly skeptical twentieth and twenty-first century philosophies from Russell to Dawkins and from Heidegger to Foucault and Rorty. Common to all of these frameworks are denials of any transcendent order of being.

7. Taylor, *A Secular Age*, 542. There is much to be said regarding the thinness or thickness of our accounts of natural reality. For Yong's accounts, see *The Spirit of Creation*.

8. Steiner, *Real Presences*, has addressed this as the "break of the covenant between word and world which constitutes one of the very few genuine revolutions of spirit in Western history and which defines modernity itself" (93). This thinning out often entails the totalizing of the social construction of meaning.

9. Note the connection between the principles of the Reformation and modern thought here.

or at least paramodern movements.[10] Many accounts of Pentecostalism tend to focus on their otherworldliness. Yet, from the start, classical Pentecostalism has been characterized by its very worldly 'canniness' in its pragmatic utilization of modern technology and methods for the furtherance of evangelistic mission, even alongside its originally 'primitivist' orientation.[11] The late twentieth and early twenty-first century blossoming of scholarship among Pentecostals has led to a growing chorus of constructive Pentecostal attempts to address the prevailing issues in the broader contemporary theological worlds.[12]

Yong has been at the forefront of this contemporary development. One helpful way of understanding his position is to read him as a Pentecostal theologian making forays that address the central intellectual problem of late modernity. Yong's theology responds to the twin (and thus closely related) late modern problems of pluralism and dissolution by providing a positive Pentecostal theological account of the pluralism of meaningful beliefs and practices. This response, in turn, provides an antidote to many popular engagements with the issue of pluralism that declare the dissolution of inherent meaning, often out of frustration or cynicism, or both.

The Problems of Late Modernity: Pluralism, Dissolution, and Globalization

To speak of the cultural situations in which theologies are produced is to do so in generalities. There are always exceptions, qualifications, caveats, to name a few. But to understand the era of late modernity, which we currently inhabit, cannot avoid generalization. If Yong's theology is considered significant, since it has been addressing a central problem of late modernity-pluralism and dissolution—it is helpful to describe in more detail the problems of the age before explaining how Yong's theology addresses them.

Sociologist James Davison Hunter sees the pluralism and dissolution of late modernity as the two most powerful challenges to the contemporary church.[13] Pluralism, as Hunter defines it, is "the simultaneous presence

10. For an example of the former take, see Anderson, *Vision of the Disinherited*. For an example of the latter, see Archer, *A Pentecostal Hermeneutic*, 9–34.

11. Wacker, *Heaven Below*, 32–34.

12. The Pentecostal Manifestos Series, which published by Eerdmans and co-edited by Yong and James K. A. Smith, exemplified this trend. For Yong's own assessment of this issue, see Yong, "Pentecostalism and the Theological Academy"; Yong, "Primal Spirituality or the Future of Faith?"

13. See Hunter, *To Change the World*, 197–212.

of multiple cultures and those who inhabit those cultures."[14] While this characterization is not unusual today, for most of human history this simultaneity has not been the norm. Although cities since ancient times have provided space for the coexistence of multiple cultures, it has not been until late modernity that global urbanization along with the advances in communication and travel have resulted in sustained contact with other cultures. Through much of modernity, a majority culture with its attendant religious faiths and meaningful accounts of reality could insulate its adherents against the claims of other cultures. With the arrival of late modernity-at least in the Western context-there seems to be no going back.[15]

The implications of cultural pluralism for religious beliefs, practices, and theology are mammoth. Following Peter Berger, Hunter advances the claim that "the credibility of one's beliefs depends on certain social conditions that reinforce those beliefs."[16] Of course, there are those who can stand firm under all kinds of intellectual, social, and political conditions. Nevertheless, most beliefs need social support and reinforcement. There are, in Berger's nomenclature, 'plausibility structures' which link societal institutions and beliefs underlying cultural life. But "when social conditions are unstable or when the cohesion of social life is fragmented, then the consistency and intelligibility of belief is undermined."[17] As Taylor puts it in his account of secularization of the West, we have gone "from a society in which it was virtually impossible not to believe in God, to one in which faith, even for the staunchest believer, is one human possibility among others. . . . Belief in God is no longer axiomatic. There are alternatives."[18] It is not that religious belief, specifically Christian belief, is disappearing entirely in the West.[19] Nonetheless, the plurality of cultures and beliefs in later modernity, in concert with the formative and immanentist power of contemporary media and technology, advance the dissolution of the givenness of meaning. Yong's work is driven by an engagement with the powers of pluralism and the conditions that allow for the discernment of truth and the encounter with God amidst the challenges posed by the gradual dissolution of meaning.

14. Hunter, To Change the World, 200.

15. Though some still fight to go back, hence Hunter's earlier thesis that the 'culture war' in America is "a contest for cultural ascendancy and the capacity to enforce conformity" (Hunter, To Change the World, 201). See also Hunter, Culture Wars.

16. Hunter, To Change the World, 202. See also Berger, The Heretical Imperative.

17. Hunter, To Change the World, 202.

18. Taylor, A Secular Age, 3.

19. David Martin's careful sociological work is helpful here.

The dissolution of meaning is identified by Hunter as the second and interrelated problem of the late modern world. The realist "covenant between signified and signifier, word and world is broken. The forces of dissolution, then lead us to a place of absence, a place where we can never be confident of what is real, what is true, what is good; a place where we are always left wondering if *nothing* in particular is real or true or good."[20] We are left, simply, and to the horror of even many of the great skeptics, to the will to power. Or so it seems in some circles. And in those circles there is often a sense of loss, even regret and nostalgia for times in which belief in God and meaning was a given. It is in this 'immanent frame' that we find as alternatives "Pentecostals, whose ability to meet the disciplines of contemporary life is bound up with Christian conversion, so that an order-sustaining morality is felt as inseparable from faith."[21] Pentecostalism has provided a way of sensing the spiritual and the moral, and allowing for an alternative way of life, in the face of the problems of late modernity. Put differently, Pentecostals increasingly enter into conversation with the prevalence of pluralism and the sense of meaninglessness. At this juncture, Yong's pneumatological theology builds a bridge between Pentecostalism and the concerns of late modernity.

A third essential aspect of this situation, and a key focus of Yong's theology, is the manifold developments of global Christianity in the late modern world. The majority of the action, and perhaps soon including the majority of the intellectual conversation, is taking place outside of the West. Scholars of global Christianity such as. Philip Jenkins, Lamin Sanneh, and Andrew Walls, as well as scholars of global Pentecostalism such as Allan H. Anderson and William K. Kay, provide the initial layers of documentation and analysis of Christianity's astounding growth, particularly in the global South.[22] Engagement with the empirical realities and the theologies of Christians from across the globe is characteristic of Yong's theology.[23] He continually works at the empirical and theological margins of the churches emerging across the global South, looking at Christianity's engagement with local and indigenous traditions.

20. Hunter, *To Change the World*, 206. Hunter is particularly following George Steiner, *Real Presences* in this linguistic characterization of dissolution.

21. Taylor, *A Secular Age*, 552–53.

22. Also, the Pentecostal and Charismatic Research Initiative, co-sponsored by the University of Southern California and the Templeton Foundation, is producing even more focused studies of Pentecostal communities across the world.

23. A good example of this is the first chapter of Yong, *The Spirit Poured Out on All Flesh*, 31–80, where he takes his readers on a brief empirical and theological survey of developments in global Pentecostalism.

Finding the Center: Yong's Hermeneutic

Religious pluralism is the primary theological problem addressed in Yong's first set of scholarly theological works. In *Discerning the Spirit(s)*, the published form of his doctoral dissertation, Yong offers his 'Pentecostal charismatic' approach to theology of religions, addressing especially the issue of religious pluralism in late modern context. In it, Yong draws on, dialogues with, debates, disagrees and modifies the work of a number of Christian theologians who have furthered the discussion of a contemporary theology of religions. He especially engages Clark Pinnock, Karl Rahner, Paul Tillich, Michael Lodahl, Donald Gelpi, Robert Cummings Neville and John Sanders. The philosophy of Charles Sanders Peirce looms large in this work, as it does in *Spirit-Word-Community*. Yet Yong is clearly his own theologian from the start, proposing his pneumatological approach to theology of religions as a way "beyond the impasse." This direction defined Yong's approach to the one and the many from the outset of his career.

However, Yong's central paradigm is most clearly articulated in his often-ignored work, *Spirit-Word-Community*.[24] A work on theological hermeneutics not explicitly formulated from a Pentecostal perspective, the dense book provides immediate insights in his theological and philosophical hermeneutic. *Spirit-Word-Community* offers a comprehensive yet open-ended paradigm, one that attempts to interpret human experience from a theological vantage point, while acknowledging the legitimacy of other directions. For Yong, it is "a robustly theological hermeneutic . . . that aims at interpreting the totality of human experience—and that includes God and God's relationships with human selves and the world as a whole—from a perspective that is specifically and explicitly grounded in faith."[25] While much focus has been rightly placed, as can be seen in the other essays in this volume,[26] on the 'pneumatological imagination' found in *Spirit-Word-Community* and throughout his entire corpus, the book brings to the surface a number of convictions central to Yong's theology. One central conviction is the emphasis on hermeneutics. In late modernity, hermeneutics itself is a concept that has significantly expanded in recent philosophical discourse. Kevin Vanhoozer succinctly explains this expansion:

> Traditionally, hermeneutics—the reflection on the principles that undergird correct textual interpretation—was a matter for exegetes and philologists. More recently, however, hermeneutics

24. See Oliverio, "An Interpretive Review Essay on *Spirit Word-Community*."

25. Yong, *Spirit-Word-Community*, 6.

26. Vondey and Mittelstadt, *The Theology of Amos Yong*.

has become the concern of philosophers, who wish to know not what such and such a text means, but what it means to understand.[27]

The blurring of the boundaries between hermeneutics and theological method in current times is, to a great extent, the result of the 'linguistic turn' made by a significant segment of twentieth century philosophy. With major figures like Hans-Georg Gadamer, Martin Heidegger, and Ludwig Wittgenstein emphasizing the way that language shapes our understanding, and with understanding itself taken as a matter of interpretation, hermeneutics has replaced epistemology as the key means of reflection on human knowledge or understanding among many philosophers, especially from the Continental tradition.[28] To use Heidegger's phrase, our stance toward anything is 'always already' shaped by our own linguistic tradition in its finitude and historical situatedness. This hermeneutical tradition from Continental philosophy has rivaled the traditions of both Romantic and Analytic hermeneutics, traditions which have more narrowly defined the task of hermeneutics as a quest for understanding the intention of the author through careful reading of the text and its context.[29]

Yong operates, in line with the Continental understanding of hermeneutics after the 'linguistic turn,' on the basis of a view of theological hermeneutics as 'the hermeneutics of the divine,' and he understands theological hermeneutics to be broad enough to "be indistinguishable from a viable theological method."[30] Theological hermeneutics is not equivalent to biblical or canonical hermeneutics. And against advocates of the equivalence of theological and biblical hermeneutics, Yong holds that biblical and canonical hermeneutics are only part of theological hermeneutics, not its totality.[31] Instead, he concludes that "a hermeneutics of the divine that fails to properly account for the interpretation of the extra-Scriptural world will ultimately sabotage the theological task."[32] Yong's theological hermeneutic is a

27. Vanhoozer, Is There a Meaning in This Text?, 19.

28. Gadamer, Truth and Method; Heidegger, Being and Time; Wittgenstein, Philosophical Investigations.

29. The key exemplars of hermeneutics in the Romantic and Analytic traditions are, respectively, Schleiermacher, Hermeneutics and Criticism; Hirsch, Validity in Interpretation; Hirsch, The Aims of Interpretation.

30. Yong, Spirit-Word-Community, 2. Another important recent work that considers the task of doing theology in terms of theological hermeneutics is Zimmerman, Recovering Theological Hermeneutics.

31. Yong, Spirit-Word-Community, 4.

32. Yong, Spirit-Word-Community, 5.

hermeneutics of life which proceeds "from the perspective of faith toward a hermeneutics of reality as a whole."[33]

Yong holds to the important assumption that any given set of hermeneutical habits, strategies or principles is in a relationship of mutual dependence with other beliefs about reality, including theological or doctrinal, anthropological, metaphysical, and epistemological affirmations. The set of epistemic principles guiding the forms of belief for a given theological paradigm, and the ontology which sustains the paradigm, are interdependent. This holistic view of human understanding strongly resists the modern epistemological project's claim that it is *the* first philosophy, although it still recognizes the primacy that belief-forming habits can have at any given moment. Rather, the quest to know which claims to truth are trustworthy and which are not goes hand-in-hand with a preunderstanding of what is true and what is not. Yong holds that while epistemic structure guides us into how to discern what is true from what is not, these structures are sustained and informed by layers of beliefs leading all the way back to an understanding of what is ultimately real. Still, beliefs emerge from the order of knowing (*ordo cogniscendi*) in forming understanding concerning the order of being (*ordo essendi*).[34] Within his hermeneutic lays a pneumatological metaphysics that sustains Yong's entire paradigm.

Finding the One in the Many: Yong's Trinitarian and Pneumatological Metaphysics

Yong's Pentecostal pneumatology has assumed a significant place in the contemporary renaissance of pneumatology.[35] Following Irenaeus' metaphor of the Word and the Spirit (Word and Wisdom) as the 'two hands of God,' Yong holds to the interdependence and coinherence of the Son and the Spirit through the doctrine of *perichoresis/circumincessio* where the persons of the Godhead interpenetrate one another. Yong affirms that "the external works of God in the world are undivided, and belong to all three

33. Yong, *Spirit-Word-Community*, 7.

34. "Theologically, the question is that of how knowledge that is always already hermeneutical (*ordo cogniscendi*) can deliver transcendental truths about God and God's relationship to the world (*ordo essendi*). This problematic is what drives our inquiry." Yong, *Spirit-Word-Community*, 49n1.

35. This can be seen, for example, in Catholic theology in the work of Yves Congar, especially in *I Believe in the Holy Spirit*; among several major Protestant theologians including Jürgen Moltmann and Wolfhart Pannenberg, charismatic theologians such as Clark Pinnock, and among charismatic-Pentecostal theologians in general.

together."[36] He then pushes his understanding of the divine being towards a 'radically relational understanding of God.'[37] Following David Cunningham, Yong affirms:

> The goal is to transcend individualistic conceptions of the Trinity prevalent historically, and to emphasize that God is "not three persons who 'have' relations, but rather, three subsistent relations" who are self-grounded precisely in their interrelationship. God, as Cunningham says, "is the relations that God has." This move frees up space to reconsider the notion of personhood from a trinitarian and perichoretic starting point rather than from a Cartesian one. . . . My own references to the three divine persons, both in the preceding and the following, should therefore always be understood according to this notion of subsistent relationality.[38]

Yong arrives at this conclusion hermeneutically. He neither claims that this conclusion was the result of some kind of pure reading of the biblical scriptures, nor does he claim that it is a reading of his philosophical and doctrinal categories onto the revelatory texts. Instead, he implies that his reading of Scripture and the doctrine of God are mutually informative, subject to revision and ongoing reflection.[39]

For Yong, the Irenaean 'two hands' model "preserv[es] both unity and plurality in the divine life" as God, who *is* Spirit, in the Godhead's constitution as the relational ground of being, is Father, Spirit and Son who are "relations without remainder."[40] This means that when applied to divine action, "pneumatological relationality may be seen to hold the key toward the perennial mysteries of the one and the many, universality and particularity, God's relationship to the world, and vice-versa."[41] All that is created by God also has its identity in relationality. In other words, "symbiotic relationality . . . characterizes both the divine reality and the creation itself as well as the togetherness of the two."[42]

36. Yong, *Spirit-Word-Community*, 49; also, 50–59.

37. Yong, *Spirit-Word-Community*, 56.

38. Yong, *Spirit-Word-Community*, 56–57. Yong is working with Cunningham, *These Three Are One.*

39. Yong, *Spirit-Word-Community*, 57.

40. Yong, *Spirit-Word-Community*, 56–58.

41. Yong, *Spirit-Word-Community*, 59.

42. Yong, *Spirit-Word-Community*. Such a sense of the mutuality of plurality and unity applies to models and methodology even aimed at the core of Yong's paradigm. After affirming the 'two hands' model, Yong immediately affirms versions of Augustine's Trinitarian formula which do not subordinate the Spirit to the Son, seeking to

Working with biblical and classical theological themes, Yong's metaphysics and ontology are distinctively late modern. His turn to relationality is a distinctively late modern iteration of a classical concern. As Yong's former colleague, LeRon Shults, has argued, the philosophical turn to relationality, including holistic and methodologically and ontologically reciprocal thought, is characteristic of late modernity.[43] More precisely, Yong finds reality itself to be dynamically relational.

Yong draws upon the dynamic and triadic metaphysics of the American pragmatist philosopher Charles Sanders Peirce.[44] Yong correlates his reading of biblical pneumatology and his trinitarian ontology with Peirce's metaphysics, which consider the character of reality, phenomenologically read, to emerge in three basic categories: the qualities of things abstracted from experiences ('Firstness'), the concreteness of actual things or facts in their differentiation from one another ('Secondness'), and the general laws which relate these together ('Thirdness'). 'Thirdness' is dynamic and relational while 'Firstness' and 'Secondness', respectively, represent the abstract and concrete. In Peirce's philosophy, all things participate in each of these three aspects of the becoming of reality. Correlating his trinitarian ontology with Peirce's categories, Yong holds that while the Father is the "qualitative source of creative efficacy" and the Son is "the decisive sign or image of the Father through whom the Godhead is embodied and efficaciously interacts with the world," it is the Spirit who is "the interpretant of the divine relationality both ad intra and ad extra."[45] Thus Peircean 'Firstness', with its attendant abstraction, is correlated with the Father, the concreteness of 'Secondness' with the Son, and the dynamism of 'Thirdness' with the Spirit.

Yong's use of Peirce is also reflected in the pragmatic and empirical aspects of Peirce's philosophy. Human experience is used to understand

---

justify a non-hierarchical version of the *filioque* in a legitimate relational Trinity (Yong, *Spirit-Word-Community*, 59–72). I interpret this move to exemplify how Yong develops multiple models for understanding subjects of his inquiry—though the transcendent God is no mere 'subject'—yet how he still draws implicit distinctions. Further, Yong's gentleness in criticism and non-contentious tone should not be mistaken for an inability to make distinctions and to stand against certain conceptions. After all, a significant aspect of his first book, *Discerning the Spirit(s)* dealt with spiritual discernment.

43. Shults, *Reforming Theological Anthropology*, 11–36. Shults taught at Bethel Seminary in St. Paul, MN from 1997–2006. Yong taught at the undergraduate Bethel College, on the same campus, from 1999–2005.

44. See Yong, *Spirit-Word-Community*, 100–105, 151–64; Yong, *Beyond the Impasse*, 132–33. Yong's most specific work on Peirce is "The Demise of Foundationalism." See also Yong's use of Peirce in *Spirit of Creation*, 118–25, where he focuses on the dynamism of reality found in Peirce's metaphysics in advocating a regularist rather than necessitarian view of the laws of nature.

45. Yong, *Spirit-Word-Community*, 95.

reality in all its dynamism. He affirms this in Peirce's philosophy, and it can be seen in his own hermeneutics of reality:

> The logic of pragmatism is that the vagueness of perception and perceptual judgment lead us to formulate equally vague inferences (abductions), from which more specific predictions are made (deductions), which are in turn finally tested in a variety of ways (induction). As these are continuously confirmed, inductive experience is shaped into provisional habits that inform our action.[46]

This epistemology is fallibilistic but not skeptical. For Yong, "human beings do not need to be skeptical about what they know or believe insofar as the referential signs we negotiate enable us to grasp the qualities, facts, and laws of things in such a way so as to manageably predict with greater rather than lesser accuracy the way the world will respond."[47] Yong notes, however, that this is a type of pragmatism that is not merely concerned with functionality for manipulating one's environment towards desired ends, but rather "in the sense of harmonizing or comporting with the way reality is."[48] This insistence further implies that truth for Yong is not merely pragmatic but includes correspondence with reality and coherence in its accounts.[49]

What is of particular interest to this chapter is Yong's understanding of the dynamism of reality as existing alongside its concreteness and abstraction. Such a dynamic and relational metaphysic entails *both* unity and continuation in truth *and* plurality, difference, and change. Yong's metaphysics gives account of *both* the oneness *and* the plurality of things. It is the center of his account of the plural that finds in things not only the dynamic and difference in their interpretation but also their stability and constancy. It is a metaphysic that says how things are plural yet without dissolving meaning and essence. This metaphysic is, of course, abstract, but it plays out quite concretely and practically in Yong's own theology.

A Pentecostal Theology for Late Modernity

Yong's hermeneutic suggests that multiple accounts of the world can serve to illuminate reality rather than stand in opposition to one another. This

46. Yong, *Spirit-Word-Community*, 155–56.

47. Yong, *Spirit-Word-Community*, 158.

48. Yong, *Spirit-Word-Community*, 165.

49. Yong, *Spirit-Word-Community*, 164–75. Yong develops his particular notions of truth as pragmatic, correspondence, and coherence as complementary rather than contradictory to one another.

conviction is central to both *Spirit-Word-Community* and to *The Spirit Poured Out on All Flesh*. A theological hermeneutic built on such a conviction sets out to address the central late modern concern of pluralism and dissolution in a globalized context. It is also found in his most recent writings on theology of religions, political theology, and science and theology, subjects of increasing concern in late modernity.

In *Hospitality and the Other*, Yong begins his proposal for Christian. Practices toward non-Christian 'others' with concrete cases-Christians involved in ethnic conflict in Sri Lanka, Muslim-Christian conflict in Nigeria, and American Christians in the face of multiculturalism along with attendant issues in interreligious relations.[50] He then draws on historical (e.g., Athanasius) and contemporary (e.g., Kevin Vanhoozer and George Lindbeck) sources for developing an understanding of the interrelationship between Christian beliefs and practices while also drawing on Speech Act Theory (J. L. Austin).[51] Yet his proposal for what follows in engaging the religious 'other' as a Christian makes a stop at his central idea of 'many tongues, many practices.'[52] Unity and plurality are always together (it is part of the nature of reality as reality's being finds its source in the God who is dynamic relationality): "To be sure, there is a unified testimony given by the many tongues to the wondrous works of God (Acts 2:11), but make no mistake about it: the particularities of the many tongues are not obliterated in the Pentecost account; rather, they are redeemed in all of their particularity for the purposes of God."[53]

The theme of many tongues, many practices also appears centrally in Yong's political theology, *In the Days of Caesar*.[54] As he does not quite do in his theology of religions,[55] Yong here follows Clark Pinnock's principle that Spirit and Word complement one another so that Word is to be seen as the criterion for Spirit. Whereas Spirit represents the universality of divine action, the Word represents the particularity of God's action in the world. The criterion of discerning the divine in our world is Christ, his person, actions, and teachings. According to Pinnock, "Spirit is in agreement with

---

50. Yong, *Hospitality and the Other*, 1–37.

51. Yong, *Hospitality and the Other*, 38–55.

52. See the section entitled, "Performing Pneumatology in a Pluralistic World" in Yong, *Hospitality and the Other*, 56–64.

53. Yong, *Hospitality and the Other*, 58.

54. Yong, *In the Days of Caesar*.

55. Yong, *Beyond the Impasse*, 110–28, 167–83. Yong acknowledges the specifically Christian importance to Pinnock's Christological criterion; however, he argues that criteria for evaluation should include those important to other religions on their own terms as well (Yong, *Beyond the Impasse*, 179–83).

the Son and agrees with what he said and did."[56] Likewise, Word is central to Yong's Pentecostal political theology as it utilizes the pneumatological imagination: "A christological focus and commitment to the Bible as a rule of faith and practice are necessary to discipline the pneumatological imagination of Pentecostalism. On the other side, such a biblical orientation energizes rather than hinders the quest for a political theology."[57] For Yong, the many tongues of Pentecost operate in the multiplicity of Pentecostalisms worldwide, translating and indigenizing biblical, Christological faith into manifold social, economic and political realities.

> The task is to avoid either a relativism of political options or a politically correct legitimation that devolves into an ideology of the majority. Further, we must resist providing a merely pragmatic account that baptizes many theological beliefs derived from the diverse political contexts within which such beliefs are shaped. Instead, if I am successful, my thesis will not only provide a theological justification for the diversity of Christian politics, but also empower the many different practices required to bear witness to the gospel in a politically pluralistic world.[58]

Yong himself unfolds his political theology patterned after the Pentecostal motif of the five-fold 'full gospel' pattern of Jesus as savior, sanctifier, baptizer in the Spirit, healer and coming king.

The methodological impact of Yong's hermeneutical principle comes out in his understanding of the complementarity of theology and science as mutually informative disciplines of inquiry. In his *The Spirit of Creation*, Yong presses the 'many tongues' metaphor in the direction of 'many disciplines,' advocating a compatibilist, interdisciplinary approach between science and theology:

> The many Pentecostal tongues can be understood analogically as providing a theological rationale for the many scientific disciplines. In this framework, the various sciences—natural, social, and human—function like distinct languages, each with its own presuppositions, traditions of practices (inquiries), and

---

56. Pinnock, *Flame of Love*, 209. Further, he states that "Wherever, for example, we find self-sacrificing love, care about community, longings for justice, wherever people love one another, care for the sick, make peace not war, wherever there is beauty and concord, generosity and forgiveness, the cup of cold water, we know the Spirit of Jesus is present. . . . Jesus uses this criterion himself for recognizing his sheep: I was hungry and you gave me food, I was thirsty and you gave me something to drink' (Matt 25:35)" (209–10).

57. Yong, *In the Days of Caesar*, 108.

58. Yong, *In the Days of Caesar*, 111.

explanations. The many tongues analogy thus underwrites, theologically, both the multidisciplinary and interdisciplinary character of the theology and science encounter. Multiple disciplines are involved, and we have to heed the relative autonomy of each discipline. At the same time, there is an increasing interdisciplinarity as well in terms of the ways in which various disciplines influence and inform others.[59]

Yong seeks to respect the domains of various forms of inquiry and finds places for integration in holistic, theological understanding. It is a deep reversal of Pentecostal anti-intellectualism, and it presses the 'many tongues' of Acts 2:11 in the more general direction of human existence. As Yong states, "the tongues of Pentecost are a polyvalent testimony to the beautiful artistry of the Creator God."[60] In the paradigm of Pentecost, the one is found in the many.

Conclusion

The heart of Yong's overall theological project is his development of the Pentecostal intuition of multiplicity in the one reality. Yong extends this biblical theme and correlates it with his relational doctrine of the Trinity, an ontology and metaphysics that builds on the work of Peirce, and concrete, empirical phenomenological accounts of the subjects which he investigates. In Yong's project, the plurality of things does not entail dissolution but is a reflection of the nature of the reality of the whole which finds its source of being in the triune God. Yong is a realist. Reality has a 'thickness' which can be uncovered and not merely constructed. Yet he is a realist through being a pluralist. Reality is dynamic, abstract and concrete, and this entails its being known in manifold ways from manifold perspectives. Yong's work calls Christians to discern where and how the Spirit of God is at work. This task is central to the task of the Christian life, even if it is a tall one within the complexities of the late modern world.

The global scope of Yong's theology is a significant contribution to Christian theology in the late modern world; it provides a seminal contribution on behalf of the global Pentecostal communities. His work resonates with the present concerns for pneumatology, Pentecostalism, and the renewal of the age. The integration of Yong's broader work hinges upon a greater reception and response to his metaphysical program and theological hermeneutics. The question remains how Yong's theological forays relate

59. Yong, *Spirit of Creation*, 29.
60. Yong, *The Spirit Poured Out on All Flesh*, 169n63.

to the Pentecostal traditions that Yong seeks to represent and to whose particularities he attends. If Yong is a true representative of Pentecostal thought, then his work suggests that Pentecostalism offers a viable solution to the problems of late modernity. Yong claims that a hermeneutics of tradition is a necessary object of theological interpretation.[61] Further, he affirms that the audiences for theological work are the public, the academy, and the church.[62] The latter has yet to engage with Yong's forays in any substantive manner. Inundated with information in this present age, the church needs her theologians to frame situations and provide navigational guidance through the complex issues of late modernity. That is to say, it is time to engage and not simply to be impressed or intimidated by Yong's work. It is time to see if his proposals resonate with the lived faith of Christian communities and if they can be integrated in the task of forming Christian disciples today.

61. Yong, *Spirit-Word-Community*, 196n63.
62. Yong, *Spirit-Word-Community*, 275–77.

II

The Theological Hermeneutic of Amos Yong

There is no more influential Pentecostal theologian in the academic world today than Amos Yong. The breadth of his influence is now in full bloom, and the depth of his contributions have left a wake in which many have only begun to swim. This article identifies and explains central aspects of his theological approach to interpreting human life and all of reality, that is, his theological hermeneutic, at a moment where Yong continues to produce his theological work in the prime of his career. While doing so, the essay adds a comparative twist by relating Yong's project to two of the most influential thinkers in the Catholic theological tradition, the twentieth century German Jesuit theologian Karl Rahner, and the great doctor, the thirteenth century Dominican Thomas Aquinas. The breadth of Yong's contribution to global Pentecostal theology now deserves to be treated analogously to those who have made orienting contributions to other Christian traditions. While it is entirely premature to make long-term historic judgments on Yong's influence, as that is in the midst of becoming and the future unknowable, this comparison might be considered more along the lines of a midterm assessment of that influence, while he remains in the prime of his theological career.

A Brief Comparison with Rahner: Karl and Amos

Yong's intellectual contribution on behalf of the relatively young Pentecostal tradition is in some ways analogous to that of Karl Rahner's on behalf of the Catholic. Remaining orthodox to the Christian tradition, Yong has explored the boundaries and interiorities of his Pentecostal tradition to release the depths of what has been embedded in Pentecostal spirituality, and he has made forays into the liminal space where theological reflection has moved beyond its previous boundaries on account of the great questions of the day. Rather than staying safely within the prescribed boundaries of Classical Pentecostal questions, Yong has taken the path of theological courage in engaging the serious questions of the day, ones which Pentecostal Christians wrestle with, often on their own or in other contexts, but are not often addressed within the confines of their communities. Like Rahner, Yong's exploration of the borders and depths of his tradition of Christianity, beyond the reigning doctrinal articulations, has meant both appreciation[1] and critique.[2] However, beyond the volume on his theology edited by Vondey and Mittelstadt, Yong's work has been insufficiently engaged, with too few in the Pentecostal academy or in church leadership having the theological and philosophical acumen or the time and will to engage his huge corpus.[3]

1. For an initial sampling of works which primarily appreciate Yong's theology, see Vondey, "Pentecostalism and the Possibility of Global Theology"; the thirteen chapters in Vondey and Mittelstadt, *The Theology of Amos Yong*; and the panel discussion edited by Christopher Stephenson in the April 2016 issue of *Evangelical Review of Theology* on Yong's *Renewing Christian Theology*, with responses from Lisa Stephenson, Chris E. W. Green, Mark H. Mann, Thomas Jay Oord, and a response from Yong.

2. For an initial sampling of works which primarily critique Yong's theology, see Olson, "A Wind that Swirls Everywhere"; Stronstad, "A Review Essay"; Menzies, "The Nature of Pentecostal Theology."

3. As of 2020, that included over two dozen monographs, over two dozen edited or co-edited volumes, co-editing five book series, over two hundred scholarly articles and book chapters, over five hundred book reviews and book notes, and around four hundred scholarly presentations. These can be seen in his CV at Yong, "Complete Curriculum Vitae." While this version of his CV, updated to August 2020, shows sixty-four responses directly on his work, the response to Yong's work from the academy has been understated thus far. There are a number of reasons for this, including: (1) Yong's theological loci diverging from standard Classical Pentecostal ones, thus locating him, again like Rahner here, as both highly influential and yet sometimes treated like an outsider within; (2) his philosophical and theological robustness outstrip common knowledge in a Pentecostal academy still predominantly filled with biblical scholars, historians, social scientists, and pastoral theologians; (3) the continued but lessening effects of Pentecostal marginalization in the wider theological and religious studies academy; (4) that the sheer quantity of his work combined with the quality of his intellect seem to have intimidated some at further engagement with his work; and (5) closely related to this previous reason, that the breadth and multi-disciplinarity of his work has created a

Like Rahner, Yong has pushed the boundaries as he has teased out the spiritual essence of the tradition. That this has been properly faithful to that spiritual essence has been, at times, contested for each, as several of the above-noted critiques show. His interreligious engagement, ecumenical theology, and multidisciplinary work have been forays into a Pentecostal theology that has not been merely content to serve as an apologetic or doctrinal explication for Classical Pentecostalism, neither for particular cultural instantiations of Pentecostal and Christian life, but his purpose has been to explore the multiplicity of these and their potentials for spiritual life in the last modern, globalized world.[4] In a certain sense, Yong has been introducing and explaining we global Pentecostals to one another, finding commonalities, and philosophically and theologically resourcing Pentecostals through providing numerous interdisciplinary and integrative theological works.

As also for Rahner, Yong's hard-won results are often best remembered through notable concepts which symbolize a complex body of work. This would suggest that as Rahner gave Catholic Christianity the 'supernatural existential,'[5] Yong's 'many tongues' principle is similarly a conceptual coinage and gift to Pentecostal Christianity. In the conclusion of this essay, I will work this principle from Yong back around to the noetic agenda of another great Catholic, Thomas Aquinas, and there point to how Yong's principle does some of the work in the late modern context which Thomas' *Summa* did in the high medieval for Christian approaches to the integration of divine revelation with general human knowledge, though, of course, with some significant theological and philosophical differences, not least in Yong's postfoundationalist epistemology in relation to Thomas' foundationalism.[6]

Analogies are limited, so it is important to clarify that this initial comparison between Rahner and Yong, which I offer here, is centered around the broad orientations which they provide. That is, Rahner and Yong each

---

sense that to engage Yong in one area is to miss other areas that are related and necessary to understanding the whole of his work.

4. I present this claim in a fuller manner in an earlier assessment of Yong in "The One and the Many."

5. See Coffey, "The Whole Rahner on the Supernatural Existential." A comparison between Rahner's "supernatural existential" and Yong's "foundational pneumatology," especially in the area of divine grace, would be a helpful study.

6. While the majority understanding of Thomas has been that he and the Thomism which follows him are epistemically foundationalist, there is a minority report, or at least a caveat for some that his reliance on divine revelation and figurative language in Scripture has led to questions that, at least in some considerations, such an interpretation of his approach is anachronistic or, more potently, that this claim fails to sufficiently account for underlying mystery or grace in that which serves as foundational in his project, as in Williams, "Is Aquinas a Foundationalist?"

provide a key axis for the faith which seeks to be understood within their respective Christian traditions. In Rahner's *magnum opus*, his *Foundations of Christian Faith: An Introduction to the Idea of Christianity*—which he famously considered merely "an introduction" to the idea of Christianity—Rahner distinguished yet connected the realization of Christian faith in everyday life with its abstract ideation in theology, and he did so through considering the existential conditions of Christian faith, relating historical and everyday life to transcendental ideas as their conditions.[7]

This is the key point of comparison, that Rahner and Yong each provide a novel development in a philosophical-theological synthesis which seeks to account for the very spiritual essence and lived experience of their respective Christian traditions. That is, they are each providing a philosophical-theological account of what is going on within, again respectively, what are now Christianity's two largest traditions. These are major contributions. As this article focuses on Yong, if the reader will forgive the length of this quote (and its lack of gender inclusive language), it will stand in for a more sufficient account of the Jesuit's project:

> For a Christian, his Christian existence is ultimately the totality of his existence. This totality opens out into the dark abysses of the wilderness which we call God. When one undertakes something like this, he stands before the great thinkers, the saints, and finally Jesus Christ. The abyss of existence opens up in front of him. He knows that he has not thought enough, has not loved enough, and has not suffered enough. There have always been attempts like this [*Foundations of Christian Faith*] to express the structure of Christianity, of Christian faith and of Christian life, as a single whole, even if only in theoretical reflection. . . . But there must always be new attempts at such reflection upon the single whole of Christianity. They are always conditioned, since it is obvious that reflection in general, and all the more so scientific theological reflection, does not capture and cannot capture the whole of this reality which we realize in faith, hope, love, and prayer. It is precisely this permanent and insurmountable difference between the original Christian actualization of existence and reflection upon it. . . . The insight into this difference is a key insight which represents a necessary presupposition for an introduction to the idea of Christianity. Ultimately what we want to do is merely reflect upon the simple question: "What is a Christian, and why can one live this Christian existence today with intellectual honesty?" The question begins with the fact of

7. Rahner, *Foundations of Christian Faith*.

Christian existence, although this existence looks very different today in individual Christians. This difference is conditioned by personal levels of maturity, by very different kinds of social situations and hence also of religious situations, by psychological differences, and so on. But we also want to reflect here upon this fact of our Christian existence, and we want to justify it before the demands of conscience and of truth by giving an "account of our hope" (1 Pet. 3:15).[8]

Rahner's articulation of his theological project is demonstrative of the tension that can be seen in the type of theologian that he and Yong both are, where their work, on the one hand, is expansive in both quantity and in terms of the borders of the tradition, yet, on the other, it is still also 'faith seeking understanding' in the Augustinian-Anselmian tradition of Christian theology, working out the faith that is being practiced and sought. In this regard, while Rahner's methodology is that of a modern Catholic existential theology, a transcendental Thomism, Yong's is that of a late modern global Pentecostal interdisciplinary hermeneutical theology in which the 'many tongues' of Pentecost resound together. Yet both are seeking in faith to understand better, and thus lay out the groundwork for better becoming, in the multiplicities of Christian existence, yet in mutuality and with an ecumenical spirit to account for our hope in Christ and the Spirit. Practically speaking, then, Rahner did what Catholics have referred to as foundational theology, while Yong provides a philosophical theology for Pentecostalism, one which seeks to unpack the idea of Pentecostal Christianity more so than to describe what is in Pentecostalism. In a certain sense, Yong unveils the potential of Pentecostalism for itself and global Christian theology. This can perhaps be understood better through considering the topic of this essay, his theological hermeneutics.

Methodological and hermeneutical questions are important because methodological-hermeneutical approaches represent the powerful further belief-forming mechanisms within personal, communal, and cultural habits which are embedded within a hermeneutical paradigm, as in a theological hermeneutic.[9] Examining hermeneutics brings the humanity and locality of theologians and Christian communities to bare upon Christian understanding. This is because it is best to be self-aware of one's or one's community's location rather than relying on populist and naïve claims which assume only a negligible (or even no) influence of one's humanity, community, location, traditions upon one's understanding of Christian faith, which sometimes

---

8. Rahner, *Foundations of Christian Faith*, 2.

9. I have further articulated this point in *Theological Hermeneutics*, 2–5, 319–53.

results in being blithely unaware of the linguistic, epistemic/hermeneutical, cultural, and ontological dynamics of the human knowing process, and simply claiming 'the truth' for one's own cultural-communal understanding and appropriation of faith, experience, and Scripture.[10] Rather, theological truths might better be understood as a way of knowing in dialectical tension between knowers and the known, in which locations and hermeneutics contribute greatly to theological agendas and claims.[11]

Rahner and Yong's methodological approaches each self-consciously embed theological, philosophical, and other content into their methodologies. In the former case, Rahner developed a transcendental Thomism under the influence of Heideggerian existentialism, and these were integrated with his social-linguistic location in mid- to late-twentieth century Europe, pre- and post-Vatican II, with certain Catholic, and, of course, given his uniqueness, his certain Rahnerian theological emphases. This powerful combination of philosophical theology, existential philosophy, social-linguistic location, and theological affirmations formed a hermeneutical nexus which formed the axis through which Rahner provided his theological influence on twentieth and now twenty-first century Catholic thought. Yong's theological project provides a deep intellectual reexamination of the realities involved in Christian life and ideas, both broadening and deepening the account of his tradition's contribution to the world, and prescribing contours for a guiding theological program. Each has seen at least some success in influencing the wider traditions as a whole, though much greater success in influencing the theological discourse.

Yong's Hermeneutical Trajectories

This article focuses on key aspects of Yong's hermeneutics as providing the contours for his project. My assumption here is that hermeneutics and methodology begin with the embodied conditions of the theological person and persons in community, so that theology begins with these historically-situated realities described above, even though theology becomes the naming of the existential-transcendental conditions of reality, an ontic-naming so that such comes to form future historically-situated realities, especially,

10. Smith's *The Fall of Interpretation* narrates this well. For more on specifically Pentecostal approaches and for the importance of traditioned approaches, see Frestadius, *Pentecostal Rationality*.

11. I articulate how such hermeneutical awareness might work for Pentecostal hermeneutics in a hermeneutical realist mode in "Contours of a Constructive Pentecostal Philosophical-Theological Hermeneutic."

in this case, in the form of religious experiences, in a linguistic-naming of experiential-theological realities. For Yong, historically-situated revelation, that is, Scripture, is the primary (re)source for theological understanding, as authorizing and correcting and furthering Christian understanding, though he continually also embraces, integrates, and acknowledges other resources for Christian theological understanding, as such generalized knowledge is also always already assumed in biblical interpretation and in doing theology.

In his *Learning Theology*, Yong explicitly embraces the Wesleyan quadrilateral of Scripture, tradition, reason, and experience to explicate the dynamics of theological understanding.[12] On the level of authority, Yong respects Scripture as having the primacy for theological knowledge. On another level, though he tends to acknowledge his own tendencies as Wesleyan, Yong's Thomistic-like move concerning general knowledge as having its own rights within disciplines not theology. Being informed by all kinds of other disciplines in his reading of Scripture influences Yong's readings of Scripture in interpretations that often run outside of certain Classical Pentecostal norms, much on account of their tendencies to invoke the common sense realism of the Anglo-American world, often in folk forms. This is part of the rub between Yong and some of his Pentecostal and Evangelical critics.[13] The assumptions about general knowledge are powerful in interpreting what is revealed in the biblical texts, and such a realization affirms the hermeneutical nature of all human knowing, of human understanding what is through our linguistic-conceptual assumptions and their development, and of our experiential feeling about and embodied knowing.

Yong's resultant theological hermeneutic might be quickly oriented to through a reading of the opening of his *Who Is the Holy Spirit? A Walk with the Apostles*, which, at the very least, triples as a devotional guide to Acts, a Pentecostal social ethics and political theology, and an enactment of what Yong means when he refers to a 'pneumatological imagination.'[14] In this text, he considers Luke-Acts theologically as not only narrating a model for, as he initially understood his religious identity, a Pentecostal pilgrim who saw the work of the Holy Spirit as purifying him from the world and involved in the work of the Spirit 'out there' in the world. In this understanding, the Spirit's role can be seen especially in convicting unbelievers of sin and turning them to Christ, and otherwise the work of the Spirit is largely restricted to the life

12. The Wesleyan quadrilateral structures the first four chapters of the eight chapters in Yong, *Learning Theology*.

13. Common sense realism's influence on Pentecostal hermeneutics plays a starring role in my account of Pentecostal interpretive practices and rationality in *Theological Hermeneutics* as well as Archer's *A Pentecostal Hermeneutic*.

14. Yong, *Who Is the Holy Spirit?*

of the church. This was the Pentecostalism in which Yong was raised, as the son of a Malaysian (Chinese-)American pastor.[15]

Not denying these aspects, though loosening the boundaries they may place on certain aspects of the Spirit's work, in *Who Is the Holy Spirit?*, Yong rereads Acts as the Spirit at work transforming all aspects of life—including the social, political, and religious. As he puts it, "In other words, I now think that the world of the Holy Spirit is much wider than I'd guessed, and that the work of the Spirit is to redeem and transform our world as a whole along with all of its interconnected parts, systems, and structures."[16] Yong's pneumatological hermeneutic thus involves a broadening understanding of where the Spirit is at work into domains sometimes reduced to a remaining creational common grace.

Yong's hermeneutic represent multiple interpretive trajectories which address concerns for theological hermeneutics. Because his works are so many, the whole is difficult to account for, and especially because he engages in the use of multiple disciplines within theological and biblical studies, and his training and development in philosophy moves his work into that disciplinary mode in which only a smaller but increasing contingent of Pentecostals are trained. Interpretations of Yong's hermeneutics, rationality, and methodology have provided orienting work which provide first layers of interpretation and evaluation of his work while Yong remains squarely in the prime of his theological career.[17]

15. Of Chinese ancestry, Yong grew up near Kuala Lumpur in Malaysia prior to his family's migration to California during his early adolescence.

16. Yong, *Who Is the Holy Spirit?*, x.

17. I have previously assessed Yong's hermeneutics as centering around three locations: (1) the nexus of his Trinitarian theology, his fallibilistic epistemology, Peircean metaphysics, and pneumatology; (2) the discernment of Spirit(s); and (3) the trialectic movement of Spirit-Word-Community (Oliverio, *Theological Hermeneutics*, 227–46). For interpretation of the first and third, see my "An Interpretive Review Essay on *Spirit-Word-Community*." Simo Frestadius emphasizes three overlapping points in considering Yong's 'Pentecostal rationality': (1) his 'pneumatological imagination'; (2) the sources of knowledge and acquiring knowledge; and (3) the justification or warrant for beliefs (Frestadius, *Pentecostal Rationality*, 9–20). Christopher Stephenson has addressed his theological method in the opening of *An Amos Yong Reader* in the areas of (1) metaphysics and foundational pneumatology; (2) epistemology and pneumatological imagination; and (3) hermeneutics and communal interpretation (2–7). Stephenson also addressed this trilogy in his "Reality, Knowledge, and Life in Community."

Pneumatological Imagination

Yong's hermeneutical circle (or spiral) might be understood as driven by the interaction between the text of Luke-Acts and the rest of Scripture with what he has called the 'pneumatological imagination.' Luke-Acts especially exemplifies the Spirit's work in the economy of salvation so that "The Spirit enables the reconciliation between God and humankind; the Spirit empowers the new relationship established through Jesus Christ; the Spirit is the relational medium that makes the incarnational and paschal mysteries."[18] Yet this Spirit is the one which Christian believers, though not just, encounter as God's presence in the world. The Spirit is most closely identified by love and brings salvation, goodness, creativity, and peace to the world. The Spirit mediates prevenient grace for the experience of God that leads to salvation, but also prevenient grace for the experience of God in general.[19]

The pneumatological imagination is important for Yong's theological hermeneutic for several reasons. It is funded by Luke-Acts, though not just, as, for example, in his *Spirit of Love* he develops it further from a (William) Seymourian theology of Spirit baptism into divine love, engagement with several other Pentecostal theologians (Steven Land, Samuel Solivan, and Frank Macchia), and draws on Johannine and Pauline pneumatologies as well. It is, thus, a biblical hermeneutic. Second, it accounts for the point of experience in which persons and persons in communities interpret their worlds as they interpret in various 'spirits.'[20] Yet, third, these 'spirits' participate in what has elsewhere been called the 'social imagination,' through which human ideas and conceptualizations are mapped onto embodied experiences in the hermeneutical 'fusion of horizons' in which socially conditioned interpretations through the human faculty of the shared imagination map onto human experiences.[21] Yong has referred to the historical-linguistic sourcing of these, in a dialectic of experience and understanding, in terms of 'root metaphors' which provide sourcing for the pneumatological imagination. In a turn that is, in the end, an anti-nominalist move, this sourcing engages the real content of dynamic spiritual realities. For the

18. Yong, *Spirit-Word-Community*, 30.

19. Yong, *Spirit of Love*, develops this. On salvific prevenient grace, in particular Yong says, "The Day of Pentecost outpouring of the Spirit upon all flesh is God's prevenient gift that makes possible the repentance of individuals hearts so that any who call upon the name of the Lord will experience for him or herself the forgiveness of sins and receive the Holy Spirit" (96).

20. This is especially developed in each of his three early monographs: *Discerning the Spirit(s)*, *Spirit-Word-Community*, and *Beyond the Impasse*.

21. For a brief philosophical explanation of the "social imaginary," see Taylor, *Modern Social Imaginaries*, esp. 23–30.

Christian, this imagination is holistic in its affective, volitional, and spiritual dimensions, and it is the means of engaging the world, but it is only properly "nourished by the image and mind of Jesus through the Spirit."[22] This is the pneumatological imagination that is put forth to, we might say, remembering Rahner the Jesuit, in the words of Ignatius of Loyola, "go, set the world on fire" with it, as perhaps the growth of global Pentecostalism, with its now 450–650 million adherents, may be thought of as having done—with its pneumatological imagination.[23]

Hermeneutical Trialectic

Key interpretations of Yong's theology have sought to explain his realism that is closely connected to his Peircean pragmatism, as the philosophical handmaiden to his theology. Yong's early work developed this, and it remains implicit in the core of Yong's theological interpreting of human existence in relationship to all that is and called to be. His very early essay, "The Demise of Foundationalism and the Retention of Truth: What Evangelicals Can Learn from C. S. Peirce," set the stage for his theological project as a whole, followed up and further explicated in detail in his *Spirit-Word-Community*.[24] This is a relational-pragmatic realism, a hermeneutical-dynamic realism, one that considers rationality in light of the becoming of what is and what is interpreted from those who are becoming with those realities. This contrasts with a scholastic approach to knowledge, which has a tendency to freeze or provide still-life imagery of dynamic being, for both knowers and that which is known. In a broad way of understanding Yong's engagement with Charles Sanders Peirce (1839–1914)—often considered the founder of American pragmatist philosophy, also a noted logician, and mathematician—so that Yong's Peircean pragmatic-realism allowed him to move past foundationalism without succumbing to relativism.

In this early essay, Yong found contemporary evangelical foundationalism wanting for assuming that objective propositional truth can be infallibly known, in line with the correspondence theory of truth.[25] Decon-

22. Yong, *Spirit-Word-Community*, 133–41.

23. The historian of global Christianity, Douglas Jacobsen, accounts for 450 million Pentecostals and Charismatics, with an additional two hundred million Pentecostal-influenced Christians worldwide right now in *The World's Christians*.

24. Yong, "The Demise of Foundationalism." The material from this essay is embedded throughout *Spirit-Word-Community*, though particularly in 84–109. The significance of this essay can be seen in its reprinting in Yong's *The Dialogical Spirit* and *The Hermeneutical Spirit* as the opening essay.

25. Yong defends the use of correspondence, along with coherence and pragmatic

structive, postmodern, pragmatist, linguistic, hermeneutical, process, and other critiques have been negatively decisive. The naïve fusing of the epistemic and the ontic in a non-fallibilistic foundationalism, assumed often enough in popular evangelical theologies, has led to widespread scholarly repudiation of this approach. As Yong succinctly simplifies the objection to this approach to knowledge, in a repudiation of the unqualifiedness of its corresponding theological claims, "All knowledge is undoubtedly tradition dependent."[26] The demise of strong foundationalism, however, has not led to the loss of truth, as the title of this essay indicates. In the North American Christian theological world of the late-twentieth century (this essay was published in 2000), two alternatives had emerged in the forms of weak foundationalism, especially among Christian philosophers like Alvin Plantinga and William Alston, and postliberalism, which represents a wide array of contemporary Christian theologians and theologies. This is to paint with broad brush strokes, of course, of a wide-ranging, detailed, and important set of debates for Christian theology today.

Yong's Peirceanism does build its accounts of reality upon certain strong affirmations about what is, yet it gives a special place for criticism of these foundations or 'perceptual facts' about reality, while retaining a critical realism, where human understanding of these imperfectly and critically speaks truths. Peirce was navigating between the unknowability of the *noumenal* from Immanuel Kant and the common sense realism of Thomas Reid and his ilk.[27] Peircean pragmatism seeks to get at the real in light of the fallible human knowing process. Yong nicely summarizes this in relation to common alternatives:

> He rejected the method of tenacity (which grasps a desired end regardless of outside influences or resulting consequences), the method of authority (which subjects itself sometimes uncritically to the powers that be), and the *a priori* method (which claims to be reasonable when oftentimes it is no more than an expression of intellectual taste). Instead, Peirce advocated a method 'by which our beliefs may be determined by nothing human, but

---

approaches, to truth, but not on the foundationalist understanding, in *Spirit-Word-Community*, 164–75. Yong has a robust understanding of correspondence in his theory of truth, but such correspondence is not a simple one between propositions and external realities, as with classical foundationalism; rather, it is a dynamic and ontic correspondence, named in ontologies and metaphysics and empirical observations and theories, but not reducible to the naming itself, in a deep and thoroughgoing hermeneutical-linguistic turn that is embedded in Yong's realism.

26. Yong, "The Demise of Foundationalism," in *The Dialogical Spirit*, 23.

27. Yong, "The Demise of Foundationalism," 26–27.

by some external permanency—by something upon which our thinking has no effect (5.384). The objective of pragmatism was to get at the truly real.[28]

Such an externalism, an out there, informs this realism. For Yong, it leads to the formation of a "relational, realistic, and social metaphysics,"[29] and it uses Peirce's semiotic triadic metaphysics to do just this, though Yong will reinterpret and operate with such an approach as a global Pentecostal theologian. Yong's summarization of Peirce's triad is worth quoting at length here as foundational for understanding Yong's postfoundationalism:

> Peirce created his own technical nomenclature of Firstness, Secondness, and Thirdness to account for the distinct but interrelated universes of lived human experience. Firstness is the quality of things which enable them to be experientially present. It is the evaluated particularity—the thisness or suchness—of a certain type of texture, taste, color, smell, perception, affection, emotion, image, concept, etc., which makes that experience what it is and nothing else. Abstraced from everything but its own meaning, Firstness is pure possibility. Our thinking it in terms of its various qualities make real possibility present to us. Secondness is the facticity or factuality of things as they resist and oppose each other. It is the decisive concreteness of things in their environmental rootedness signifying their over-and-againstness and their relatedness to each other. Human experience consists most vividly of Secondness: brute physical interactions, resistance and struggle—hence our experience of actuality. Thirdness is that which mediates between (F)irst and Secondness, what Peirce called the activity of law or real generality. It is the habitual disposition or tendency to act in specific ways thus orienting experience dynamically toward the future. As real universals, Thirdness provides the impulses that drive both the evolution of the world and the trajectories of lived-experience, thereby structuring our experience of the emergence of actualities from possibilities—hence our experience of legality and continuity within development. Finally, Thirdness is the interpretant which makes meaningful Secondness' otherness over and against Firstness. Alternatively said, Thirdness is the interpretation of actual or concrete signs or symbols (Secondness) with regard to their objects (Firstness). Note that in this metaphysical scheme there are not different three [sic] kinds of

28. Yong, "The Demise of Foundationalism," 28. The in-text citation of Peirce is from *Pragmatism and Pragmaticism*.

29. Yong, *Spirit-Word-Community*, 101.

> things or experiences in the world. Rather everything presents
> itself to us experientially through the three elemental modes of
> Firstness, Secondness, and Thirdness.[30]

Peircean metaphysics plays off of or against historic Western philosophical metaphysics, especially the Platonic-Aristotelian, but also the modern, as in the Cartesian, Kant's critical project, various idealisms, and common sense realism.

Amos Yong is a Peircean, and he is to be understood as such. He has explicitly and expressly developed his theology in a Peircean philosophical approach and mode, and he is misunderstood, often enough, by those who do not understand him on his own terms, difficult, in some ways, as this may be, a point that is also applicable to other areas of his work. Yong's pneumatological foundationalism should be understood in relation to his Peirceanism. It is a foundation of spirit, of the fluidity of the becoming of being in relationship to God, of the interpretation of life that is always a movement of spirits.

Yong develops this metaphysics in ontic and epistemic directions, in a hermeneutical holism where his epistemology works in relationship to his metaphysics with an at least attempted coherence.[31] This is especially correlated with the doctrine of the Trinity, for Yong. Firstness in metaphysics is like the First Person of the Trinity, providing meaning, possibility, and sourcing to all things, as the Father represents the breadth of all that is among abstract realities. The Second Person of the Trinity correlates with Peircean Secondness, as the Incarnate Son has come and dwelt among us in particular concreteness, as historical reality, and as the Word continues in particular presences of the person and teaching of Jesus of Nazareth. The dynamism of mediation, the movement of life in Thirdness is correlated with the Spirit and all that is as spirit, as the Third Person of the Trinity elicits actualities from possibilities in calling humanity and the world to God-given purposes. The Trinity is a dynamic relationship so that God is spirit.

This triadic metaphysics images the Triune God. The community interprets the concrete realities in dynamic spirit, as the collective image of God. *Spirit-Word-Community* puts forth Yong's hermeneutical paradigm. We begin as spirits, and we ought to with the Spirit; we interpret concrete signs, and we ought to turn to the Word; and we do so in self-discovery of

---

30. Yong, *Spirit-Word-Community*, 92–93.

31. This statement is not a criticism but rather an acknowledgment of the vastness of his project, and the difficulty of keeping coherence in his large body of work as it has manifested from this paradigm.

who we are as a community, and we ought to receive in grace the knowledge of the Father who is the source of all that is dynamically becoming.

Biblical Theology: Theological (Pneumatological) Interpretation of Scripture

Though primarily a philosophical and systematic theologian, Yong is also a biblical theologian and theological interpreter of Scripture. Whereas, for example, Rahner begged off of the functional task of exegetical work on account of the functional specialization of the modern disciplines in religious studies,[32] Yong has embraced the interpretation of Word throughout his works. Almost all of his book-length works could be said to include dimensions of biblical theology and theological interpretation of Scripture, with some exegetical work, and sometimes he employs these fairly heavily. His methodology often includes narration of key biblical texts which inform the theological topics he is engaging. In some regards, he might be considered as more akin to Aquinas, who wrote a number of commentaries on Scripture beyond his scholastic theological summations and treatises, and who continually 'on the other hand' (*sed contra*) turned to Scripture, than the kind of scholastic who systematizes based on numerous assumptions concerning Scripture, the type who effectively systematizes one's own tradition. Rather, Yong's hermeneutic has both a 'from below' of exegetical reading and hearing of the text and a 'from above' of theological interpretation of the text, which move dialectically.

If there is a point of demarcation for Yong's turn to theological (pneumatological) interpretation of Scripture approach, it might be found in a 2017 review article in *The Journal of Theological Interpretation* in which he worked through three commentaries on the book of Revelation by Pentecostal commentators and provided a brief typology of these before offering his own proposal.[33] Locating one's Pentecostalism in biblical interpretation can occur implicitly and authorially, where one is a Pentecostal yet the influence on the generalized argument concerning Scripture is far less specified to such an identity and its attendant understanding of Scripture and life.[34] There is, on the other hand, a particularist hermeneutic which explicitly reads the text from within the Pentecostal tradition and often with a particular motif or loci within that.[35] The third model he recounts is what

32. As in Rahner, *Foundations of Christian Faith*, 3–14.
33. Yong, "Unveiling Interpretation."
34. Yong's exemplar here is Newton, *The Revelation Worldview*.
35. Yong's exemplar here is Archer, *'I Was in the Spirit on the Lord's Day.'* Yong's

he calls the hybridic, one in which the interpretation is both particularist and generalist (or implicit-authorial in its Pentecostalism), where some of the particularity of Pentecostal reading of the text finds a pneumatology there, it is also treated as one theological loci among others "and thereby is inhibited from being theologically generative."[36] What Yong suggests as being particularly theologically generative for Pentecostal interpretation of Scripture is a thoroughgoing pneumatological trajectory, that is, "Third Article theology . . . from a pentecostal standpoint . . . grounded centrally in the Day of Pentecost narrative of the Spirit's outpouring on all flesh."[37] Again, this is not a new motif in Yong but the maturation of a hermeneutic of 'the Spirit poured out on all flesh,' of the development of theological interpretation of Scripture that explicitly considers interpretation in light of the implications of a pneumatology that assumes a Pentecostal theology in which Acts 2:17–18 (and thus Joel 2:28–29) indicate a foundational pneumatology. Yong's third major work, *The Spirit Poured Out on All Flesh* might be understood as his early foray into such a theology and pneumatological approach to Scripture, one that has come to maturation in his later works.[38] A key aspect of this maturation has been a more thoroughgoing outworking of this pneumatology as representing a post-Pentecost hermeneutic.[39]

---

reference here is clearly and more broadly here to the 'Cleveland School,' which comes out of Pentecostal Theological Seminary and the Church of God (Cleveland, TN) biblical theologians who have developed their own Pentecostal theological interpretation of Scripture movement, often focusing on reception history. Yong specifically references John Christopher Thomas and Robby Waddell, beyond Archer, here, "Unveiling Interpretation," 146–47, esp. n19.

36. Yong, "Unveiling Interpretation," 151. Yong's exemplar he is the co-authored Two Horizons New Testament Commentary volume from Thomas and Macchia, *Revelation*. Yong does not significant appreciation for Thomas and Macchia as two leading Pentecostal scholars here, constraining his criticism of this as "a missed opportunity" (Yong, "Unveiling Interpretation," 151).

37. Yong, "Unveiling Interpretation," 152.

38. Yong, *The Spirit Poured Out on All Flesh.*

39. "The most important aspect of any pentecostal approach to Scripture that aspires to be ecumenically relevant, I suggest, is less that it derives from the particularity of the Pentecostal ecclesiality (although this is certainly important) but that it builds on the pentecostal story itself, the work of the Spirit unleashed in and through the Day of Pentecost outpouring. The credentials of such a Pentecostal hermeneutic, then, are founded not in the idiosyncrasies of Pentecostal spirituality but in the scriptural narrative's attestations regarding the foundational and universal work of the Spirit poured out 'upon all flesh'. . . . In this respect, the proposal for a pneumatological reading of scripture after Pentecost not only strives to understand how the NT authors read their sacred texts after the Spirit's gifting but also seeks to receive all of these early Christian writings as pentecostal treatises written *in* and carried *by* the Spirit. I suggest that such provides a more radical Pentecostal grounding, based not only on contemporary

Yong's *Mission after Pentecost* (2019) thus represents a later maturation of his biblical-theological hermeneutic, a 'pneumato-missiological interpretation of Scripture'; that is, the entirety of this text is a theological hearing of the Old and New Testaments, utilizing a 'pneumatological reading of Scripture' approach,[40] which has been developing in his works over the past twenty years.[41] This approach has been present since his first writings appeared at the turn of the twenty-first century, and his use of biblical theology a constant presence in his systematic-interdisciplinary theologies, that one is hard-pressed to make the claim that this is anything more than the culmination of an approach that has been building throughout his theological career, one that has culminated in a more robust move toward the theological (for Yong, especially pneumatological) interpretation of Scripture.

Yet Yong might also be considered as doing biblical theology, if we take it to mean "seeking to articulate the inner unity of the Bible."[42] For example, Yong finds canonical unity in *Mission after Pentecost*, unity in Luke-Acts in *Who Is the Holy Spirit?*, and he identifies continuities in Johannine, Pauline, and Lukan pneumatologies of love in *Spirit of Love*. Thus, on a certain level, this functions as recognizing a unity 'from below' that arises from Scriptural revelation in Yong's hermeneutics. On the other hand, Yong's approach here embarks on more of a 'from above' in (re)interpreting texts in light of theological convictions which have emerged from other (and perhaps that very) scriptural text. Yong's colleague—and predecessor as dean at Fuller Seminary, Joel B. Green, puts the dynamic this way:

> Biblical theology locates meaning in the past; theology is "contained" within the biblical text; and the text's potential ongoing significance is discerned through a process that moves from

---

Pentecostal experience but on *the* Pentecostal character of Christian life and faith after Easter. At the same time, the normativity of this primordial Pentecost begs for elucidation and this can arise out of any community that is formed by the ongoing work of the pentecostal Spirit. Put in other terms, such a pneumatological hermeneutic welcomes the specificity of pentecostal situatedness but only as one among many expressions of the 'fellowship of the Holy Spirit' (2 Cor 13:13 NRSV) in this dispensation, each strand adding something important and significant to the overall 'choir' of the Spirit. As such, then, it is poised to promote a pneumatological and pentecostal reading of Scripture that has wider purchase, for the church catholic and also for the theological academy" (Yong, "Unveiling Interpretation," 153). It might be noted that Yong's 'choir of the Spirit' here may be another indicator of the 'many tongues' principle noted below.

40. Yong, *Mission after Pentecost*, xv, 1.

41. This approach may be identified as having clearly and self-reflectively emerged in Yong, "Unveiling Interpretation."

42. This is how Craig Bartholomew puts it in his article on "Biblical Theology" in *Dictionary for Theological Interpretation of the Bible*.

left to right (historical description → theological synthesis → constructive theology) or from bottom to top (foundation → superstructure). Theological interpretation locates meaning in the dynamic interaction of the past and present (and expectations of the future); theology (and thus ongoing significance) is the outcome of that interaction. Undertaken from different locations, conceptualizing the same data yet doing so differently, these interpretive approaches serve different aims and so order their questions differently.[43]

Yong does take and interpret the biblical texts 'from below' in their inner unity, and he occasionally performs some (lighter) exegetical work, and he further regards and utilizes the results of historical-critical approaches fairly regularly. What is significant here is that he circles back around through the implications of pneumatology after Pentecost.

Yong himself explicitly considers that we "can and do read scripture also [beyond biblical studies] from a theological posture of faith that invites interaction with biblical content as communicating God's word for human benefit."[44] This has meant engagement from within his own Pentecostal tradition and its spirituality, but, as he has sought to go beyond the particularist and hybridic approaches, this has meant a more ecumenical orientation,[45] yet one that also brings a deeper pneumatological orientation:

> The proposal is that Christians, at least—those who are followers of Jesus the Messiah, meaning those also filled with the same spirit that anointed Jesus—can read scripture only after Pentecost. The controlling Christian vision therefore is Jesus the Christ, the Messiah anointed by the divine spirit, including his life, death, resurrection, ascension, and then giving of his spirit (Acts 2:33), not just to the church institutionally conceived (and effectively controlled in many cases), but to all flesh understood as the people of God gathered from every tongue, tribe, and nation (cf. Rev. 5:9 and 7:9) . . . the Pentecost narrative is itself essentially a missiological account, concerned as it is with the

43. Green, "What You See Depends on What You Are Looking For," 457. For additional work on these distinctions there is Vanhoozer's "Introduction" in *Dictionary for Theological Interpretation of the Bible*.

44. Yong, *Mission after Pentecost*, 12.

45. While I find that Yong's criticism, in "Unveiling Interpretation," of Frank Macchia's contribution to his joint commentary, *Revelation*, with John Christopher Thomas, in the hybridic-type as perhaps cogent, Macchia has, on the other hand, made a similar move to both deepen Pentecostal theology while simultaneously broadening ecumenically in a theology for the whole church as part of his *modus operandi*, especially in his *Baptized in the Spirit*.

gift or economy of the spirit as enabling witness from Jerusalem and Samaria to the ends of the earth.[46]

Yong, however, perhaps does better at performing pneumatological interpretation of Scripture than he does describing it, at least to date. This can be found in *Mission after Pentecost*, *Who Is the Holy Spirit?*, the heavy amounts of biblical interpretation in *Renewing Christian Theology*—a one-volume systematic theology based off of the Assembly of God World Fellowship's Statement of Faith, and embedded in numerous works, which provide abundant examples of the hermeneutical strategy in its implementation.[47] These exemplars each also include two other centers of his theological hermeneutic—inclusion of sources of understanding beyond theology and continual acknowledgment of the legitimacy of different understandings from different locations in Yong's 'many tongues' principle.

Interdisciplinary Theology

Yong's theological hermeneutic is especially interdisciplinary. I would contend that it is far more interdisciplinary, which means it is actually integrative, rather than multidisciplinary, which indicates sourcing from multiple disciplines but falling short of integration. Yong is constantly, at worst, attempting to integrate sources from across the disciplines of knowledge, into theological understanding; at best, he is a successful pioneer in this realm, particularly for Pentecostals, who has explored far ahead of the field of his religious fellows. This interdisciplinarity is pervasive in his work. For instance, in *Spirit of Love*, after providing a historical summarization of theologies of love from Augustine, Aquinas, and Tillich, he turns to empirical research on altruism—that is, before he also goes on to examine Pentecostal praxes and then theologies of love, drawing on Steven Land, Samuel Solivan, and Frank Macchia in the latter, prior to drawing on Lukan, Pauline, and Johannine pneumatologies of love, all before ending with nine theological conclusions on love. His theological projects seem to be attempts at developing pneumatologically-driven interdisciplinary *tours de force*. Illustrative is his opening to the chapter, and justification, of his inclusion of empirical research on altruism in *Spirit of Love*:

> The preceding theological reflections invite us to understand
> love as woven into the basic structure of the cosmos that we

46. Yong, *Mission after Pentecost*, 12–13. This post-Pentecost approach resembles the approach of Craig Keener in biblical studies in *Spirit Hermeneutics*.

47. Yong, *Revelation*.

inhabit. Beyond these ontological considerations, Tillich's theology of love also identifies its existential dimensions, especially love's role in healing and salvaging a fragmented world. Both of these aspects of love—the ontological and existential—invite other, not strictly theological questions and analyses. Further, the long legacy left by the medieval understanding of theology as science (*scientia*) suggests that contemporary scientific perspectives may be fruitfully brought to bear on illuminating the phenomenon of love. Might it be possible that the contemporary natural sciences could shed light on the ontological character of love while the social and human sciences could inform our existential experience of love?[48]

Yong's answer is, of course, in the affirmative to this final dual question. This interdisciplinarity has been fairly broad.

Yong's work in theology of disability, or perhaps better, his theology of ability, is another key location for integration and interdisciplinarity. Beyond other writings and a number of presentations on the subject, he published two major works in this area, *Theology and Down Syndrome*[49] and *The Bible, Disability, and the Church.*[50] Perhaps few things drill deeper down into the 'unthought,' those deep cultural assumptions than assumptions about human ability. Yong draws on scientific, social science, medical research, psychological, and moral philosophy, in the latter text, while drawing heavily on reflections from key biblical texts to reread them in light of an anti-exclusionary interpretation that rereads Scripture in this light, and comes to theological conclusions in light of the integration which then emerges. This interdisciplinary center is highly integrative with his pneumatological interpretation of Scripture center, for example, as his Lukan (and highly pneumatological) reflections on disability in Luke's (the physician's) and other New Testament texts, reconsider ministry practices in

---

48. Yong, *Spirit of Love*, 21. Yong goes on to explain, "I advocate a theological approach to the natural world and a dialogical understanding of the relationship between theology and science in the conviction that all truth is God's truth and that Christian theological self-understanding can illuminate the natural world and contribute to the scientific enterprise in ways that do not undermine the integrity of science" (22).

49. Yong, *Theology and Down Syndrome*.

50. Yong, *The Bible, Disability, and the Church*. On a biographical note here, one might wonder if Mark Yong, younger brother of Amos, and a person with Down Syndrome, beyond all the other things God has done through him, has been a gift to the Pentecostal theological world through his influence on his oldest brother's journey, leaving us to wonder if we would have the Amos we have without Mark, including if the Yong family even immigrates to California in Amos' early adolescence if not for their experience after Mark's birth in Malaysia (1–5).

light of multiple aspects of sensory experience, rather than just seeing and hearing.[51] Such interdisciplinarity provokes reconsiderations of assumed approaches to all kinds of subject matters.

Yong has also made forays into theology and science as well as political theology with interdisciplinary integration.[52] His major work in political theology, *In the Days of Caesar: Pentecostalism and Political Theology*,[53] performed interdisciplinary interpretation with a focus on political theory and underlying philosophical and moral philosophies. Yet here he employed both his 'many tongues' principle, in terms of accounting for the many-ness of (and differences within) global Pentecostalism in relation to the political, and also a more distinctly Pentecostal theological grid on the subject matter, structuring much of the volume through the fivefold version of the Pentecostal gospel tradition: Jesus as savior, sanctifier, Spirit baptizer, divine healer, and soon coming King. In a certain sense, Yong was constructing and mapping Pentecostal theology (really, theologies) back onto the political, in a case for appropriate multiplicities of Pentecostal political theologies, calling for commonality in a post-Pentecost imagination which he spelled out in five domains, a liturgical, sanctified, pneumatological, charismatic, and eschatological imagination, of course correlated with the five-foldness of full-gospel politics.[54] Yong's *The Spirit of Creation* not only takes into account the domains of physics, philosophical and theological reflection on late modern science, and history of Pentecostalism on the doctrine of creation, but it also includes psychological and sociological reflection on the topic in a quickly moving work that exemplifies an interdisciplinary theological modality which centers around the questions of divine and human action.[55]

The 'Many Tongues' Principle

A key centerpiece for Yong is his 'many tongues' principle. A landmark for this was Yong's publication of "Many Tongues, Many Senses: Pentecost, the

51. Yong, *The Bible, Disability, and the Church*, 49–81.

52. Of the five sections of Stephenson's recent editing of Yong's works into a (relatively) short reader, three of the five are in these interdisciplinary areas, with part 2 as "Religion and Science," part 3 as "Theology and Disability," and part 4 as "Political Theology," in Yong, *Amos Yong Reader*.

53. Yong, *In the Days of Caesar*. This text originated in Yong's Edward Cadbury Lectures in Theology at the University of Birmingham (UK) in 2007.

54. Yong, *In the Days of Caesar*, 361–62. The characterization of this as 'post-Pentecost' or 'after Pentecost' was not quite coined by Yong, as such, at this point, but it is clear from this text that he was moving, or had already implicitly moved, to such a stance.

55. Yong, *The Spirit of Creation*.

Body Politic, and the Redemption of Dis/Ability" in *Pneuma* in 2009.[56] As aforementioned, concerning the book-length theology of disability that followed this in 2011, Yong recognizes the multiplicity of knowing in human sensory experience, beyond sight and hearing as dominant. He finds the Lukan texts in the New Testament to recognize God's work inclusive of the human somatic sensory capabilities, in a receptive capacity, so that those limited in one or more may still receive from the Lord in the others. This, however, turns outward. "Glossolalic utterances, the dance, the shout, the laying on of hands, prostrations, tarrying at the altar, being slain in the Spirit, and so on—each of these are affective-somatic signs of the Spirit's presence and activity in Pentecostal contexts," he notes, with focus on their restorative and reconciling functions.[57] Here, Yong is moving towards the insight that the seemingly 'weak,' as well as the seemingly 'strong,' have a tongue to speak. That is, this key insight that Yong had begun developing several years earlier was moving deeper into theological anthropology, and it moved, to borrow Charles Taylor's metaphor, which he has used to describe the modern proliferation of beliefs and options to the even more exponential late modern, from a nova to a supernova.[58] In 2005, in *Journal of Pentecostal Theology*, Yong's article, "Academic Glossolalia?" started developing this idea that engagement in various endeavors, such as the academic disciplines, that receives from the Holy Spirit and works to the benefit of others, is an implication of the Pentecost-event, in its diversity.[59] Between 2005 and 2009, Yong goes deeper, exponentially, into the multiplicity of human noetic experience that legitimately works in concert with the Spirit of God.

As I have argued elsewhere, Yong holds together unity and plurality, difference and change, continuity and change, in his metaphysics and hermeneutic.[60] The 'many tongues' principle holds down the vast, pluralistic supernova of all graced encounter with the Spirit of God in the world. Yong has been working out the implications of 'the Spirit poured out on all flesh' since very early in his theological career. The 'many tongues' principle is a Pentecostal take on difference, plurality. Yong is an ontic realist yet a vast pluralist in terms of the vastness of humanity, the vastness of the *imago Dei*. A *missio Dei*, then, requires this recognition.

---

56. See also, Yong, "Many Tongues, Many Senses."

57. Yong, "Many Tongues, Many Senses," 182.

58. This is a key metaphor throughout Taylor, *A Secular Age*.

59. Yong, "Academic Glossolalia?" Another key earlier development in this 'many tongues' metaphor is his explicit reflection on it in interreligious encounter in Yong, *Hospitality and the Other*, 62–64.

60. Oliverio, "The One and the Many."

To reference two other Catholic theologians, Yong's 'many tongues' principle does similar work to David Tracy's 'analogical imagination' and Hans Urs von Balthasar's 'symphony.'[61] Since around 2010, Yong's 'many tongues' principle is littered throughout his works, often implied and occasionally explicitly reflected upon. The result is a bit of an interdisciplinary mashup of resourcing theological reflection and argumentation, drawing on 'many tongues' in almost all instances. As any reader of Yong knows, he rarely fails to be complex. If Yong's logic is analyzed, it would be assessed more along the lines of convergent affective-pneumatic and manifold general premises forming multi-layered complex argumentation, rather than the inductive analytical reasoning and deductive syllogisms of scholastic theologies. Thus, while he is constructing a noetic approach in his theological hermeneutic that holds the kind of potential for a broad integration of all forms of human knowledge together, like Thomas, to whom I will briefly compare him below, what is, as we moderns say, "under the hood" of this vehicle is wired and built otherwise.

A Brief Comparison with Aquinas: Thomas and Amos

Thomas has been rarely engaged by Pentecostals, and when this is the case, it has often been for the sake of engaging his work on the biblical charisms or reviewing his contribution to received Western theological categories.[62] As just stated, the comparison between Yong and Thomas is limited, especially in that Yong is clearly not an Aristotelian nor a scholastic theologian as Thomas was, although Yong has clearly still worked within many of the received categories of Western theology and scholasticism as influenced by Thomas. Yong's Peirceanism moves away from the substance metaphysics of the Platonic-Aristotelian tradition while holding to the continuity of the abstraction and concreteness in Peircean Firstness and Secondness, which works to account for what is form-matter on the Platonic-Aristotelian register, while adding the dynamism of Thirdness, of spirit. Yong's engagement

61. Tracy, *The Analogical Imagination*, esp. 446–56; Balthasar, *Truth Is Symphonic*, esp. 43–64. Of course, there are differences between Yong, Tracy, and von Balthasar here. The point is that they each are accounting for the unity-plurality dynamic with a significant degree of adequacy.

62. For example, King, "Thomas Aquinas and Prophecy"; Blankenhorn, "The Metaphysics of Charisms." Some typical examples of Pentecostal engagement would be Yong's review of Thomas' theology of love in the *Summa Theologiae* in *Spirit of Love*, 9–14; Frank Macchia's review of Thomas on habitual grace in *Justified in the Spirit*, 18–22; and Steven Studebaker's review of Thomas' Trinitarian theology in *From Pentecost to the Triune God*, 111–18.

with more dynamic approaches to causation and divine action marks a large difference between the contemporary Pentecostal and the medieval Dominican. He is interested in considering divine action in terms of late modern science and the theological turn to the future where God's action is understood eschatologically and the laws of nature are considered regularities for this epoch of history, not in terms of a static metaphysical order.[63] There are, however, some key points of continuity between Yong and Thomas, and they are worth recounting, especially as Pentecostalism, at times, has some tendencies which more closely resemble Catholic tendencies than classical Protestant ones.

First, differing from certain forms of Protestantism, there is a positivity towards general knowledge in both Thomas and Yong. For the former, grace fulfills or completes nature. Still, the fall has damaged human nature.[64] Yong has similar tendencies, more in the Irenaean trajectory in theological anthropology in regard to the human noetic function, where human fallenness has not erased the ability to know truthfully, even as it is diminished through sin. Broad knowledge from multiple disciplines illuminates human understanding. For Yong, it is also especially funded through the Incarnation and the calling ahead of eschatology in its redemption.[65]

63. Yong, "How Does God Do What God Does?"

64. The medieval scholastic clarifies that "The good in human nature is threefold. First there are the principles constitutive of nature together with the properties derived from them, for example the powers of soul and the like. Secondly, since it is from this nature itself that man has an inclination to virtue, as previously indicated, this inclination is itself a good of nature. Thirdly, the gift of original justice can be termed a good of human nature in the sense that in the first man it was bestowed as a gift to all humankind. Of these goods, the first is neither destroyed nor lessened through sin. The third has been totally removed by the sin of the first parents. But the middle one, man's connatural inclination to virtue is lessened through sin" (Aquinas, *Summa Theologiae*, I-II.85.1).

65. Yong, *Renewing Christian Theology*, 283. "In fact, these features of theological anthropology are illuminated also by the biological, cognitive, psychological, anthropological, and sociological sciences, and we neglect them to our ignorance.... From a theological perspective, we might agree with the Roman Catholic hierarchy ... that human souls are uniquely implanted into human lives by God. From a scientific perspective, any kind of 'emergent anthropology' would suffice that see these intellectual, moral, and psychical capacities as arising unpredictably from out of a sufficiently complex nexus of constituent parts (like how the features of water, H_2O, are novel and are unforeseeable merely as hydrogen and oxygen taken separately). Both the theological and scientific views are, to varying degrees, postures of faith, complementary in outcome but derived from different starting points. But whatever is refracted dimly about humanity in a fallen world grows in brilliance when illuminated in the light of Christ. Life in Adam reveals the frailty of the present human condition; life in Christ projects and even makes present what is possible, what is emerging, what is promised in the gospel. Thus Irenaeus' instincts are sound, indicative of the fact that we know about the image of God not necessarily from what we see present in ourselves, but from what is

This relates to habit, of course, in "the exercise of human acts," in habituating virtue or sin. Thomas considers that the rational nature cannot be taken away completely, "for sin to cause man to cease to be rational is impossible, since he would then no longer be capable of sinning. It is not possible, then, that this good be totally taken away."[66] This means that there is still left a natural capacity for good that remains in the human,

> The good of nature lessened by sin, as has been said, is man's natural bent to virtue. Because he is rational, it belongs to man to act in accord with reason, which is to act virtuously. For sin to cause man to cease to be rational is impossible, since he would then no longer be capable of sinning. It is not possible, then that this good be totally taken away.[67]

Yong's dialogical approach to those of all kinds of people, including of other faiths, presumes something along these very lines. Yong's sense of something like a pneumatological common grace upon humanity, even amidst other religions, through which some truth might be known likewise provides not just a leftover creational common grace that remains, but one that includes the dynamic and present reality of the Spirit of God in the world, not limited to the Spirit's presence in the Church.[68]

Second, this all results in a more thoroughgoing and implemented theological hermeneutic that includes a Thomistic-like understanding of the interaction between general or philosophical knowledge and theological

---

revealed eschatologically in Christ: 'Just as we have borne the image of the man of dust, we will also bear the image of the man of heaven' (1 Cor 15:49)."

66. Aquinas, *Summa Theologiae*, I-II.85.2.

67. Aquinas, *Summa Theologiae*, I-II.85.2.

68. "According to the Christian theological tradition, the *imago Dei* in human beings derives in part from our having received the divine breath of life. This breath sets us apart from other creatures. We are distinguished from them by our rational, volitional, moral, and interpersonal and relational capacities. Because human beings subsist through the expression of these capacities, we are all, in the words of Lyle Dabney, 'otherwise engaged in the Spirit' (cf. Acts 17:28). To choose freely, to act morally, to relate to others intentionally, to experience interpersonal subjectivity—these are the pneumatological features of human living in the world. Thinking itself, in this fundamental sense, is thus intrinsically pneumatological. Our processes of reasoning, whether in terms of imagining, hypothesizing, deducting, inferring, and so on, constitute, in part, our life in the Spirit. From this perspective, the Spirit is the means of thought in general and perhaps the object of thought when focus is placed specifically upon the Spirit's presence and activity. Any and all who think are therefore potentially addressed when discussing pneumatology; they become an actual part of the conversation when they accept our invitation to theologize about the Spirit or about human life and spirituality. In this sense, foundational pneumatology, by nature of its content, requires a universal horizon and involves a universal audience as well" (Yong, *Beyond the Impasse*, 131).

knowledge funded by special revelation, furthered and enlivened by a robust pneumatology and its attendant pneumatological imagination. In effect, this is the key point of comparison between Yong and Thomas here, and the center for the comparison. Academic and thoroughgoing human glossolalia means that Pentecostalism can actually address all realms of human knowledge. Thomas' attraction to the Dominican order and its broadening of what high medieval Christianity could address provides a parallel, as he and they turned to the arrival of Aristotelian philosophy via Islamic interlocutors, as a discovery made through interreligious encounter.

Given the dominance of ecclesial powers in his day, and the dominance of religious knowledge in his context, the opening of Thomas' greatest work provides what may appear to be a surprising question. In his answer to the originating question of the *Summa Theologiae*, Thomas defends the very need for a theological discipline in concert with the philosophical, which, for him, was human rationality understood in line with Aristotelianism. For Aristotle, theology was a sub-discipline of philosophy referring to the divine.[69] Thomas does so by holding to the actuality and beneficence of special revelation in Scripture, as that which "is no part of the branches of philosophy traced by reasoning"; God provides this "above all because God destines us for an end beyond the grasp of reason."[70] Yet this does not deny but, in fact, affirms the convergence of human philosophy and divine revelation which the human rational facility, in turn, proceeds to utilize its faculties in forming theological knowledge. Knowledge of things provided by divine revelation assist the frail realities of human existence, as humans rarely have the ability to spend extensive time in philosophical reflection about the divine, yet also since many of these divine truths surpass the human rational capacity for cognition. Both knowledge that comes through philosophy and knowledge that comes through divine revelation, that is, the theology that comes from it and is a science in its own right, serve in the diversification of sciences which are together unified in human knowledge, two interrelated yet differentiable genuses.[71] This does not mean that philosophy was

69. Aquinas, *Summa Theologiae*, I.1.1 draws on Aristotle's *Metaphysics* and 2 Tim 3:16, Isa 64:4, and the apocryphal *Ecclesiasticus* 3:25 in formulating his response.

70. Aquinas, *Summa Theologiae*, I.1.1.

71. Aquinas, *Summa Theologiae*, I.1.1.2: "The diversification of the sciences is brought about by the diversity of aspects under which things can be known. Both an astronomer and a physical scientist may demonstrate the same conclusion, for instance that the earth is spherical; the first, however, works in a mathematical medium prescinding from material qualities, while for the second his medium is the observation of material bodies through the senses. Accordingly there is nothing to stop the same things from being treated by the philosophical sciences when they can be looked at in the light of natural reason and by another science when they are looked at in the light of

altogether positive for the medieval doctor; his writings include a number of negative verdicts about the inabilities of pagan philosophies, and he exempted Christian writers from his occasional epitaph that a given statement was mere philosophical opinion.[72] Nevertheless, for Thomas and Amos, the Christian tradition needs to make this critical move of expanding both the topics of knowledge and those from whom truth might be known.

Third, Thomas and Amos share an approach towards dialoguing with and engaging religious others in a mode that is unafraid to learn from them and include knowledge gleaned from them, while also providing a Christian

divine revelation. Consequently the theology of holy teaching differs in kind from that theology which is ranked as a part of philosophy."

72. Jordan, "Theology and Philosophy," 233–36; Jordan summarizes the negative side of Thomas' judgment of philosophy here: "Pagan philosophy presented itself as the love of the best knowledge of the highest things, that is, as a way toward happiness. Yet philosophy was incapable of providing happiness. The ancient philosophers multiplied views on the human good, but they could not achieve it. Philosophers were unable to convince even their fellow citizens, because they could not offer a teaching about life that was firm, comprehensive, and useful. No philosophers had enough wisdom to call men back from error; instead they led many into error. The philosophers could not avoid sin, because they could not undergo the unique purification of the true worship of God, which begins in the philosophically unknowable coming of Christ" (Jordan, "Theology and Philosophy," 234–35). Fergus Kerr considers that the *Summa Theologiae* "might have been composed (though we don't know) to persuade admirers of Aristotle that his *philo-sophia*, 'love of wisdom', was not only quite compatible with Christian assumptions about nature, truth, goodness, and the soul, but greatly illuminated them. Thomas did once say that philosophy is a kind of revelation: 'the study of philosophy is in its own right allowable and praiseworthy, because God revealed to the philosophers the truth which they perceive, as the Apostle [Paul] says' (*ST* 2/2.167.1). On the other hand, in one of his last sermons at the University of Paris, he said this: 'A little old lady (*vetula*) of today knows more about things concerning the faith than all the philosophers of antiquity'—quite a significant remark (we might think) to his assembled colleagues and students at the height of the crisis over the effects on Catholic Christian doctrine of the study of the pagan Aristotle" (Kerr, *Thomas Aquinas*, 35).

For Thomas, cognition is his "fundamental epistemic category," with intellect as that through which the human soul (Thomas held to the Aristotelian hylomorphic anthropology, where the soul is the substantial form of the body) assimilates the corporeal substances it encounters to itself. Thomas reserves *scientia* for complete and certain cognition of the truth of a thing, with cognition remaining the broader intellectual power of the human (MacDonald, Theory of Knowledge," 160–63). MacDonald notes that Thomas does account for probabilistic *scientia*, noting a passage that explicitly states this in Thomas' *Posterior Analytics* II.12.5. As Thomas moves from inferences about reality, which establish premises, to deductive conclusions about such, his systemic theological and philosophical system produces a foundationalism. Thomas developed a faculty psychology where the active intellect, together with the will, marked the distinctive feature of the human rational capacity for cognition and action, For appreciation of Thomas' faculty psychology which evaluates it and otherwise relates it to contemporary neuroscientific developments as well as contemporary philosophy of language, see Murphy, *A Philosophy of the Christian Religion*, 224–35.

apologetic towards them. While Aquinas did so primarily in the mode of an apologist, as in his *Summa Contra Gentiles*, Yong's pragmaticism recognizes the importance of dialogue with religious, cultural, and philosophical others which would require a recognition that they, too, are witnessing to truth in the world. This is because we are meant to flourish together:

> Dialogue with others, Christians and religious or unreligious others, informs faithful Christian praxis. How then do we live faithfully in the complicated postfoundationalist, post-Christendom, post-secular, postmodern, and pluralist context of our present situation? Faithful living means, in part, being able to flourish with others, and such flourishing requires that we know our neighbors in order that we can develop common cause toward a more just and humane world. Dialogue enables such vital praxis to emerge. The Christian theological endeavor contributes to such an important objective when it proceeds dialogically in and with the company of others.[73]

Such a dialectic is funded by the pneumatological imagination which mediates a back-and-forth and represents a spirit of understanding between persons and communities. For the Christian, such dialogue entails inclusion of the Spirit in it, as the Spirit is necessarily present for the Christian as the Spirit of Christ.[74] Insofar as the Spirit's presence is explicitly understood as such for the Christian, it is easy to speak about. However, Yong is often dealing with other types of common human experiences in daily experience, like ones where those at various places in their Christian discipleship are encountering others of some or little or no or other faith. In cases like these, Christians may be encountering the witness of the Spirit within them and from others just as others are encountering the Spirit. Despite some qualifications concerning this in his earlier work, particularly *Beyond the Impasse*, where, in dealing with discernment of spirits, he focused on the phenomenology of discernment and cultural-linguistic frameworks for such,[75] Yong's work past his early works most often points to the Christological criterion for such discernment.[76]

---

73. Yong, *The Dialogical Spirit*, 284.

74. Despite Yong's early dabbling with a denial of the *filioque* in *Spirit-Word-Community*, even as such was even then significantly qualified by his engagement with mediating positions to the Eastern-Western debate, such as that of David Coffey, Yong's subsequent work has often affirmed that the Spirit is the Spirit of Christ, even as the human encounter with the Spirit may not and often does not include thematic recognition that this is the Spirit of Christ.

75. Yong, *Beyond the Impasse*, 129–61.

76. "First and foremost, the dialogue enabled by the Holy Spirit will ultimately point

Operating from convergent affective-pneumatic premises rather than deductive syllogisms, with a pneumatological imagination, Yong's theological hermeneutic has developed to the point that it can handle some of the heavy lifting for the Pentecostal tradition, the way that Thomas' work has for the Catholic, that is, it is a serious foray, the most serious to date, for Pentecostals to handle the breadth of human knowledge in experience. In its "many tongues," it is, to borrow from another leading Pentecostal thinker, J. Aaron Simmons, a "mashup" approach. Like contemporary musical "mash-ups" where musical genres are mixed yet identifiable, and they each provide something the other could not, Yong puts for a theological hermeneutic that can handle the "mashup" of disciplines and human abilities and cultures and approaches to life, a theological hermeneutic of unity-plurality for the late modern world.[77]

---

to Jesus Christ. This means that Christians who are dialogically engaged will inevitably, even if also incessantly, revolve around Christ. Here the life of Christ, his teachings, and his selfless and atoning death are the normative shape of the Spirit's presence and activity. Voices, behaviors, and phenomena that are contrary to this Christic and cruciform character are those of the antichrist and hence opposed also to the spirit of Jesus. Those that manifest the fruits of the spirit of Christ (Gal 5:22–24) and are consistent with the values of the shalom Jesus, proclaimed and embodied, can be said to at least anticipate, if not also participate in, the coming reign of God. At the same time, because Christ is the one who is also yet to come and we see through a glass dimly (1 Cor 13:12). . . . We may find ourselves transformed into greater Christlike-ness only in hindsight, even as others come into more consciously thematized knowledge of Christ only eschatologically. On the other hand, if we gradually or otherwise cease to bear the fruits of the spirit of Christ in the course of our dialogical encounter, then the conversation will be animated by other spirits—at least our own, certainly—rather than the spirit of Jesus" (Yong, *The Dialogical Spirit*, 285).

77. Simmons, "On Shared Hopes."

12

Reading Craig Keener

Craig Keener's Spirit Hermeneutics: Reading Scripture in the Light of Pentecost is now the most significant and comprehensive text to have been written on Pentecostal hermeneutics. The 2016 monograph published by Eerdmans with a foreword by Amos Yong is a landmark in the communal development of hermeneutics for global Pentecostalism, broadly construed, as the volume plays out the more general ecumenical implications of a disciplined pneumatic hermeneutic—a hermeneutic that has its cultural and practical roots in Pentecostal interpretive habits as they meet believing modern historical studies of Scripture. *Spirit Hermeneutics* is set to become to charismatic-pentecostal biblical hermeneutics what Anthony Thiselton's *The Two Horizons* has been to Christian hermeneutics in general in the English-speaking world, and what Kevin Vanhoozer's *Is There a Meaning in This Text?* has been to American evangelical hermeneutics.

A charismatic Baptist who has worshipped and ministered at predominantly African-American churches throughout his adult life—ordained in the National Baptist Convention—Keener received his first biblical-theological training at what was the Assemblies of God's flagship ministerial training institution, Central Bible College, and he earned his MA and MDiv from the Assemblies of God Theological Seminary, both in Springfield, Missouri and both now encompassed into Evangel University there. After he completed his PhD from Duke University (1991), he taught at Hood Theological Seminary (Salisbury, NC) and then at Palmer Theological Seminary of Eastern University (near Philadelphia) before becoming the F. M. and Ada Thompson Professor of Biblical Studies at Asbury Theological Seminary

(Wilmore, KY) in 2011. He is known to broader audiences through his work that bring his scholarship to use in study of the Bible as well as through his personal website (craigkeener.com) and his popular writings published on internet sites.

Keener has provided some of the most significant contributions from the charismatic-pentecostal scholarly community in his scholarship on the New Testament and related subjects. He has authored over two dozen full-length scholarly works. These include Keener's often dense and carefully noted commentaries, work on the historical Jesus and miracles, as well as more pastorally and spiritually oriented books on the role of women in the church and the black church, plus a popular autobiographical work on his relationship with his then future wife Médine as she was caught in a life-and-death struggle during war in her native Congo. *Spirit Hermeneutics* lays out a practiced hermeneutical paradigm with which those who know his works will already be familiar. Rather than a proposal for a hermeneutical program, this theoretical work on hermeneutics is the result of long hermeneutical practice and experience.

The typical pair of human hands has enough fingers to count those who might be qualified to address the breadth of subjects with the depth of *Spirit Hermeneutics*, at least if the scope is limited to those in the charismatic-pentecostal tradition. Keener is uniquely gifted to do so with his renowned detail. His documentation throughout, in the form of endnotes here (304–88), is the work of an erudite lover of biblical and ancient cultural studies. This erudition is met by scholarly competency and cogent reasoning in his philosophical and theological hermeneutics, a combination that results in a work that addresses biblical, theological, and philosophical hermeneutics with sufficient adequacy, even as its focus remains the interpretation of Scripture.

Spirit Hermeneutics thus includes geological layers of Keener's developed understanding and research, on top of which his hermeneutical approach surfaces as a developed pentecostal hermeneutical paradigm that is now the foremost constructive effort in the field. With due respect to the manifold contributions made to contemporary pentecostal hermeneutics and several particularly influential ones,[1] I can only concur with Amos

1. I would list as the other major works: Archer, *A Pentecostal Hermeneutic*; Yong, *Spirit-Word-Community*; among other leading works, some might consider my *Theological Hermeneutics*. Three recent edited collections on hermeneutics among Charismatic-Pentecostals provide some recent contributions on the topic: Archer and Oliverio, *Constructive Pneumatological Hermeneutics*; Martin, *Pentecostal Hermeneutics*; Spawn and Wright, *Spirit and Scripture*. There are dozens of monographs from pentecostal scholars that address hermeneutics in a sustained manner in works that primarily address other topics, especially in the area of biblical studies, along with hundreds of

Yong's consideration in the Foreword that this is "by far the most comprehensively articulated" book on the matter (xviii). Even so, Keener's boldness in his scholarly and spiritual convictions throughout is met by humility in the recognition of his own limits, exemplified by the modal strength by which he oftentimes prefaces the strength of his statements.[2]

Yet, Keener's boldness and breadth of understanding are essential aspects of his success. Hermeneutics as an encompassing and basic place of beginning for human inquiry, as a supersession of epistemology and the latter's dominance over human thought as the 'first philosophy' of modernity, requires the theorist to have broad understanding concerning philosophical, linguistic, anthropological, and ontological issues.[3] Such understanding goes beyond the focal point of the study here in charismatic-pentecostal biblical interpretation, though a well-developed hermeneutic requires it. This breadth can perhaps best be seen in the numerous secondary comments in the endnotes or in Appendixes A and B, where his compulsion for thoroughness provides his readers with succinct if developed responses to twentieth-century continental hermeneutics (Appendix A) and a sensitive response to postcolonial hermeneutics (Appendix B). The extensive bibliography (389–456) is likewise demonstrative, and his use of those sources goes far beyond awareness of published works in the filed as he moves toward the limits of the human ability to stay abreast of work in related disciplines. And while he makes hermeneutics the encompassing discipline for inquiry, he still recognizes the formative importance of epistemology for hermeneutics, developing an 'epistemology of Word and Spirit' that is both informed by and focused on understanding Scripture in its epistemic-anthropological implications in part 4 (153–204). He does so because "the theological sphere requires an epistemic approach appropriate to it. The infinite God

---

articles and hook chapters. Keener's bibliography at the end of *Spirit Hermeneutics* (389–456) notes most of them. A few additional works not found in his nearly comprehensive one can be found in the bibliography of my *Theological Hermeneutics*, 363–76.

2. For example, this can be seen in his conclusions concerning the contemporization of the hermeneutics of Jesus (italics mine to note his modal humility): "*I still surmise that* if Jesus were doing the same sort of ministry today, he would not start by cultivating favor with our denominational leaders or scholars; certainly not with political or academic establishments either. *I believe that* he would start with children in the projects, with teenagers on the most impoverished Native American reservations, or the world's shantytowns. *He might* look more like a street outreach worker in Teen Challenge than a political activist. He would start from the bottom up" (216). Throughout, a general air of humility towards Keener's own interpretation meets the strengths of his claims.

3. On hermeneutics as a supersession of epistemology, see Taylor, "Overcoming Epistemology"; Westphal, *Overcoming Onto-theology*.

is known only where he reveals himself, and theological epistemology must thus begin with those places of revelation" (153).

Keener writes *Spirit Hermeneutics* as one whose life has been deeply immersed in Scripture, both as a scholar and in Christian devotion. It may not even be bold to consider Keener's commentaries and other works on the New Testament, Jesus, Paul, and other themes related to the Christian Scriptures—now including *Spirit Hermeneutics* as an articulation of his hermeneutical paradigm—not only as leading works in biblical scholarship today but even as classic works for future generations. Here, my goal is to provide an initial interpretation and evaluation of *Spirit Hermeneutics* as it begins its influence on its audiences, though my own interpretation here has had to choose between many important themes that I would likely concede criticisms from those who may find that I have missed an important idea in *Spirit Hermeneutics* in this essay.

Pentecostal Hermeneutics and *Spirit Hermeneutics*

Most changes in societies and cultures happen gradually, and thus even major trends can go unnoticed when they do not fit into regnant or championed narratives. While the regnant script on the future of religion in the West has often told us that the religious future is, at least in the main, a diminishing one, and that this future will be more secular, insufficient notice has been paid to the manifold growth of global Pentecostalism and its implications.[4] That this script is regnant does not, however, mitigate the reality that global Pentecostalism has grown to five-to-six hundred million adherents worldwide and now ranks as the second largest global Christian tradition. That is Pentecostalism is at least co-second to global Protestantism, after the Roman Catholic tradition, and is in the process of surpassing global Protestantism.[5] This is the new and present reality, even as this shift and its implications are being digested—or, more often, ignored—by an academy struggling to account for it, one still dominated by philosophical assumptions built into it by certain modes of Enlightenment philosophy. Pentecostalism has, for instance, as a practical religious reality, countered the three modes of secularity spelled out by Charles Taylor in his *A Secular Age*: secularization

4. For some helpful surveys here, see: Anderson, *An Introduction to Pentecostalism*; Miller and Yamamori, *Global Pentecostalism*; Vondey, *Pentecostalism*. For an up-to-date sociological assessment, see Wilkinson, "Pentecostals and the World."

5. For a recent history that accounts for this, see Jacobsen, *Global Gospel*; pentecostal demographic developments are also well accounted for by the continuing work of the *World Christian Encyclopedia* and The Pew Forum on Religion and Public Life.

in the public place of religion, actual religious belief and the practices of religion, and the underlying cultural structures and plausibility conditions of religious belief.[6] Pentecostalism is thus more often treated as anomaly than as the religious future, even if that conclusion may be well criticized as one built more upon philosophical assumptions than on present realities. So when Craig Keener writes *Spirit Hermeneutics* as a constructive effort at pentecostal hermeneutics, he is not merely representing an odd species of American Evangelicalism, he is representing and building upon a now leading global Christian movement that is an outgrowth of an already century-old hermeneutical tradition that itself has undergone development in various types and approaches.[7]

Yet, Pentecostalism itself was originally an ecumenically oriented revival movement, and global Pentecostalism has brought its experiential hermeneutic to the contemporary global church as a major contribution to ecumenism.[8] Further, Keener develops *Spirit Hermeneutics* as an ecumenical hermeneutic in which the charismatic influence of charismatic-pentecostal Christianity has leavened much of contemporary Christianity and its hermeneutics today. Thus, a reading of Keener that considers *Spirit Hermeneutics* a partisan or communal hermeneutic would misinterpret not only his ecumenical orientation but also his prioritization of Scripture as the authority for charismatic-pentecostal interpretation of Scripture above the interpretive traditions of charismatic-pentecostal communities.[9] Keener contends that charismatic-pentecostal communities have been born out of the desire for having experiences that alight with what is taught and modeled in the New Testament texts, even if, in his estimation, Pentecostals have

6. Taylor, *A Secular Age*, esp. 15–20. Here, I claim that Pentecostalism has provided a counternarrative to the mainstream stories of western secularization concerning all three of these modes of secularism.

7. My *Theological Hermeneutic in the Classical Pentecostal Tradition* accounted for four major types of hermeneutics among North American Classical Pentecostals: the original classical type, early and contemporary versions of the evangelical-pentecostal hybrid type, the contextual-pentecostal type, and the ecumenical-pentecostal type. These types are orientations that continue to form new hybridizations and developing paradigms in contemporary pentecostal hermeneutics. Further work is needed to account for broader global pentecostal hermeneutical types, though many have contributed toward works that could develop these broader accounts.

8. Robeck has considered the original revival at Azusa Street as an ecumenical revival in *The Azusa Street Mission and Revival*. Wolfgang Vondey has considered Pentecostalism, in part, "an ecumenical melting pot" (*Pentecostalism*, 49) throughout his works.

9. Keener specifically addresses the role of community in interpretation in chapter 18, "Global Pentecostal Community as a Safety Net?" of *Spirit Hermeneutics*, 277–85. This comes after he has argued in the previous chapter that genuinely pentecostal, as differentiated from naïve "pentecostal" readings (Keener's scare quotes) are "biblically sensitive."

not always had accurate historical grids—that is, good historical information *and* good historical-theological accounts—for interpreting these texts in their historical contexts (21–38).

Few have been more careful students of Scripture and the attendant historical and cultural background.[10] Yet, Keener does not consider ancient context and present experience in an oppositional manner. He instead champions an experiential-believing pneumatic hermeneutics of Scripture driven by the continuity between the historical situations of biblical revelation and the present work of God. Here it is worth allowing his own words to testify:

> As followers of the risen Messiah, we are people of the era of the Messiah and the Spirit, inaugurated at Pentecost, a prophetic, eschatological people. Referring to events that began at Pentecost, Acts announces the era of the Spirit that God had earlier promised: "In the last days . . . I will pour out my Spirit on all flesh, and your sons and daughters will prophesy." A 'Spirit hermeneutic' seems an apt title for that interpretive location. Moreover, it is one shared by the first Pentecostals and most global Pentecostals and charismatics, including myself. This means that we are interested in biblical texts not simply for what they teach us about ancient history of ideas (intriguing as that is to me), but because we expect to share the kind of spiritual experience and relationship with God that we discover in Scripture. (5)

Keener's pneumatic hermeneutics is an experiential-spiritual hermeneutic fused together with great attention to the historical and literary. Of course, certain spiritual-theological-ontological affirmations can be seen as underlying what he brings to the texts, but he contends, and works to demonstrate, that these are themselves formed by an experiential reading of Scripture, a "reading by the Spirit and with the heart" (219). While "grammar is valuable because it helps us to hear and obey the message," it is not sufficient for our hermeneutic, as linguistic and conceptual understanding "is not the same as embracing the heart of God that the text is designed to communicate" (257).

Hermeneutical Theory in *Spirit Hermeneutics,* and Pentecost as the Reversal of Babel

In *Spirit Hermeneutics,* Keener is a master builder of a hermeneutic. He does so with many materials that are ready to hand, already present in the living

10. Keener is coeditor (with John H. Walton) of the *NIV Cultural Background Study Bible* and editor of the *InterVarsity Press Bible Background Commentary: New Testament.*

hermeneutics of the global pentecostal and charismatic community and her scholars (see the "Index on Authors," 458–75), yet *Spirit Hermeneutics* is nevertheless his own construction, a landmark work in charismatic-pentecostal hermeneutics at that.

Spirit Hermeneutics cultivates an approach to scriptural interpretation that accounts for *both* the always traditioned and enculturated second nature involved in human interpretation—the hermeneutical turn—*and* the historical actualities given to historical actualities given to interpreters in texts, which give us their own parameters for what is legitimate and illegitimate interpretive possibilities—the ontic, the real. In this way, Keener's hermeneutics attends to what I have argues is the critical both-and in hermeneutical theory for the future of pentecostal hermeneutics, in a hermeneutical realism that recognizes both of these sets of concerns in a way that does not deny, neglect, mute, or suffocate the other, as some current hermeneutical approaches do.[11] What further distinguishes Keener from many other hermeneutic theorists, including those who address biblical and theological hermeneutics, is how much he turns to Scripture itself in developing his scriptural hermeneutics. He has an entire chapter on the hermeneutics of Jesus (chapter 14, "How Jesus Invites Us to Hear the Bible," 207–18), a rich if relatively brief study. Keener's hermeneutical circle—or spiral, if that is a more adequate metaphor, as suggested by Grant Osborne—heavily sources from Scripture itself.[12] Scripture forms Keener's hermeneutic even as his interpretation of Scripture is itself formed by what he has already taken to be the case about the biblical texts and the way he ought to go about interpreting them.

In developing this hermeneutic, Keener has gotten over the modern aversion to recognizing the role that experience and situation, culture and generation, play in interpretation; thus he eschews the idea that there is anything like a single proper or neutral standpoint for interpreting texts, one that often latches onto the concept of objectivity. Such a position often follows a logical non sequitur where realism—that is, the affirmation that our language concerning reality actually speaks of reality as it is *to some degree of adequacy or another*—entails a kind of ideal vantage point or propositional articulation that speaks 'the truth' (the definite article giving the definitive articulation) on the matter. Keener is operating on a different conceptual plane in *Spirit Hermeneutics*. He affirms the text, its realities, and the parameters it gives for interpretation, while nonetheless he also affirms

---

11. I have addressed this pair of concerns in "Towards a Hermeneutical Realism in Pentecostal Theological Hermeneutics," chapter 7 of *Theological Hermeneutics*, 315–62; and "Introduction" in Archer and Oliverio, *Constructive Pneumatological Hermeneutics*, 1–14.

12. Osborne, *The Hermeneutical Spiral*.

the humanness—the enculturation and finitude and volition, the unrecognized assumptions and that which primes our assumptions moving beyond self-awareness—involved in all understanding. For Keener, "People read texts with interests and agendas" so that the questions we pose to and about the texts lead to what we find in and about them. Human finitude is not an obstacle to interpretation but its inevitable condition: "Personal experience inevitably shapes how texts of communications affect us" (30).

Keener does not simply press this point because of late modern or postmodern concerns. Though he is undoubtedly influenced by cultural-philosophical assumptions, his primary reasons for stressing this point have to do with Scripture itself and the fruitfulness found in the experiential readings of God's people today. In so doing, he develops his hermeneutic crossculturally, finding that greater insight comes from listening to the interpretations of Scripture from the many tongues of the global church today. Much of the contemporary global church's biblical interpretation is experiential reading, yet Keener finds that Scripture itself invites experiential reading. Similar to how Lee Roy Martin has emphasized the affective hearing of Scripture in pentecostal scholarly circles, Keener holds that readings that seek to be affected by Scripture are usually closer to the origination and original situation of a biblical text and its audience than are modern technical, critical readings—even though Martin and Keener are both specialists in the skills involved in those technical and critical approaches.[13]

Contextualization and being formed by experiences are ubiquitous aspects of all human understanding, and Keener's emphasis on the cultural backgrounds of the original contexts is not used to deemphasize contemporary culture but to bring about awareness of contemporary as well as ancient or original contexts. *Contexts* are just that, they are what the text and the interpreter(s) bring *with* them to the conveying and understanding of meaning. They are always already there, whether recognized or not. Keener's emphasis on culture comes as an affirmation of Scripture as revelation:

> Those of us who embrace Scripture as divine revelation must recognize that God communicated cross-culturally. All communication has a cultural context; no one communicates or hears in a cultural vacuum. Insofar as we wish to hear the Bible as communication, then, we need to take into account its cultural context. (73)

Scripture is divine revelation—originating in particular contexts and in human language and in culturally laden communication, and always

---

13. A summary of his affective approach as it meets technical biblical scholarship can be found in Martin, "Longing for God."

interpreted in the same. There is no escaping this. The basic problem posed by Lessing's broad and ugly ditch between the truths of history and eternal truths is denied. Particularity as a possible condition for divine revelation is not only affirmed but taken to be the necessary condition for a Christian—a pentecostal—understanding of revelation.

Keener, here and elsewhere (for example, regarding miracles), moves past some of the seeming dilemmas of modern thought concerning spiritual things. With less philosophical and theological articulation, though none the lesser in practice, Keener operates with the affirmation developed by James K. A. Smith in *The Fall of Interpretation* that genuinely Christian hermeneutics do not buy into those modern Enlightenment or other episte-mologies which seek to overcome the finitude and situatedness of humanity to attain some ideal state of knowledge and the often attendant quest for some meta-articulation of truth that can somehow move beyond cultures and traditions; yet neither Smith nor Keener lapses into a hermeneutics led by suspicion or despair.[14] Rather, Keener is more in line with the 'many tongues' principle for which Amos Yong advocates throughout his works, where a Christian plurality of voices and interpretations in the global church better speak the truth and meaning found in and revealed to us through Scripture. Even further for Keener, and this in line with his previous work in *The Historical Jesus of the Gospels* and *Miracles*, the cultural and linguistic plurality of the church birthed at Pentecost that witnesses the truth of God stands as a reversal of the empires of Babel, including the reductionistic-empirical academic empire and its hegemony over what can be counted as real and true in Scripture. Instead, Keener finds a thicker, revelatory, and empowering Bible:

> If we read from the vantage point of Pentecost, we recognize that God speaks all languages and reaches out to all cultures. Different cultures may hear different aspects of the Spirit's voice more readily. A reading from the vantage point of Pentecost, then, invites us to trust the Spirit's work in the global church enough that we dialogue with one another, listen to one another, and share with one another. The Spirit speaks through differ-ent gifts in the local church, and we all provide a safety net of discernment for one another's blind spots (1 Cor. 14:29). (66)

This is even as Keener strongly grounds meaning in the original text and the communicative work of the authors—though he is comfortable with a broader semantic range of the meaning of 'meaning' while prioritizing the

---

14. Smith, *The Fall of Interpretation*. Westphal, *Whose Community? Which Interpre-tation?*, addresses these issues from a largely Gadamerian approach.

origination of the text and gravitating all other senses of meaning in their relation to it. He does not see authority over meaning as coming from the global Christian community that gives the text its meaning but from the Lord who communicates to us. Together we hear and see and interpret this communication, which comes in and through the text itself.

Meaning(s), Contexts, Authors, and Texts and Readers—and "Keener's Hammer"

To summarize, Keener holds that the textual and revelatory meaning of biblical texts adheres to contexts, that is, the original contexts. The contexts of historical and contemporary interpreters are then productive of interpretations whose meanings are accountable to the original texts themselves, which are properly understood only in relation to these original contexts. Contrasting with the more modern than biblical approach often adhered to by some strands of contemporary Christian hermeneutics, a multicultural hermeneutics that has Pentecost as its exemplary moment better understands the original text—both in its original meaning and present meaningfulness—than could a single vantage point:

> Welcoming a multicultural range of perspectives to the table checks biases far better than welcoming only a single perspective, but the ideal is that, once at the table, dialogue can help all of us to hear more clearly not simply ourselves or even (more helpfully) one another but the biblical text and how it speaks to our various situations. (85)

Keener holds the interpreter accountable to the text's origination, linking the text to its origination while eschewing the concept that a singular contemporary articulation of its meaning functions as the properly correct one for all. This does not, however, relativize original meaning.

Key to Keener's approach is the affirmation that biblical texts all communicate to us today through ancient voices, so that we can hear the texts as Scripture only as much as we hold to their originality. It is thus the hermeneutic responsibility of the interpreter to regard the text in its originality, and the originality of any text cannot be had without context and historicity. At the heart of Keener's theological-hermeneutical approach is the central conviction that "it is when we hear most clearly what the biblical writers communicated, often forcefully, to their own generations that we can hear most clearly what these texts speak to us in our very different contexts" (126). This then implies that "modern contextual readings that are most faithful to that original sense as their foundation will have the greatest common ground ability to dialogue with other contextual readings" (126–27). That is, "Culture makes a difference on both ends of interpretation: understanding the ancient context and relating to the interpreter's context" (127). This means that "appropriate application is generally indigenous, and is varied as the contexts to which the principles are meant to be applied. One cannot produce *universal* application except in a generalized and usually obvious form" (247).

Though Keener especially engages the matter of authorial intention through the oft discussed work of E. D. Hirsch Jr., and the debate around the discovery of authorial intention as textual meaning, among philosophical hermeneutic theorists Keener's hermeneutic might come closer to that of the philosopher Jürgen Habermas's consideration of texts as communicative actions, and even closer to his fellow Christian theologian Kevin Vanhoozer's revision of Hirsch and resourcing of Habermas. Habermas and Vanhoozer, and Keener here, avoid the Romantic hermeneutic consideration of authorial intention as psychological knowledge of the author in consonance with the interpreter's own psychology. The notions of intention as known only through communicative action follows a more chastened approach that avoids a psychological mysticism of sorts—though Keener, of course, has no problem with attending to realities that go beyond what normally goes by the empirical.[15]

Yet, the pneumatic-experiential is not license to ignore history. Keener the historian considers authorial intention as "not fully recoverable," but "this limitation does not prevent us from examining the text's design and inferring from such strategies relevant aspects of the text's *implied* author's interests. The approximation is imperfect but usually sufficient for communication to work" (140).[16] While Keener implies openness to the HIrschian distinction between 'meaning' as original textual meaning and 'significance' or 'application' as reserved for subsequent use of the original meaning, he is less concerned with oft-debated 'semantics.' Rather, the originality of the text gravitates meaning; yet—and there is a special sense for which this is true in Scripture—it does not entirely limit meaning. Keener clarifies his understanding:

---

15. Key works here for each would be Habermas, *Moral Consciousness and Communicative Action*; Vanhoozer, *Is There a Meaning in This Text?*

16. A common related objection to 'meaning' as the discovery of authorial intention is whether authors really even 'intend' in any strict rational sense, that is, whether authors even know their own motives with clarity. The inspiration of Scripture raises further complexities for this issue.

Of course, we cannot perfectly reconstruct the original meaning. We have access neither to everything authors thought nor to the full original contexts that they assumed their ideal audiences shared, the information needed to fill lacunae in secondary communication. But whatever else a biblical text might mean, it usually means *at least* what it meant to the inspired author, who understood his own language, idioms, and cultural allusions better than we do. Offering historical reconstructions as responsibly as possible (given the limits of the evidence and our own horizons) is a reasonable objective that need not be discounted simply because it cannot be perfectly achieved. (141)

Still, the turn to communicative actions seeks to enter the hermeneutical circle through priority given to the communicative actions of the author rather than the presumed psychological consonance with the same. Then there are the situations in which texts are layered in composition by the work of multiple persons, in edits and editions.

Of course, there is some presumed consonance about meaning and understanding, or no communication could ever take place. That is part of the importance of Schleiermacher's psychological emphasis, while the critique of Schleiermacher and Romantic hermeneutics has been that this all goes too far, and that the focus on texts as communicative action chastens interpreters from overinterpreting the psychology of others in presumptuous projectionism. In the matter of interpretation of Scripture, there are of course additional issues, especially the matter of divine authorship. Those who focus on communicative actions of authors, however, look to the givenness of the texts to speak correctively to the interpreter's understanding. The texts correct the interpreter as to the implied intent involved in the composition, for Keener here its 'design.' So, if the interpreter's goal is to understand what is communicated, the interpreter must give precedence to the communication itself. Of course, there is much to say, then, about literary devices in communication, from jokes and sarcasm to communication under duress as well as varieties of genres and literary forms. These, however, only further illustrate how important context is, and for Keener all good interpretation attends to context.

Keener's estimation of the reality of the original text may be the critical point at which he breaks with the great hermeneutic theorist Hangs-Georg Gadamer, whose famous statement that "writing is self-alienation" in his great masterwork *Truth and Method* detached the relationship between authorship and the otherness of texts.[17] While Gadamer accounted for the

17. Gadamer, *Truth and Method*.

becoming of being (following Heidegger's *Dasein*, or 'being there') as necessitating that we only experience a text through its history of effect, and
that only through our own 'historically effected consciousness' (*wirkungsge-
schichtliches Bewusstsein*) in a 'fusion of horizons' (*Horizontverschmelzung*),
Keener operates with a different albeit tact view of history and its relationship to texts, here biblical texts, and their meaning. In an approach to history that affirms memory of the past as guiding our understanding for the
future, like the memory of God's salvific action in the Exodus informing
subsequent Israelite history, the biblical texts have a past that is not merely
the becoming of their being into the present. There seems to be a greater ontic existence to the past for Keener than in Gadamerian hermeneutics—that
past is *there*, communicated in and through presently experienced texts and
able to be differentiated from its history of effect. The Aristotelian definition of truth is put in a past tense so that "to say of what was not, that it
was, or of what was, that it was not, is false; while to say of what was that it
was, or what was not that it was not, is true." Keener operates with a theory
of correspondence between truth and the past—hermeneutically, and with
attention to context and semantic range, of course, but nevertheless. Still,
these past events of revelation come to us in and through the biblical texts
as part of the work of the Spirit in calling humanity to salvation and God's
eschatological purposes. We are joined to the original texts by the Spirit
who spoke in and through them then and is doing so now.

Keener holds a high regard for intention or, as part 3 of *Spirit Hermeneutics* uses in the title, the 'designed sense,' in this chastened sense of
understanding intention. Against detachment of the text from its original
history, however, Keener contends, on the grounds of a theological conclusion, that "the incarnation would show us that history and historical particularity matter" (99). Yet, whose design?

Throughout, the implication seems to be that it is the dual design of
human biblical authors and the revelatory Spirit, that the human authors
have their intentions with the biblical texts, and that the Spirit brings these
and a surplus of divine intention to bear upon them as well. The extended
implications of this approach are manifold for particular cases in Scripture,
and Keener provides plenty of examples throughout. The importance of
seeking the design of a text has practical implications for the goals of biblical hermeneutics. Keener's hammer illustration exemplifies this. A hammer,
Keener points out, can be employed

> as a weapon, a doorstop, or a prop, but the specific design of
> the handle, face, and claws fit its designed function in pounding
> in and removing nails. The goals for which texts were designed

point us toward these uses for which they will usually be most relevant. We cannot infallibly recover an author's thought processes; we can, however, seek to recognize the "implied author's" design in the text. (100)

Further, Keener considers that canonical texts are 'measuring sticks' and not texts to be exploited for ideological agendas. The main reason so much effort has been spent on Scripture is that Christians hold it to be God's chosen medium for divine disclosure to us. Therefore, Keener is also concerned to deny a variety of readings of Scripture that seek to use Scripture in what that run contrary to its implied design rather than resourcing its messages anew—from political-ideological readings to "preachers . . . more committed to evoking particular audience responses than to hearing God's message in the text" (102). Keener is an advocate for a legitimate pluralism of readings and perspectives over and against *both* singular articulations that claim full sufficiency *and* irresponsible readings that seek to (ab)use the authority of the biblical texts instead of honoring it. Part 4, the final part, of *Spirit Hermeneutics* play this out in more detail as it addresses some popular and theoretical examples in the contemporary charismatic-pentecostal world, and it includes some takeaways for those more interested in the practical-theological implications of his hermeneutic.

Developing Keener's Hermeneutical Paradigm

Where might charismatic-pentecostal hermeneutics go from here? How might others in the tradition pick up on Keener's paradigm and further it? What are other related issues to address, beyond the many that Keener has in *Spirit Hermeneutics*? Here, I would suggest a few areas for hermeneutical development around this magnificent and carefully constructed tome. To employ a metaphor of this hermeneutical work as a monumental building—how might we also develop or revitalize the pentecostal hermeneutical neighborhood surrounding it?

First, Keener advocates reading experientially, though he focuses on the original contextualized biblical texts, where his own work has functioned as a gift to he scholarly community and the church. For Keener, historical understanding of both the original context and ourselves is now essential. Even as Keener develops an 'epistemology of Word and Spirit' (153–204) that develops his anti-Enlightenment hermeneutical ontological realism, he heavily employs western scholarly historiographical methods and the traditional western correspondence theory of truth. He works with a version of western historiography that rejects the dismissal of the supernatural, yet he not only retains but exemplifies excellence in history as a discipline, including the affirmation of honesty about evident that emerges in contrast to the historian's own prejudices. Yet, Keener argues that this kind of concern for understanding historicity, context, and a text's origination is not essentially modern. Rather, these are concerns found among the ancients, including much of Greco-Roman literature, rabbinic Judaism, and patristic and medieval Christianity. The Reformers, deeply influenced by humanism's *ad fontes*, esteemed the primacy of the historical and grammatical sense about the medieval 'four senses' (119–32). Still, Keener's historical approach has been shaped by modern western historiography, for her is a western scholar and a contemporary biblical historian par excellence, even as his approach to history represents and enlarging and opening of this paradigm in a way that incorporates a Christian ontology and 'majority world insights' to craft a historiographical approach that affirms the realities testified to in Scripture, thereby completing the hermeneutical circle-spiral (88–98).

This paradigm might seem comprehensive enough. But what of those in the Body of Christ whose gifts are to relate scriptural meaning that goes further, focusing on the effects of the text's meaning in the present in more philosophical or existential or theological readings? What of, for example, Barth's *Römerbrief* as a hermeneutic in comparison and as a companion to Keener's commentary on Romans? Would this then lead down a slippery slope right back to ideological and naïve or manipulative interpretations of Scripture?

I see Keener's work as at least implying a rejoinder here. That is, the very grain of Scripture, incarnationally embedded in historical context, is productive of and corrective to theological understanding. His hermeneutic affirms that Scripture is giving out spiritual-theological, perhaps even certain philosophical-existential understanding, in a historical-ontic realism provided by the text's inspired nature. In this sense, it might be said that Scripture operates as a communicative grace, as a relational gift of God. For instance, when Keener addresses Bultmann's approach to Scripture as in many ways deeply flawed, he sees Bultmann's existential hearing from God in Scripture as nevertheless a positive, as a way of hearing from the text primarily rather than getting stuck in technical or secondary questions, even historical ones (125). There are many ways forward here for a Keenerian charismatic-pentecostal hermeneut (better, I would say, than looking to anything from Bultmann), whether the Barthian approach that hears the Word of God in encounter with Scripture, the philosophical hermeneutic of George Steiner's 'real presences,' a pentecostal personalism that draws from Martin Buber's 'I-Thou' in encounter with the Absolute Thou, or Lee Roy Martin's 'hearing' of the text. There are ways to develop a theology of encounter that becomes constructive or systematic theology or even a Christian philosophy that is held within the orbit of the gravitational pull of the historical biblical text found in Keener's hermeneutics.

Second, others will want to revisit the attention to the second horizon, that of the present interpreters, for further development. This is where the focus and work of some, like Ken Archer, has gone, on interpretive communities. Keener addresses them in his final, brief chapter (277–85). Yet, the formation of this horizon is a matter of great attention for contemporary hermeneutics. Consideration of the contemporary interpreters and their purview of interpretation has often dominated the contemporary conversation, and Keener's work may be seen as corrective to just that. On the other hand, studies of how particular biblical interpretations are happening as matters of present culture, language, human nature, and so on are important to our self-understanding, as Keener himself advocates. While Archer has focused on how narratives shape meaning for modern pentecostal communities, Mark Cartledge has studied pentecostal hermeneutics in practice through empirical studies. Others have examined philosophical or cultural assumptions of present interpreters. Just because the narratives and cultural histories that inform the second horizon are not Keener's focus does not mean that the pentecostal hermeneutical neighborhood does not need responsible reconstructions of our present horizons. What we take to be the original horizon is itself informed by the horizons of our contemporary situations, shaped by multiple sources, hopefully including the biblical text and its history of interpretation.

Third, it is important to identify that the above and other issues blend the prescriptive and the descriptive together. This blending of prescriptive and descriptive is inevitable in our biblical hermeneutics, often occurring moment by moment as interpreters work with Scripture. Yet, all of this also demonstrates the need for philosophical clarity, as, for example in Pol Vandevelde's distinction between the *act* and *event* of interpretation.[18] I applied this key philosophical distinction in *Theological Hermeneutics in the Classical Pentecostal Tradition* as helpful for analyzing contemporary theological hermeneutics. Vandevelde contends that hermeneutic camps tend to talk past one another because some tend to focus on hermeneutics as *acts* for which we are responsible, such as in Hirsch, while others focus on hermeneutics as *events* that we describe, as in Gadamer. The former operates with a primarily prescriptive orientation and the latter primarily descriptive. The task of hermeneutical theory is to account for both. The need for making such a distinction is critical to hermeneutical self-understanding,

18. Vandevelde, *The Task of the Interpreter*.

and failing to understand it leads to confusion even if we understand the distinction implicitly, as commonly occurs. This is analogous to, say, an athlete or musician who can adjust a technique because s/he is aware of the process. It is not that a Keenerian hermeneutic always needs to stop and identify its descriptive or prescriptive posture; it is to say that it is occasionally very helpful.

Fourth, the relationship between Keener's Christian approach to knowledge and history, on the one hand, and modernism on the other is an important underlying matter for his hermeneutic. As I have indicated earlier in this essay, Keener, along with other Christians, including charismatic-pentecostal Christians, finds the typical epistemic approach in the academic world reductionistic, often wrongly closed to examining what should be open questions about spiritual realities. Perhaps this is less the case today than it was a generation ago. A multitude of discussions of modern and postmodern or late modern epistemologies and cultures have addressed this issue.

Here, however, I find Keener's postmaterialism notable. His hermeneutic includes an open epistemology, in the sense that it is open to 'majority world insights' about spiritual realities over and against western Enlightenment materialisms. Yet, I find that his postmaterialism and his partial postmodernism have some further implications, one of which I find particularly important: Keener breaks with the modernist package against the modern principle of novelty as inherently good, by reverting not to any kind of traditional authoritarianism or conservatism but to faith in the God of Pentecost. Or, employing the notion of the great historian and philosopher of modernism Peter Gay, Keener breaks with the modern affinity for 'heresy.' Keener is a heretic to the modern affirmation of 'heresy'—"absolute artistic autonomy, all guidance emerging solely from within . . . [the] assertion of personal sovereignty"[19]—breaking from the atheistic and autonomous stance of his youth toward an attitude of faithfulness to the text and the Lord and the many tongues of God's pentecostal people.

This may lead to a fifth hermeneutical issue for the pentecostal neighborhood. A theology of culture, or better, a theological hermeneutics of culture is a necessary complement to Keener's biblical hermeneutics, even if he has an implicit theological hermeneutics of culture working in *Spirit Hermeneutics*. And perhaps this is a broader and more general point that would be true of almost any text that develops a scriptural hermeneutic: it ought to have a hermeneutics of culture as a companion to it. This is not to call Keener to write another book. It is to say that charismatic-pentecostal

19. Gay, *Modernism*, 4.

hermeneutics needs to develop cultural theological hermeneutics as companions to *Spirit Hermeneutics*. The need for this kind of development is exactly what Duane Loynes illustrated in his essay "Pentecostal Hermeneutics and Race in the Early Twentieth Century," when he identified how the lack of a theological hermeneutic of culture failed to accompany the developing biblical and spiritual hermeneutics of the early movement and could be considered an important factor in why early pentecostal racial reconciliation failed after some initial success.[20]

Sixth, against poor popular hermeneutics in the charismatic-pentecostal world, Keener's work here may serve as an extended hermeneutical catechism for many. *Spirit Hermeneutics* offers the kind of hermeneutical wisdom and breadth that is helpful for educated Christians in ministry. It makes for a rich seminary text. Still, like many skyscrapers, other useful buildings are needed in the neighborhood, and texts—say, a Keenerian hermeneutical primer for undergraduates or the layperson—might provide needed hermeneutical goods and services. Following Keener's basic hermeneutical parameters and insight would do so much good on the popular level for the way Charismatic-Pentecostals understand Scripture and life.

Seventh, and finally, Spirit hermeneutics is essentially a hermeneutic of the Spirit and power, of faith and hope and love in the triune God. As such, the practice of this kind of hermeneutics moves in opposition to the 'works of the flesh' and the exertion of power on behalf of self-seeking ideologies and destructive movements in the world. Spirit hermeneutics occur on behalf of the good and creative agencies that are aligned with the Spirit of God's purposes for the world. That this is the stance of a Christian hermeneutic might be taken for granted. In practice, that a Spirit hermeneutics is about love of God and love of neighbor is, in its moral essence, its key activity, and this is the area for which this hermeneutic will likely face the most opposition as those who follow Keener's hermeneutic program seek to implement it. It is built upon a strong foundation.

---

20. Loynes, "Pentecostal Hermeneutics."

Bibliography

Alexander, Estrelda Y. *Black Fire: One Hundred Years of African American Pentecostalism.* Downers Grove, IL: IVP Academic, 2011.

Anderson, Allan H. *An Introduction to Pentecostalism: Global Charismatic Christianity.* 2nd ed. Cambridge: Cambridge University Press, 2014.

———. *To the Ends of the Earth: Pentecostalism and the Transformation of World Christianity.* Oxford: Oxford University Press, 2013.

Anderson, Gordon L. "Pentecostal Hermeneutics: Part I." *Paraclete* 28 (1994) 1–11.

———. "Pentecostal Hermeneutics: Part II." *Paraclete* 28 (1994) 13–22.

Anderson, Robert Mapes. *Vision of the Disinherited: The Making of American Pentecostalism.* New York: Oxford University Press, 1979.

"Annual Statistics." https://www.gordonconwell.edu/center-for-global-christianity/resources/status-of-global-christianity/.

Aquinas, Thomas. *Commentary on Aristotle's Posterior Analytics.* Translated by Richard Berquist. South Bend, IN: St. Augustine's, 2008.

———. *Summa Theologiae: Latin Text and English Translation, Introductions, Notes, Appendices, and Glossaries.* Translated and edited by Blackfriars. New York: McGraw-Hill, 1964–81.

Archer, Kenneth J. *A Pentecostal Hermeneutic for the Twenty-First Century: Spirit, Scripture, and Community.* Journal of Pentecostal Theology Supplement 28. London: T. & T. Clark, 2004.

———. "Pentecostal Story: The Hermeneutical Filter for the Making of Meaning." *Pneuma* 26 (2004) 26–59.

———. "A Pentecostal Way of Doing Theology: Method and Manner." *International Journal of Systematic Theology* 9 (2007) 301–14.

Archer, Kenneth J., and L. William Oliverio Jr. eds. *Constructive Pneumatological Hermeneutics in Pentecostal Christianity.* Christianity and Renewal Interdisciplinary Studies. New York: Palgrave Macmillan, 2016.

Archer, Melissa L. *'I Was in the Spirit on the Lord's Day': A Pentecostal Engagement with Worship in the Apocalypse.* Cleveland, TN: Center for Pentecostal Theology, 2015.

Arrington, French L. "Hermeneutics." In *Dictionary of Pentecostal and Charismatic Movements,* edited by Stanley M. Burgess and Gary B. McGee, 376–89. Grand Rapids: Zondervan, 1988.

Azusa Street Mission. "Beginning of the World Wide Revival." *The Apostolic Faith,* January, 1907.

———. "The Elder Brother." *The Apostolic Faith,* October, 1906.

———. "The Pentecostal Baptism Restored." *The Apostolic Faith,* October, 1906.

Balthasar, Hans Urs von. *Truth Is Symphonic: Aspects of Christian Pluralism*. San Francisco: Ignatius, 1987.

Barth, Karl. *Church Dogmatics*. Translated by G. T. Thomson. Edinburgh: T. & T. Clark, 1936.

Bartholomew, Craig. "Biblical Theology." In *Dictionary for Theological Interpretation of the Bible*, edited by Kevin J. Vanhoozer, 84–90. Grand Rapids: Baker Academic, 2005.

Bartleman, Frank. *Another Wave Rolls In! What Really Happened at Azusa Street*. Monroeville, PA: Whitaker, 1970.

Berger, Peter L. *The Heretical Imperative*. New York: Anchor Doubleday, 1979.

Berlin, Isaiah. *The Hedgehog and the Fox: An Essay on Tolstoy's View of History*. New York: Mentor, 1957.

Blankenhorn, Berhard. "The Metaphysics of Charisms: Thomas Aquinas, Biblical Exegesis, and Pentecostal Theology." *Angelicum* 91 (2014) 373–424.

Blumhofer, Edith Waldvogel. *The Assemblies of God: A Chapter in the Story of American Pentecostalism*. Vol. 2. Springfield, MO: Gospel Publishing House, 1989.

———. *Restoring the Faith: The Assemblies of God, Pentecostalism, and American Culture*. Urbana: University of Illinois Press, 1993.

Brown, Raymond E. "Hermeneutics." In *The Jerome Biblical Commentary*, edited by Raymond E. Brown et al., 605–23. Vol. 2. Englewood Cliffs, NJ: Prentice-Hall, 1968.

Brown, Robert E. *Jonathan Edwards and the Bible*. Bloomington: Indiana University Press, 2002.

Brunner, Emil. *The Christian Doctrine of God*. Philadelphia: Westminster, 1949.

Byrd, Joseph. "Paul Ricoeur's Hermeneutic Theory and Pentecostal Proclamation." *Pneuma* 15 (1993) 203–14.

Camery-Hoggat, Jerry. *Reading the Good Book Well: A Guide to Biblical Interpretation*. Nashville: Abingdon, 2007.

Cargal, Timothy. "Beyond the Fundamentalist-Modernist Controversy: Pentecostals and Hermeneutics in a Postmodern Age." *Pneuma* 15 (1993) 163–87.

Cartledge, Mark. "Renewal Ecclesiology in Empirical Perspective." *Pneuma* 36 (2014) 5–24.

Chan, Simon. *Liturgical Theology: The Church as Worshipping Community*. Downers Grove, IL: InterVarsity, 2006.

———. "Mother Church: Towards a Pentecostal Ecclesiology." *Pneuma* 22 (2000) 177–208.

———. *Pentecostal Ecclesiology: An Essay on the Development of Doctrine*. Journal of Pentecostal Theology Supplement 38. Blandford Forum, UK: Deo, 2011.

———. *Pentecostal Theology and the Christian Spiritual Tradition*. Sheffield: Sheffield Academic Press, 2000.

———. *Spiritual Theology: A Systematic Study of the Christian Life*. Downers Grove, IL: InterVarsity, 1998.

Cherry, Conrad. "Symbols of Spiritual Truth: Jonathan Edwards as Biblical Interpreter." *Interpretation* 39 (1985) 263–71.

Clemmons, Ithiel C. *Bishop C. H. Mason and the Roots of the Church of God in Christ*. Bakersfield, CA: Pneuma Life, 1996.

Coffey, David. *Deus Trinitas: The Doctrine of the Triune God*. New York: Oxford University Press, 1999.

————. "The Whole Rahner on the Supernatural Existential." *Theological Studies* 65 (2004) 95–118.

Congar, Yves. *I Believe in the Holy Spirit.* Translated by David Smith. 3 vols. New York: Crossroad Herder, 1979–80.

Cox, Harvey. *Fire from Heaven: The Rise of Pentecostal Spirituality and the Reshaping of Religion in the Twenty-First Century.* Cambridge: Da Capo, 2001.

Cross, Terry. "The Rich Feast of Theology: Can Pentecostals Bring the Main Course or Only the Relish?" *Journal of Pentecostal Theology* 16 (2000) 27–47.

Cunningham, David S. *These Three Are One: The Practice of Trinitarian Theology.* Malden, MA: Blackwell, 1998.

Dabney, D. Lyle. "Saul's Armor: The Problem and Promise of Pentecostal Theology Today." *Pneuma* 23 (2001) 115–46.

Daniels, David D., III. "God Makes No Difference in Nationality: The Fashioning of a New Racial/Nonracial Identity at the Azusa Street Revival." *Enrichment* 11 (2006) 72–76.

Davies, Andrew. "What Does It Mean to Read the Bible as a Pentecostal?" *Journal of Pentecostal Theology* 18 (2009) 216–29.

Dayton, Donald. *Theological Roots of Pentecostalism.* Metuchen, NJ: Scarecrow, 1987.

Dempster, Murray W. "Paradigm Shifts and Hermeneutics: Confronting Issues Old and New." *Pneuma* 15 (1993) 129–35.

Deppe, Dean. "Comparing *Spirit Hermeneutics* by Craig Keener with Classical Pentecostal Hermeneutics." *Calvin Theological Journal* 52 (2017) 265–76.

Derrida, Jacques. *Of Grammatology.* Translated by G. C. Spirak. Baltimore: Johns Hopkins University Press, 1975.

Dreyfus, Hubert, and Charles Taylor. *Retrieving Realism.* Cambridge: Harvard University Press, 2015.

Dupré, Louis. *Passage to Modernity: An Essay in the Hermeneutics of Nature and Culture.* New Haven: Yale University Press, 1993.

Edwards, Jonathan. "A Divine and Supernatural Light." In *Works of Jonathan Edwards* 17, edited by Mark Valeri, 408–26. New Haven: Yale University Press.

————. *Freedom of the Will.* In *Works of Jonathan Edwards* 1, edited by Paul Ramsey. New Haven: Yale University Press.

————. *The Great Awakening.* In *Works of Jonathan Edwards* 4, edited by C. C. Goen. New Haven: Yale University Press.

————. "Harmony of the Scriptures." In *Works of Jonathan Edwards* 29, edited by Jonathan Edwards Center. New Haven: Yale University Press.

————. "History of Redemption" *Notebooks.* In *Works of Jonathan Edwards* 31, edited by Jonathan Edwards Center. New Haven: Yale University Press.

————. "Images of Divine Things." In *Works of Jonathan Edwards* 11, edited by Wallace E. Anderson et al., 51–143. New Haven: Yale University Press.

————. "Of Insects." In *Works of Jonathan Edwards* 6, edited by Wallace E. Anderson, 154–63. New Haven: Yale University Press.

————. *Original Sin.* In *Works of Jonathan Edwards* 3, edited by Clyde A. Holbrook. New Haven: Yale University Press.

————. *Religious Affections.* In *Works of Jonathan Edwards* 2, edited by Paul Ramsey. New Haven: Yale University Press.

————. "Resolutions." In *Works of Jonathan Edwards* 16, edited by George S. Claghorn, 753–59. New Haven: Yale University Press.

Ervin, Howard M. "Hermeneutics: A Pentecostal Option." *Pneuma* 3 (1984) 11–25.

Faupel, D. William. "Whither Pentecostalism? 22nd Presidential Address of the Society for Pentecostal Studies, November 7, 1992." *Pneuma* 15 (1993) 9–27.

Feuerbach, Ludwig. *The Essence of Christianity*. Translated by George Eliot. New York: Harper, 1957.

Frankel, David, dir. *The Devil Wears Prada*. Fox 2000 Pictures, 2006.

Frestadius, Simo. *Pentecostal Rationality: Epistemology and Theological Hermeneutics in the Foursquare Tradition*. T. & T. Clark Systematic Pentecostal and Charismatic Theology. London: T. & T. Clark, 2020.

Gadamer, Hans-Goerg. *Truth and Method*. 2nd rev. ed. Translated by Joel Weinsheimer and Donald G. Marshall. New York: Continuum, 2002.

Gay, Peter. *Modernism: The Lure of Heresy, from Baudelaire to Beckett and Beyond*. New York: Norton, 2008.

General Council of the Assemblies of God. "Minutes of the General Council of the Assemblies of God in the United States of America, Canada, and Foreign Lands." Bethel Chapel, St. Louis, Missouri, October 1–7, 1916.

Green, Chris E. W. *Sanctifying Interpretation: Vocation, Holiness, and Scripture*. Cleveland, TN: Center for Pentecostal Theology, 2015.

———. *Towards a Pentecostal Theology of the Lord's Supper: Foretasting the Kingdom*. Cleveland, TN: Center for Pentecostal Theology, 2012.

Green, Joel B. "What You See Depends on What You Are Looking For: Jesus's Ascension as a Test Case for Thinking about Biblical Theology and Theological Interpretation of Scripture." *Interpretation* 70 (2016) 445–57.

Grenz, Stanley J. *Renewing the Center: Evangelical Theology in a Post-Theological Era*. 2nd ed. Grand Rapids: Baker Academic, 2006.

Grenz, Stanley J., and John R. Franke. *Beyond Foundationalism: Shaping Theology in a Postmodern Context*. Louisville: Westminster John Knox, 2001.

Grenz, Stanley J., and Roger E. Olson. *20th Century Theology: God and the World in a Transitional Age*. Downers Grove, IL: InterVarsity, 1992.

Habermas, Jürgen. *Moral Consciousness and Communicative Action*. Translated by Christian Lenhardt and Shierry Weber Nicholsen. Cambridge: MIT Press, 1990.

Heidegger, Martin. *Being and Time: A Translation of "Sein und Zeit."* Translated by Joan Stambaugh. Albany, NY: State University of New York Press, 1996.

Hirsch, E. D., Jr. *The Aims of Interpretation*. Chicago: University of Chicago Press, 1976.

———. *Validity in Interpretation*. New Haven: Yale University Press, 1967.

Hocken, Peter. "The Meaning and Purpose of 'Baptism in the Spirit.'" *Pneuma* 7 (1985) 125–34.

Holifield, E. Brooks. *Theology in America: Christian Thought from the Age of the Puritans to the Civil War*. New Haven: Yale University Press, 2003.

Hollenweger, Walter. *Pentecostalism: Origins and Developments Worldwide*. Peabody, MA: Hendrickson, 1997.

Horkheimer, Max, and Theodor W. Adorno. *The Dialectic of Enlightenment*. Translated by John Cumming. New York: Herder and Herder, 1972.

Horton, Stanley. *What the Bible Says about the Holy Spirit*. Springfield, MO: Gospel Publishing House, 1976.

Hunter, James Davison. *Culture Wars: The Struggle to Define America*. New York: Basic, 1991.

—————. *To Change the World: The Irony, Tragedy, and Possibility of Christianity in the Late Modern World.* Oxford: Oxford University Press, 2010.

Huyssteen, J. Wentzel van. *Essays in Postfoundationalist Theology.* Grand Rapids: Eerdmans, 1997.

International Roman Catholic-Pentecostal Dialogue. "Final Report: Perspectives on *Koinonia* (1985–89)." *Pneuma* 12 (1990) 97–142.

Irvin, Dale T. "'Drawing All Together in One Bond of Love': The Ecumenical Vision of William J. Seymour and the Azusa Street Revival." *Journal of Pentecostal Theology* 3 (1995) 25–53.

Israel, Richard D., et al. "Pentecostals and Hermeneutics: Texts, Rituals and Community." *Pneuma* 15 (1993) 137–61.

Jacobsen, Douglas. "Global Christianity: Pentecostalism. *YouTube,* November 28, 2013. https://www.youtube.com/watch?v=-TxnfOxeIjg.

—————. *Global Gospel: An Introduction to Christianity on Five Continents.* Grand Rapids: Baker Academic, 2015.

—————. "Knowing the Doctrines of Pentecostals: The Scholastic Theology of the Assemblies of God, 1930–1955." In *Pentecostal Currents in American Protestantism,* edited by Edith L. Blumhofer et al., 90–107. Urbana: University of Illinois Press, 1999.

—————. *Thinking in the Spirit: Theologies of the Early Pentecostal Movement.* Bloomington: Indiana University Press, 2003.

—————. *The World's Christians: Who They Are, Where They Are, and How They Got There.* Malden, MA: Wiley-Blackwell, 2011.

—————. *The World's Christians: Who They Are, Where They Are, and How They Got There.* 2nd ed. Hoboken, NJ: Wiley-Blackwell, 2021.

Jeanrod, Werner. *Theological Hermeneutics: Development and Significance.* New York: Crossroad, 1991.

Johns, Cheryl Bridges. "The Adolescence of Pentecostalism: In Search of a Legitimate Sectarian Identity." *Pneuma* 17 (1995) 3–17.

—————. *Pentecostal Formation: A Pedagogy among the Oppressed.* Journal of Pentecostal Theology Supplement 2. Sheffield: Sheffield Academic Press, 1993.

Johnson, Todd, and Gina A. Zurlo. *The World Christian Encyclopedia.* 3rd ed. Edinburgh: Edinburgh University Press, 2020.

Jordan, Mark D. "Theology and Philosophy." In *The Cambridge Companion to Aquinas,* edited by Norman Kretzmann and Eleonore Stump, 233–36. New York: Cambridge University Press, 1993.

Kahneman, Daniel. "A Perspective on Judgment and Choice: Mapping Bounded Rationality." *American Psychologist* 58 (2003) 697–720.

—————. *Thinking: Fast and Slow.* New York: Farrar, Straus, and Giroux, 2011.

Kärkkäinen, Veli-Matti. *An Introduction to Ecclesiology: Ecumenical, Historical, and Global Perspectives.* Downers Grove, IL: InterVarsity, 2002.

Keener, Craig, ed. *InterVarsity Press Bible Background Commentary: New Testament.* Downers Grove, IL: InterVarsity, 2014.

—————. *Spirit Hermeneutics: Reading Scripture in Light of Pentecost.* Grand Rapids: Eerdmans, 2016.

Kerr, Daniel Warren. "Facts on Fire." *The Pentecostal Evangel,* April, 1925.

—————. "Spontaneous Theology." *The Weekly Evangel,* April 17, 1915.

—————. *Waters in the Desert.* Springfield, MO: Gospel Publishing House, 1925.

Kerr, Fergus. *Thomas Aquinas: A Very Short Introduction*. Oxford: Oxford University Press, 2009.

King, James G., Jr. "Thomas Aquinas and Prophecy." *Pneuma* 1 (1979) 50–58.

Kuhn, Thomas S. "Objectivity, Value Judgment, and Theory Choice." In *Introductory Readings in the Philosophy of Science*, edited by E. D. Klemke et al., 435–50. 3rd ed. Amherst, NY: Prometheus, 1998.

———. *The Structure of Scientific Revolutions*. 3rd ed. Chicago: University of Chicago Press, 1996.

Lakatos, Imre. *The Methodology of Scientific Research Programmes: Philosophical Papers, Volume 1*. Edited by John Worrall and Gregory Curie. Cambridge: Cambridge University Press, 1978.

Land, Steven J. *Pentecostal Spirituality: A Passion for the Kingdom*. Journal of Pentecostal Theology Supplement 1. Sheffield: Sheffield Academic Press, 1993.

Lindbeck, George A. *The Nature of Doctrine: Religion and Theology in a Postliberal Age*. Philadelphia: Westminster, 1984.

Lonergan, Bernard. *Method in Theology*. New York: Herder and Herder, 1972.

Long, D. Stephen. *Speaking of God: Theology, Language, and Truth*. Grand Rapids: Eerdmans, 2009.

———. *Theology and Culture: A Guide to the Discussion*. Eugene, OR: Cascade, 2008.

Loynes, Duane T., Sr. "Pentecostal Hermeneutics and Race in the Early Twentieth Century: Towards a Pentecostal Hermeneutics of Culture." In *Constructive Pneumatological Hermeneutics in Pentecostal Christianity*, edited by Kenneth J. Archer and L. William Oliverio Jr., 229–48. New York: Palgrave Macmillan, 2016.

Lyotard, Jean-François. *The Postmodern Condition: A Report on Knowledge*. Minneapolis: University of Minnesota Press, 1984.

Macchia, Frank. *Baptized in the Spirit: A Global Pentecostal Theology*. Grand Rapids: Zondervan, 2006.

———. *Justified in the Spirit: Creation, Redemption, and the Triune God*. Pentecostal Manifestos. Grand Rapids: Eerdmans, 2010.

———. "Sighs Too Deep for Words: Toward a Theology of *Glossolalia*." *Journal of Pentecostal Theology* 1 (1992) 47–73.

MacDonald, Scott. "Theory of Knowledge." In *The Cambridge Companion to Aquinas*, edited by Norman Kretzmann and Eleonore Stump, 160–63. New York: Cambridge University Press, 1993.

MacIntyre, Alasdair. *After Virtue*. 3rd ed. Notre Dame: University of Notre Dame Press, 2012.

———. *Whose Justice? Which Rationality?* London: Duckworth, 1988.

Margolis, Joseph. *Art and Philosophy*. Brighton: Harvester, 1980.

———. "Works of Art as Physically Embodied and Culturally Emergent Entities." *British Journal of Aesthetics* 14 (1974) 187–96.

Marsden, George. *Fundamentalism and American Culture*. New York: Oxford University Press, 2006.

———. *Jonathan Edwards: A Life*. New Haven: Yale University Press, 2003.

Martin, David. *A General Theory of Secularization*. Oxford: Blackwell, 1978.

———. *Pentecostalism: The World Their Parish*. Oxford: Blackwell, 2002.

———. *On Secularization: Towards a Revised General Theory*. Aldershot, UK: Ashgate, 2005.

———. *Tongues of Fire: The Explosion of Protestantism in Latin America*. Oxford: Blackwell, 1990.

Martin, Lee Roy. "Longing for God: Psalm 63 and Pentecostal Spirituality." *Journal of Pentecostal Theology* 22 (2013) 54–76.

———, ed. *Pentecostal Hermeneutics: A Reader*. Leiden: Brill, 2013.

———. *The Unheard Voice of God: A Pentecostal Hearing of the Book of Judges*. Blandford Forum, UK: Deo, 2008.

Mason, Mary, comp. *The History and Life Work of Elder C. H. Mason and His Co-Laborers*. Memphis, TN: Church of God in Christ, 1987.

McClymond, Michael J., and Gerald R. McDermott. *Theology of Jonathan Edwards*. New York: Oxford University Press, 2012.

McDermott, Gerald R. *Jonathan Edwards Confronts the Gods: Christian Theology, Enlightenment Religion, and Non-Christian Faiths*. New York: Oxford University Press, 2000.

McPherson, David, and Charles Taylor. "Re-Enchanting the World: An Interview with Charles Taylor." *Faith and Philosophy* 24 (2012) 275–94.

Menzies, Robert P. *Empowered for Witness: The Spirit in Luke-Acts*. Journal of Pentecostal Theology Supplement 6. Sheffield: Sheffield Academic Press, 1994.

———. "The Nature of Pentecostal Theology: A Response to Veli-Matti Kärkkäinen and Amos Yong." *Journal of Pentecostal Theology* 26 (2017) 196–213.

Menzies, William W. "The Methodology of Pentecostal Theology: An Essay on Hermeneutics." In *Essays on Apostolic Themes: Studies in Honor of Howard M. Ervin*, edited by Paul Elbert, 1–14. Peabody, MA: Hendrickson, 1985.

———. "The Non-Wesleyan Origins of the Pentecostal Movement." In *Aspects of Pentecostal-Charismatic Origins*, edited by Vinson Synan, 81–98. Plainfield, NJ: Logos International, 1975.

Meyering, Theo C. *Historical Roots of Cognitive Science*. Dordrecht: Kluwer, 1989.

Miller, Donald E., and Tetsunao Yamamori. *Global Pentecostalism: The New Face of Christian Social Engagement*. Berkeley: University of California Press, 2007.

Miller, Perry. *Jonathan Edwards*. American Men of Letters Series. New York: Sloane, 1949.

Moltmann, Jürgen. *The Trinity and the Kingdom: The Doctrine of God*. San Francisco: Harper and Row, 1981.

Murphy, Nancey. "Non-Reductive Physicalism: Philosophical Issues." In *Whatever Happened to the Soul? Scientific and Theological Portraits of Human Nature*, edited by Warren S. Brown et al., 127–48. Minneapolis: Fortress, 1998.

———. *A Philosophy of the Christian Religion*. Louisville: Westminster John Knox, 2018.

———. *Theology in the Age of Scientific Reasoning*. Ithaca, NY: Cornell University Press, 1990.

Murphy, Nancey, and Brad J. Kallenberg. "Anglo-American Postmodernity: A Theology of Communal Practice." In *Cambridge Companion to Postmodern Theology*, edited by Kevin J. Vanhoozer, 26–40. Cambridge: Cambridge University Press, 2003.

Newton, Jon K. *The Revelation Worldview: Thinking in a Postmodern World*. Eugene, OR: Wipf & Stock, 2015.

Nichols, David. R. "The Search for a Pentecostal Structure in Systematic Theology." *Pneuma* 6 (1984) 57–76.

Noel, Bradley Truman. *Pentecostal and Postmodern Hermeneutics: Comparisons and Contemporary Impact*. Eugene, OR: Wipf & Stock, 2010.

Noll, Mark. *The Scandal of the Evangelical Mind*. Grand Rapids: Eerdmans, 1994.

Oliverio, L. William, Jr. "Breaking Out of the Immanent Frame: A Review Essay of James K. A. Smith's *How (Not) to Be Secular: Reading Charles Taylor*." *The Pentecostal Educator* 2 (2015) 7–19.

———. "Contours of a Constructive Pentecostal Philosophical-Theological Hermeneutic." *Journal of Pentecostal Theology* 29 (2020) 35–55.

———. "An Interpretive Review Essay on Amos Yong's *Spirit-Word-Community: Theological Hermeneutics in Trinitarian Perspective*." *Journal of Pentecostal Theology* 18 (2009) 301–11.

———. "The Nature of Theology and Pentecostal Hermeneutics: On the Relationship Among Scripture, Experience of the Spirit, and Life in Spirit-Filled Community." In *Pentecostal Theology and Ecumenical Theology: Interpretations and Intersections*, edited by Peter Hocken et al., 157–79. Leiden: Brill, 2019.

———. "The One and the Many: The Theology of Amos Yong and the Dissolution and Pluralism of Late Modernity." In *The Theology of Amos Yong and the New Face of Pentecostal Scholarship*, edited by Wolfgang Vondey and Martin Mittelstadt, 45–61. Leiden: Brill, 2013.

———. "Pentecostal Hermeneutics and the Hermeneutical Tradition." In *Constructive Pneumatological Hermeneutics in Pentecostal Christianity*, edited by Kenneth J. Archer and L. William Oliverio Jr., 1–6. New York: Palgrave Macmillan, 2016.

———. "Reading Craig Keener: On *Spirit Hermeneutics: Reading Scripture in Light of Pentecost*." *Pneuma* 39 (2017) 126–45.

———. "Spirit Baptism in the Late Modern World: A Pentecostal Response to *The Church: Towards a Common Vision*." In *The Holy Spirit and the Church: Ecumenical Reflections with a Pastoral Perspective*, edited by Thomas Hughson, 44–70. London: Routledge, 2016.

———. "The Theological Hermeneutic of Amos Yong, in the Prime of His Theological Career." *Australasian Pentecostal Studies* 21 (2020) 4–28.

———. "Theological Hermeneutics: Understanding the World in Encounter with God." In *Routledge Handbook of Pentecostal Theology*, edited by Wolfgang Vondey, 140–51. London: Routledge 2020.

———. *Theological Hermeneutics in the Classical Pentecostal Tradition: A Typological Account*. Global Pentecostal and Charismatic Studies 12. Leiden: Brill, 2012.

———. "Toward a Hermeneutical Realism for Pentecostal Theological Hermeneutics." In *Theological Hermeneutics in the Classical Pentecostal Tradition: A Typological Account*, 315–54. Leiden: Brill 2012.

———. "'True Religion, in Great Part, Consists of Holy Affections': A Comparison of the Biblical Hermeneutics of Jonathan Edwards and Pentecostals." In *From Northampton to Azusa: Pentecostals and the Theology of Jonathan Edwards*, edited by Steven Studebaker and Amos Yong, 23–39. London: T. & T. Clark, 2020.

Olson, Roger E. "A Wind That Swirls Everywhere." *Christianity Today*, March 1, 2006. https://www.christianitytoday.com/ct/2006/march/38.52.html.

Osborne, Grant. *The Hermeneutical Spiral: A Comprehensive Introduction to Biblical Interpretation*. 2nd ed. Downers Grove, IL: InterVarsity, 2006.

Pannenberg, Wolfhart. *An Introduction to Systematic Theology*. Grand Rapids: Eerdmans, 1991.

Peirce, Charles Sanders. *Collected Papers of Charles Sanders Peirce, Volumes V and VI: Pragmatism and Pragmaticism and Scientific Metaphysics.* Edited by Charles Hartshorne and Paul Weiss. Cambridge: Harvard University Press, 1935.

Pew Forum on Religion and Public Life. "Spirit and Power—A 10-Country Survey of Pentecostals." *Pew Research Center,* October 5, 2006. https://www.pewforum.org/2006/10/05/spirit-and-power/.

Pinnock, Clark. *Flame of Love: A Theology of the Holy Spirit.* Downers Grove, IL: InterVarsity, 1996.

Plantinga, Alvin. *Warranted Christian Belief.* New York: Oxford University Press, 2000.

Plüss, Jean-Daniel. "Azusa and Other Myths: The Long and Winding Road from Experience to Stated Belief and Back Again." *Pneuma* 15 (1993) 189–201.

Polanyi, Michael. *Personal Knowledge: Towards a Post-Critical Philosophy.* Chicago: University of Chicago Press, 1962.

Porter, Stanley E., and Jason C. Robinson. *Hermeneutics: An Introduction to Interpretive Theory.* Grand Rapids: Eerdmans, 2011.

Rahner, Karl. *Foundations of Christian Faith: An Introduction to the Idea of Christianity.* Translated by William V. Dych. New York: Seabury, 1978.

Ramsey, Paul. "Editor's Introduction (*Religious Affections*)." In *Works of Jonathan Edwards* 2, edited by Paul Ramsey, 1–83. New Haven: Yale University Press, 2009.

Reid, Thomas. *An Inquiry into the Human Mind on the Principles of Common Sense.* Edited by Derek R. Brookes. Edinburgh: Edinburgh University Press, 1997.

Robeck, Cecil M., Jr. *The Azusa Street Mission and Revival: The Birth of the Global Pentecostal Movement.* Nashville: Nelson, 2006.

Rorty, Richard. *The Linguistic Turn: Recent Essays in Philosophical Method.* Chicago: University of Chicago Press, 1967.

Rose, Matthew. "Tayloring Christianity: Charles Taylor Is a Theologian of the Secular Status Quo." *First Things,* December, 2014. https://www.firstthings.com/article/2014/12/tayloring-christianity.

Saussure, Ferdinand de. *Course in General Linguistics.* Translated by Wade Baskin. New York: McGraw Hill, 1959.

Schleiermacher, Friedrich D. E. *Hermeneutics and Criticism and Other Writings.* Translated and edited by Andrew Bowie. Cambridge: Cambridge University Press, 1998.

Sheppard, Gerald T. "Pentecostals and the Hermeneutics of Dispensationalism: The Anatomy of an Uneasy Relationship." *Pneuma* 6 (1984) 5–34.

Shults, F. LeRon. *The Postfoundationalist Task of Theology: Wolfhart Pannenberg and the New Theological Rationality.* Grand Rapids: Eerdmans, 1999.

———. *Reforming Theological Anthropology: After the Philosophical Turn to Relationality.* Grand Rapids: Eerdmans, 2003.

Simmons, J. Aaron. "On Shared Hopes for (Mashup) Philosophy of Religion: A Reply to Trakakis." *Heythrop Journal* 55 (2014) 691–710.

Smith, James K. A. *Awaiting the King: Reforming Public Theology.* Cultural Liturgies Volume 3. Grand Rapids: Baker Academic, 2017.

———. *Desiring the Kingdom: Worship, Worldview, and Cultural Formation.* Cultural Liturgies Volume 1. Grand Rapids: Baker Academic, 2009.

———. "The Devil Reads Derrida: Fashion, French Philosophy, and Postmodernism." In *The Devil Reads Derrida: And Other Essays on the University, the Church, Politics, and the Arts,* 134–36. Grand Rapids: Eerdmans, 2009.

———. *The Fall of Interpretation: Philosophical Foundations for a Creational Hermeneutic.* Downers Grove, IL: InterVarsity, 2000.

———. *How (Not) to Be Secular: Reading Charles Taylor.* Grand Rapids: Eerdmans, 2014.

———. *Imagining the Kingdom: How Worship Works.* Cultural Liturgies Volume 2. Grand Rapids: Baker Academic, 2013.

———. "Scandalizing Theology: A Pentecostal Response to Noll's *Scandal.*" *Pneuma* 19 (1997) 225–38.

———. *Speech and Theology: Language and the Logic of Incarnation.* London: Routledge, 2002.

———. *Thinking in Tongues: Pentecostal Contributions to Christian Philosophy.* Pentecostal Manifestos. Grand Rapids: Eerdmans, 2010.

———. *Who's Afraid of Postmodernism? Taking Derrida, Lyotard, and Foucault to Church.* Grand Rapids: Baker, 2006.

Spawn, Kevin L., and Archie Wright, eds. *Spirit and Scripture: Exploring a Pneumatic Hermeneutic.* New York: Bloomsbury, 2012.

Stein, Stephen J. "Editor's Introduction (*Blank Bible*)." In *The Blank Bible: The Works of Jonathan Edwards* 24, edited by Harry S. Stout, 1–4. New Haven: Yale University Press, 2006.

———. "Editor's Introduction (*Notes on Scripture*)." In *Notes on Scripture: The Works of Jonathan Edwards* 15, edited by Harry S. Stout, 1–46. New Haven: Yale University Press, 1998.

———. "The Quest for the Spiritual Sense: The Biblical Hermeneutics of Jonathan Edwards." *Harvard Theological Review* 70 (1977) 99–113.

Steiner, George. *Real Presences.* Chicago: University of Chicago Press, 1989.

Stephenson, Christopher A. "Reality, Knowledge, and Life in Community: Metaphysics, Epistemology, and Hermeneutics in the Work of Amos Yong." In *The Theology of Amos Yong and the New Face of Pentecostal Scholarship*, edited by Wolfgang Vondey and Martin Mittelstadt, 63–82. Leiden: Brill, 2013.

———. *Types of Pentecostal Theology: Method, System, Spirit.* Oxford: Oxford University Press, 2013.

Stronstad, Roger. *The Charismatic Theology of St. Luke.* Peabody, MA: Hendrickson, 1984.

———. "Pentecostal Experience and Hermeneutics." *Paraclete* 26 (1992) 14–30.

———. "A Review Essay on Amos Yong, *Who Is the Holy Spirit? A Walk with the Apostles.*" *Journal of Pentecostal Theology* 22 (2013) 295–300.

Studebaker, Steven. *From Pentecost to the Triune God: A Pentecostal Trinitarian Theology.* Pentecostal Manifestos. Grand Rapids: Eerdmans, 2012.

Sweeney, Douglas A. *Edwards the Exegete: Biblical Interpretation and Anglo-Protestant Culture on the Edge of the Enlightenment.* New York: Oxford University Press, 2015.

Taylor, Charles. "Explanation and Practical Reason." In *Philosophical Arguments*, 34–60. Cambridge: Harvard University Press, 1995.

———. *Human Agency and Language: Philosophical Papers.* Vol. 1. Cambridge: Cambridge University Press, 1985.

———. "The Importance of Herder." In *Philosophical Arguments*, 79–99. Cambridge: Harvard University Press, 1995.

———. *The Language Animal: The Full Shape of the Human Linguistic Capacity.* Cambridge: Belknap, 2016.

———. *Modern Social Imaginaries.* Durham: Duke University Press, 2004.

———. "Overcoming Epistemology." In *Philosophical Arguments*, 1–19. Cambridge: Harvard University Press, 1995.

———. *Philosophical Arguments.* Cambridge: Harvard University Press, 1995.

———. "A Philosopher's Postscript: Engaging the Citadel of Secular Reason." In *Reason and the Reasons of Faith*, edited by Paul J. Griffiths and Reinhard Hütter, 339–53. New York: T. & T. Clark, 2005.

———. *A Secular Age.* Cambridge: Belknap, 2007.

———. *Sources of the Self: The Making of the Modern Identity.* Cambridge: Harvard University Press, 1989.

———. *Varieties of Religion Today: William James Revisited.* Cambridge: Harvard University Press, 2003.

Taylor, Charles, et al., eds. *Multiculturalism: Examining the Politics of Recognition.* Edited by Amy Gutmann. Princeton: Princeton University Press, 1994.

Thiselton, Anthony. *Hermeneutics: An Introduction.* Grand Rapids: Eerdmans, 2009.

———. *The Two Horizons: New Testament Hermeneutics and Philosophical Description with Special Reference to Heidegger, Bultmann, Gadamer, and Wittgenstein.* Grand Rapids: Eerdmans, 1980.

Thomas, John Christopher, ed. *Toward a Pentecostal Ecclesiology: The Church and the Fivefold Gospel.* Cleveland, TN: Center for Pentecostal Theology, 2010.

———. "Women, Pentecostals, and the Bible: An Experiment in Pentecostal Hermeneutics." *Journal of Pentecostal Theology* 5 (1994) 41–56.

Thomas, John Christopher, and Frank Macchia. *Revelation.* Two Horizons New Testament Commentary. Grand Rapids: Eerdmans, 2016.

Toulmin, Stephen. *Cosmopolis: The Hidden Agenda of Modernity.* Chicago: University of Chicago Press, 1990.

Tracy, David. *The Analogical Imagination: Christian Theology and the Culture of Pluralism.* New York: Crossroad, 1981.

Vandevelde, Pol. *The Task of the Interpreter: Text, Meaning, and Negotiation.* Pittsburgh: University of Pittsburgh Press, 2005.

Vanhoozer, Kevin J., ed. *Dictionary for Theological Interpretation of the Bible.* Grand Rapids: Baker, 2005.

———. *The Drama of Doctrine: A Canonical-Linguistic Approach to Christian Theology.* Louisville: Westminster John Knox Press, 2005.

———. "Introduction: What Is Theological Interpretation of the Bible?" In *Dictionary for Theological Interpretation of the Bible*, edited by Kevin J. Vanhoozer, 19–25. Grand Rapids: Baker Academic, 2005.

———. *Is There a Meaning in This Text? The Bible, the Reader, and the Morality of Literary Knowledge.* Grand Rapids: Zondervan, 1998.

———. "Theology and the Condition of Postmodernity: A Report on Knowledge (of God)." In *The Cambridge Companion to Postmodern Theology*, edited by Kevin J. Vanhoozer, 3–25. Cambridge: Cambridge University Press, 2003.

Volf, Miroslav. *Exclusion and Embrace: A Theological Exploration of Identity, Otherness, and Reconciliation.* Nashville: Abingdon, 1996.

Vondey, Wolfgang. *Beyond Pentecostalism: The Crisis of Global Christianity and the Renewal of the Theological Agenda*. Pentecostal Manifestos. Grand Rapids: Eerdmans, 2010.

———. "Introduction: The Presence of the Spirit as an Interdisciplinary Concern." In *The Holy Spirit and the Christian Life: Historical, Interdisciplinary, and Renewal Perspectives*, edited by Wolfgang Vondey, 1–20. Christianity and Renewal Interdisciplinary Studies. New York: Palgrave Macmillan, 2014.

———. "Pentecostal Perspectives on *The Nature and Mission of the Church*." In *Receiving "The Nature and Mission of the Church": Ecclesial Reality and Ecumenical Horizons for the Twenty-First Century*, edited by Paul M. Collins and Michael A. Fahey, 55–68. London: T. & T. Clark, 2008.

———. *Pentecostal Theology: Living the Full Gospel*. T. & T. Clark Systematic Pentecostal and Charismatic Theology. London: T. & T. Clark International, 2017.

———. *Pentecostalism: A Guide for the Perplexed*. London: Bloomsbury, 2013.

———. "Pentecostalism and the Possibility of Global Theology: Implications of the Theology of Amos Yong." *Pneuma* 28 (2006) 289–312.

———. "Pentecostalism as a Theological Tradition: An Ideological, Historical, and Institutional Critique." *Pneuma* 42 (2020) 521–35.

———, ed. *The Routledge Handbook of Pentecostal Theology*. London: Routledge, 2020.

Vondey, Wolfgang, and Martin Mittelstadt, eds. *The Theology of Amos Yong and the New Face of Pentecostal Scholarship: Passion for the Spirit*. Global Pentecostal and Charismatic Studies 14. Leiden: Brill, 2013.

Wacker, Grant. *Heaven Below: Early Pentecostals and American Culture*. Cambridge: Harvard University Press, 2001.

Walton, John H., and Craig Keener, eds. *NIV Cultural Background Study Bible*. Grand Rapids: Eerdmans, 2016.

Wariboko, Nimi. *The Charismatic City and the Public Resurgence of Religion: A Pentecostal Social Ethics of Cosmopolitan Urban Life*. Christianity and Renewal Interdisciplinary Studies. New York: Palgrave Macmillan, 2014.

———. *Economics in Spirit and Truth: A Moral Philosophy of Finance*. Radical Theologies. New York: Palgrave Macmillan, 2014.

———. *Nigerian Pentecostalism*. Rochester, NY: University of Rochester Press, 2014.

———. *The Pentecostal Principle: Ethical Methodology in New Spirit*. Pentecostal Manifestos. Grand Rapids: Eerdmans, 2012.

———. *The Split God: Pentecostalism and Critical Theory*. Albany, NY: SUNY Press, 2018.

Warner, Michael, et al., eds. *Varieties of Secularism in a Secular Age*. Cambridge: Harvard University Press, 2010.

Weinandy, Thomas G. *The Father's Spirit of Sonship: Reconceiving the Trinity*. Edinburgh: T. & T. Clark, 1995.

Westphal, Merold. "Spirit and Prejudice." In *Constructive Pneumatological Hermeneutics in Pentecostal Christianity*, edited by Kenneth J. Archer and L. William Oliverio Jr., 17–32. Christianity and Renewal Interdisciplinary Studies. New York: Palgrave Macmillan, 2016.

———. *Overcoming Onto-theology: Toward a Postmodern Christian Faith*. New York: Fordham University Press, 2001.

———. *Whose Community? Which Interpretation? Philosophical Hermeneutics for the Church*. The Church and Postmodern Culture. Grand Rapids: Baker, 2009.

Wilkinson, Michael, ed. *Global Pentecostal Movements: Migration, Mission, and Public Religion*. Leiden: Brill, 2012.

———. "Pentecostals and the World: Theoretical and Methodological Issues for Studying Global Pentecostalism." *Pneuma* 38 (2016) 373–93.

Wilkinson, Michael, et al., eds. *Brill's Encyclopedia of Global Pentecostalism*. Leiden: Brill, 2021.

Williams, A. N. "Is Aquinas a Foundationalist?" *New Blackfriars* 91 (2010) 20–45.

Williams, Ernest Swing. *Systematic Theology*. 3 vols. Springfield, MO: Gospel Publishing House, 1953.

Wittgenstein, Ludwig. *Philosophical Investigations*. Translated by G. E. M. Anscombe. New York: Macmillan, 1953.

World Assemblies of God Fellowship. "Statement of Faith." https://worldagfellowship. org/Fellowship/Bylaws-Membership-Position-Papers.

Yong, Amos. "Academic Glossolalia? Pentecostal Scholarship, Multi-Disciplinarity, and the Science-Religion Conversation." *Journal of Pentecostal Theology* 14 (2005) 61–80.

———. *An Amos Yong Reader: The Pentecostal Spirit*. Edited by Christopher A. Stephenson. Eugene, OR: Cascade, 2020.

———. *Beyond the Impasse: Toward a Pneumatological Theology of Religions*. Grand Rapids: Baker Academic, 2003.

———. *The Bible, Disability, and the Church: A New Vision of the People of God*. Grand Rapids: Eerdmans, 2011.

———. "Complete Curriculum Vitate." https://www.fuller.edu/wp-content/ uploads/2020/08/Amos-Yong-vita-publications0820.pdf.

———. "The Demise of Foundationalism and the Retention of Truth: What Evangelicals Can Learn from C. S. Peirce." *Christian Scholar's Review* 29 (2000) 563–88.

———. *The Dialogical Spirit: Christian Reason and Theological Method in the Third Millennium*. Eugene, OR: Cascade, 2014.

———. *Discerning the Spirit(s): A Pentecostal Contribution to Theology of Religions*. Journal of Pentecostal Theology Supplement 20. Sheffield: Sheffield Academic Press, 2000.

———. *The Hermeneutical Spirit: Theological Interpretation and Scriptural Imagination for the 21st Century*. Eugene, OR: Cascade, 2014.

———. *Hospitality and the Other: Pentecost, Christian Practices, and the Neighbor*. Maryknoll, NY: Orbis, 2008.

———. "How Does God Do What God Does? Pentecostal-Charismatic Perspectives on Divine Action in Dialogue with Modern Science." In *Science and the Spirit: A Pentecostal Engagement with the Sciences*, edited by James K. A. Smith and Amos Yong, 50–71. Bloomington: Indiana University Press, 2010.

———. *In the Days of Caesar: Pentecostalism and Political Theology*. Cadbury Lectures 2009. Grand Rapids: Eerdmans, 2010.

———. "In Search of Foundations: The *Oeuvre* of Donald L. Gelpi, S.J., and Its Significance for Pentecostal Theology, Philosophy, and Spirituality." *Journal of Pentecostal Theology* 11 (2002) 3–26.

———. *Learning Theology: Tracking the Spirit of Christian Faith*. Louisville: Westminster John Knox, 2018.

———. "Many Tongues, Many Senses: Pentecost, the Body Politic, and the Redemption of Dis/Ability." *Pneuma* 31 (2009) 167–88.

———. *Mission after Pentecost: The Witness of the Spirit from Genesis to Revelation.* Grand Rapids: Baker, 2019.

———. "Pentecostalism and the Theological Academy." *Theology Today* 64 (2007) 244–50.

———. "Primal Spirituality or the Future of Faith? The Shifting Winds of Pentecostal Studies in the Wider Academy." *Pneuma* 33 (2011) 327–29.

———. *Renewing Christian Theology: Systematics for a Global Christianity.* Waco, TX: Baylor University Press, 2014.

———. *Revelation.* Belief: A Theological Commentary on the Bible. Louisville: Westminster John Knox, 2021.

———. *The Spirit of Creation: Modern Science and Divine Action in the Pentecostal-Charismatic Imagination.* Pentecostal Manifestos. Grand Rapids: Eerdmans, 2011.

———. *Spirit of Love: A Trinitarian Theology of Grace.* Waco, TX: Baylor University Press, 2012.

———. *The Spirit Poured out on All Flesh: Pentecostalism and the Possibility of Global Theology.* Grand Rapids: Baker Academic, 2005.

———. *Spirit-Word-Community: Theological Hermeneutics in Trinitarian Perspective.* Aldershot, UK: Ashgate, 2002.

———. *Theology and Down Syndrome: Reimagining Disability in Late Modernity.* Waco, TX: Baylor University Press, 2007.

———. "Unveiling Interpretation after Pentecost: Revelation, Pentecostal Reading, and Christian Hermeneutics of Scripture." *Journal of Theological Interpretation* 11 (2017) 139–55.

———. *Who Is the Holy Spirit? A Walk with the Apostles.* Brewster, MA: Paraclete, 2011.

Ziefle, Joshua R. *David du Plessis and the Assemblies of God: The Struggle for the Soul of a Movement.* Global Pentecostal and Charismatic Studies 13. Leiden: Brill, 2013.

Zimmerman, Jens. *Recovering Theological Hermeneutics: An Incarnational-Trinitarian Theory of Interpretation.* Grand Rapids: Baker, 2004.